CHAUCER'S COMIC PROVIDENCE

Before you start to read this book, take this moment to think about making a donation to punctum books, an independent non-profit press,

@ https://punctumbooks.com/support/

If you're reading the e-book, you can click on the image below to go directly to our donations site. Any amount, no matter the size, is appreciated and will help us to keep our ship of fools afloat. Contributions from dedicated readers will also help us to keep our commons open and to cultivate new work that can't find a welcoming port elsewhere. Our adventure is not possible without your support.
Vive la open access.

Fig. 1. Detail from Hieronymus Bosch, *Ship of Fools* (1490–1500)

CHAUCER'S COMIC PROVIDENCE. Copyright © 2023 Janet Thormann and Aranye Fradenburg Joy. This work carries a Creative Commons BY-NC-SA 4.0 International license, which means that you are free to copy and redistribute the material in any medium or format, and you may also remix, transform, and build upon the material, as long as you clearly attribute the work to the authors and editors (but not in a way that suggests the authors or punctum books endorses you and your work), you do not use this work for commercial gain in any form whatsoever, and that for any remixing and transformation, you distribute your rebuild under the same license. http://creativecommons.org/licenses/by-nc-sa/4.0/

First published in 2023 by Brainstorm Books
An imprint of punctum books, Earth, Milky Way
https://www.punctumbooks.com

ISBN-13: 978-1-68571-020-0 (print)
ISBN-13: 978-1-68571-021-7 (ePDF)

DOI: 10.53288/0362.1.00

LCCN: 2023935953
Library of Congress Cataloging Data is available from the Library of Congress

Book design: Hatim Eujayl and Vincent W.J. van Gerven Oei
Cover image: Giotto, *The Seven Vices: Foolishness* (1306), fresco, 120 × 55 cm, Cappella Scrovegni (Arena Chapel), Padu, Italy.

Chaucer's Comic Providence

by Janet Thormann

with Aranye Fradenburg Joy

Brainstorm Books
Santa Barbara, California

Contents

Introduction · 9

· · ·

1. The Interminable Happiness of the Symptom:
The Merchant's Tale · 21

2. The Magician, the Squire, the Knight, and His Wife:
The Franklin's Tale · 55

3. That Elusive Object of Desire:
The Shipman's Tale · 91

4. Some Rules of the Game:
The Miller's Tale · 127

5. The Sweet Life:
The Nun's Priest's Tale · 173

· · ·

Bibliography · 1989

Acknowledgments

The book that you hold in your hand has been long in the making. Since Janet's passing in 2014, her daughter, Gabrielle Thormann, has been a driving force in seeing this book published posthumously. She worked with me on all stages of the book's editing and production. I owe her my gratitude for her support during the long trajectory of this project from its inception until its completion.

I also cannot begin to express my thankfulness to Aranye Fradenburg Joy, who through the process of working on this book has become a co-author with Janet. Through her deep familiarity and engagement with both the literary work of Chaucer and Lacanian psychoanalysis, she has made indispensible contributions to what was initially an unfinished manuscript. This work would not have been the same without her.

Finally, I have to thank John Hill, who was kind enough to add translations of the Middle English and footnotes with further clarifications.

– Eileen A. Fradenburg Joy
Director, punctum books

Introduction

Chaucer's Comic Providence presents readings of five *Canterbury Tales* that dramatize sexual division and the lack of rapport between the sexes. The readings of the tales are founded on the psychoanalytic thinking of Jacques Lacan in his rereading of Freud. They are motivated by my conviction that Chaucer understood what psychoanalysis would come to study as an unconscious operating in the subject that is independent of conscious control and desire. For psychoanalysis, the subject is interminably engaged with unconscious sexual difference and with the absence of sexual rapport. Lacan emphasizes that male and female are asymmetrical positions, and sexual rapport does not exist.[1] Chaucer's plots of sexual adventures, mishaps, and surprise in the five tales dramatize the lack of symmetry and absence of accord between the sexes.

Each of the five tales ends with a variation on a repeated type-scene. This scene, or narrative cluster, is composed of three

---

1   See Ruth Evans, "Historicism, Sexuality Studies, Psychoanalysis," *postmedieval FORUM*, October 2011, https://postmedievalforum.wordpress.com/forums/forum-i-responses-to-paul-strohm/evans/: "Sexual difference for Lacan is not reducible to cultural construction because it is a real, not a symbolic, difference .... Certainly there is no general, universal category 'heterosexuality,' only historically specific categories of sex, gender, and desire (and we need to know what they are), but this does not address the agonizing dynamics of the sexual relation that are staged in courtly fictions .... Still, Lacan insists on the historicity of the drives and on their link to 'remembering,' which includes cultural remembering."

signifying chains. Unexpected speech intrudes into the action; an enlarged perspective is suddenly introduced, an extended physical space becomes visible, or an instantaneous insight becomes accessible; finally, a consoling insight results from a shift in conscious awareness, among the characters and for the audience of the tale. The intrusion of the speech event setting off the concluding shift in awareness may be unexpected, erupting as if spontaneously, seemingly from nowhere, but is in fact motivated by the immediate dramatic situation. The scene's final effect is to offer assurance in the latent powers of thought and unconscious processes that may sponsor desire. The scene thereby projects a secure space and time into a future capable of bringing about happiness. The conclusion of each tale reasserts the desire that has been at stake from the start of the narrative; each tale ends with a conviction in the adequacy of language and social structures to fulfill desires. Since, however, fulfillment can never be anything other than transitory, the repetition of this kind of narrative work from tale to tale also fails finally to remove sexual difference. We remain "not one"; we are irreducible to "one."

The repeated formulaic scene concludes narratives that respond to the unconscious absence of sexual rapport and relation. The narratives' plots exaggerate sexual deception and dissimulation, misadventure, disloyalty, unfulfilled longing, frustration, and dissatisfaction. The effect is that whatever their characters' strategies, purposes, and goals, the narratives do not achieve harmony between men and women. Rather, they dramatize the incompatibility of the sexes, and their plots insistently demonstrate that sexual difference is not symmetrical. They show that unanticipated, unconscious processes that structure behavior and desire consistently interfere with conscious intentions and motives. Four of the five – *The Merchant's Tale, The Miller's Tale, The Franklin's Tale,* and *The Shipman's Tale* – are commonly studied among the "Marriage Group," proposed by George Lyman Kittredge,[2] while *The Nun's Priest's Tale* takes up the moral values associated with marriage in a story about a cock and a hen. My interest here is in the ways these five narratives rep-

---

2   George Lyman Kittredge, "Chaucer's Discussion of Marriage," *Modern Philology* 9, no. 4 (1912): 435–67.

resent and deal with sexual division, in their means of handling what, in any case, cannot be avoided or mastered. Consequently, the resolutions of the narratives sponsor an ethics of desire: they affirm sexual pleasure and acknowledge misprision and limitation, but they do not compromise, close down, or finish with incompatibility, contraction, and limitation.

The tales share a common emphasis on the operations of systems of social exchange. For both Chaucer's writing and for Lacan, the human is a subject of language, which is to say, a subject of exchange. Language imbricates individuals everywhere in particular systems of exchange; these forms of exchange govern both individual subjectivity and large social formations. Seth Lerer points out that "Money, language, and sex thus emerge as literary themes and social issues at the center" of the *Canterbury Tales*.[3] The narratives, whether explicitly or by implication, put in play varied functions and operations of these structures of exchange, their different modes of interpenetration, and the changes they undergo in a changing society. Related to their focus on money, sex, and language as forms of exchange is the tales' concern with ideology. They dramatize, whether in subdued or explicit forms, the ways ideology performs unconsciously, how it functions in marriage and bolsters sexual division, how it contributes to forms of identification.

My reading of the several *Canterbury Tales*, then, claims that Chaucer's poetry already reveals the unconscious that Freud is credited with discovering. As well, Chaucer not only anticipates Lacan's pronouncement that "the unconscious is structured like a language," but also his emphasis on unconscious sexual difference and the absence of rapport between the sexes. Lacanian theory approaches sexual difference and asymmetry not as matters of gender identity but as unconscious structures. Gender is socially determined and historically variable, variously adaptable by conscious agents, malleable and changing. Since sexual difference functions unconsciously and persists in spite of conscious control, it makes gender difference possible. It is understood,

3 Seth Lerer, "The Canterbury Tales," in *The Yale Companion to Chaucer,* ed. Seth Lerer (New Haven: Yale University Press, 2006), 244.

supervised, and controlled differently in different cultures. Sexual difference is a ground for ideologies; gender is a function of ideology. This is not to say that for Lacan, sexual difference is biological, however. Psychoanalytic criticism is not essentialist. It emphasizes unconscious determinants of identifications, subjectivity, behaviors, as well as unconscious operations in ideology and language generally within changing historical contexts and cultural circumstances. Because it considers both difference and continuity, change and perpetuation, and because it incorporates psychic processes, motives, functions, and dynamics operating outside of conscious awareness, psychoanalysis offers a wider range for analysis of Chaucer's tales than does gender theory alone. A psychoanalytic concern with sexual difference and the absence of sexual relation brings attention to precisely those themes and issues at stake in Chaucer's texts, especially in the tales concerned with sexual deception, incompatibility and discord, transgressive desire, self-destructive motivation, stereotypical character, and repeated patterns of behavior and thought.

Contemporary criticism of Chaucer, however, is inimical or, at the least, largely indifferent to psychoanalysis and psychoanalytically inflected criticism, although much valuable work has made use of psychoanalytic theory. In particular, H. Marshall Leicester, Jr.'s *The Disenchanted Self* is thoroughly informed by Lacanian theory.[4] L.O. Aranye Fradenburg draws on Lacan in her sophisticated examination of critical desire in *Sacrifice Your Love: Psychoanalysis, Historicism, Chaucer*;[5] her treatment of *The Book of the Duchess* in "'Voice Memorial': Loss and Reparation in Chaucer's Poetry" studies grief from a psychoanalytically-inflected perspective.[6] Erin Felicia Labbie has shown that a variety of medieval sources influenced Lacan in important

---

4   H. Marshall Leicester, Jr., *The Disenchanted Self: Representing the Subject in the Canterbury Tales* (Berkeley: University of California Press, 1990).

5   L.O. Aranye Fradenburg, *Sacrifice Your Love: Psychoanalysis, Historicism, Chaucer* (Minneapolis: University of Minnesota Press, 2002).

6   Louise Olga Fradenburg, "'Voice Memorial': Loss and Reparation in Chaucer's Poetry," *Exemplaria* 2, no. 1 (1990): 169–202.

ways.⁷ Carolyn Dinshaw's *Chaucer's Sexual Politics* foregrounds feminist revisions of exchange theory and opened Chaucer studies to the queer analytic work also exemplified by Steven F. Kruger and Glenn Burger.⁸ Elaine Tuttle Hansen, in *Chaucer and the Fictions of Gender,* provides an inclusive consideration of Chaucer's earlier poetry as well as several *Canterbury Tales*.⁹ Her feminist perspective is informed by Freudian theory even as it is sensitive to historical contexts. Especially in chapters on the *Merchant's* and *Franklin's Tales,* Hansen specifically treats the construction of masculinity from the standpoint of a recurring "feminization" while extending gender theory in close, wide-ranging textual analyses.

However, the productive deployment of Freud and Lacan in close readings and in theory during the late 1980s and 1990s, in academic feminism, queer theory, and gender studies, in studies of the formation of subjectivity, and in historical scholarship was hindered by the publication of Lee Patterson's "Case against Psychoanalysis" in *Speculum* in 2001.¹⁰ Gender studies and queer theory certainly continued, largely independent of psychoanalytic moorings. But Patterson's concentrated attack on Freud's methods, reasoning, and putatively faulty science; his close study of *The Pardoner's Tale* within the context of medieval theology and iconology; his mastery of English history, of dissent and power; and the rhetorical dismissals of academic scholars like Tuttle and international icons like Žižek – all of these amounted to an overwhelming dismissal of psychoanalytic criticism. Patterson's attack on Freud was itself open to debate, and has not held up well in the light of continuing research

7   Erin Felicia Labbie, *Lacan's Medievalism* (Minneapolis: University of Minnesota Press, 2006).
8   Carolyn Dinshaw, *Chaucer's Sexual Politics* (Madison: University of Wisconsin Press, 1989); Steven F. Kruger, "Claiming the Pardoner: Toward a Gay Reading of Chaucer's *Pardoner's Tale*," *Exemplaria* 6, no. 1 (1994): 115–39; and Glenn Burger, *Chaucer's Queer Nation* (Minneapolis: University of Minnesota Press, 2003).
9   Elaine Tuttle Hansen, *Chaucer and the Fictions of Gender* (Berkeley: University of California Press, 1992).
10 Lee Patterson, "Chaucer's Pardoner on the Couch: Psyche and Clio in Medieval Literary Studies," *Speculum* 76, no. 3 (2001): 638–80.

into the mind/brain, but because of his reputation, he put up a formidable obstacle to new engagements with psychoanalytical theory generally and with Lacanian theory in particular. References to psychoanalytic terms in work on Chaucer and other medieval authors continued to appear, but responses to Lacanian theory grew more rare and were often hostile. Patterson's own indispensible study, *Chaucer and the Subject of History,* recalibrated Chaucer scholarship by focusing on ideology, class, and class conflict, the topics of choice in the heyday of the "new historicism" and cultural materialism. Nevertheless, as has been noted by Elizabeth Scala and Aranye Fradenburg, psychoanalytically inflected language does not escape Patterson's discourse, perhaps if only because it has so penetrated contemporary thinking and habits of language.[11] For example, his analysis of the Merchant describes "the self-fulfilling dynamic of the jealous imagination,"[12] where terms from Chaucer that predate psychoanalysis take on special resonance within contemporary knowledge. His development of the Merchant's "fantasye"[13] in particular reveals powerful affective investments in moral judgments, and attributes unconscious depth to various characters, as does his condemnation of May as "grossly duplicitous"[14] and his characterization of "her depravity."[15]

Despite Patterson's negative influence, the use of psychoanalytic theory in medievalist practice has not waned altogether, and perhaps has even flourished. Elizabeth Scala, Sarah Kay, Erin Labbie, Ruth Evans, and Simon Gaunt have continued throughout to produce important work in this tradition, and many other prominent scholars, like Patricia Ingham and Bruce Holsinger, are psychoanalytically informed and friendly to psychoanalytic

---

11 See Elizabeth Scala, "Historicists and Their Discontents: Reading Psychoanalytically in Medieval Studies," *Texas Studies in Language and Literature* 44 (2002): 108–31, and *Desire in the Canterbury Tales* (Columbus: Ohio State University Press, 2015), 20n32.
12 Lee Patterson, *Chaucer and the Subject of History* (Madison: University of Wisconsin Press, 1991), 339.
13 Ibid.
14 Ibid., 338.
15 Ibid., 337.

medievalism.¹⁶ George Edmonson draws on Lacanian theory to develop an ethical understanding of the neighbor – who is also the *bon vezi,* the beloved courtly lady – in *The Neighboring Text: Chaucer, Boccaccio, Henryson.*¹⁷ His work, in turn, has recently been taken up and further developed by Emily Houlik-Ritchie.¹⁸ While my own book is not intended as an apologia for psychoanalytic theory *per se,* I do believe that some of the central concepts of Lacanian theory still provide important entry points that can open up, decenter, and renew our responses to Chaucer's works. As the readings developed in the following chapters focus on the theme of sexual division and ways of handling the absence of sexual relation, they are buttressed by Lacan's treatment of the three

16 For some examples of robust twenty-first century work on psychoanalysis, medieval literature, and medieval culture, see Nicolette Zeeman, "Medieval Dreams," in *A Concise Companion to Psychoanalysis, Literature, and Culture,* eds. Laura Marcus and Ankhi Mukherjee (London: Blackwell, 2014), 137–50; David Bakan, Dan Merkur, and David S. Weiss, *Maimonides' Cure of Souls: Medieval Precursor of Psychoanalysis* (Albany: SUNY Press, 2009); John A. Pitcher, *Chaucer's Feminine Subjects: Figures of Desire in the Canterbury Tales* (New York: Palgrave 2012); Jane Gilbert, *Living Death in Medieval French and English Literature* (Cambridge: Cambridge University Press, 2011); Karen A. Lurkhur, "Medieval Silence and Modern Transsexuality," *Studies in Gender and Sexuality* 11, no. 4 (2010): 220–38; Herman Westerink, *The Heart of Man's Destiny: Lacanian Psychoanalysis and Early Reformation Thought* (New York: Routledge, 2012); M.W. Bychowski, "Trans Textuality: Dysphoria in the Depths of Medieval Skin," *postmedieval* 9, no. 3 (2018): 318–33; Miranda Griffin, *Transforming Tales: Rewriting Metamorphosis in Medieval French Literature* (Oxford: Oxford University Press, 2015); Nicholas Ealy, *Narcissism and Selfhood in Medieval French Literature: Wounds of Desire* (New York: Palgrave, 2019); and Amy Hollywood, *Acute Melancholia and Other Essays: Mysticism, History, and the Study of Religion* (New York: Columbia University Press, 2016).
17 George Edmondson, *The Neighboring Text: Chaucer, Boccaccio, Henryson* (Notre Dame: University of Notre Dame Press, 2011).
18 Emily Houlik Ritchie, "Love Thy Neighbor, Love Thy Fellow: Teaching Gower's Representation of the Unethical Jew," in *Jews in Medieval England,* eds. Miriamne Krummel and Tyson Pugh (New York: Palgrave, 2017), 101–15.

registers of the unconscious: the symbolic register of language and social exchange; the domination of image, ego, rivalry, and meaning in the imaginary; and the Real of enjoyment beyond language. Chapter 1 on *The Merchant's Tale* focuses on the Real by way of an impossible suffering of enjoyment through the symptom. Chapter 2 approaches *The Franklin's Tale's* concerns with imaginary ideology by foregrounding a structure of interlocking, separate exchanges of language, women, and money. Chapter 3, by contrast, shows how *The Shipman's Tale* maps the circulation of desire through overlapping metonymic symbolic chains drawing equivalences between words, sex, and money. Chapter 4, covering *The Miller's Tale* and also referencing *The Friar's Tale* and *The Summoner's Tale,* examines narratives based on imaginary rivalry, aggression, and revenge, at the same time that their dependence on the lie reaffirms their dependence on the values of exchange and social being. Chapter 5 on *The Nun's Priest's Tale* explores the knotting-together of the Real, symbolic, and imaginary registers in the voice of a narrator who is an object of the unconscious; in the terms of Slavoj Žižek, the narrator is "subjectivity without subject-agent."[19]

The prototype of these tales' repeated conclusion is the final scene at the ending of Chaucer's *Troilus and Criseyde,* modeled on the *Somnium Scipionis* of Cicero. After Troilus's loss of his lover and his death in battle, his spirit ascends to the heavens' reaches to achieve a vision of cosmic sound, sight, and knowledge: he hears the celestial music of the stars, producing harmony as they rotate at different speeds; he sees the miniscule earth from the perspective of the cosmos; within this extended space and time, he gains insight into the instability of the changing world. Troilus ends by despising the "wrecched world, and held al vanite" ("the wretched world, and held everything as vanity").[20] When the narrator addresses his epic poem of romance and history as "litel myn tragedye," he affirms this spirit's judgment of the

---

19 Slavoj Žižek, "Leave the Screen Empty!," *lacanian ink* 35 (2010): 156.
20 *Troilus and Criseyde* Book V, l. 1817. Chaucer's works are hereinafter cited in the text, and are taken from Larry D. Benson, ed., *The Riverside Chaucer,* 3rd edn. (Boston: Houghton Mifflin, 1987).

world ("my little tragedy," Book V, l. 1786).[21] In the *Canterbury Tales,* the concluding scenes do not follow upon death nor lead either to tragedy or to rejection of the earthly world. But the same pattern at the conclusion of the *Troilus* appears in these tales' endings. The sound of unanticipated language suddenly emerges to change the narrative's direction and bring it to a conclusion; an expanded space opens up, whether in the psychical environment of the tale or in the unconscious of characters or reader; and time extends into the future. A perspective on sexual division emerges, together with a means of conceptualizing the lack of rapport between the sexes (Troilus's *bon vezi,* Criseyde, is a "vanity," like all objects of desire). For Chaucer's Monk, tragedy is defined as "The harm of hem that stoode in heigh degree, / And fillen so that ther nas no remedie / To brynge hem out of hir adversitee" ("the harm that befell those who stood in high prosperity yet fell so that there was no remedy for bringing them out of their adversity," *The Monk's Tale,* ll. 1992–94). In contrast, the five tales' trajectories move from confusion, error, and ignorance to an expansive insight and perspective.

Another definition, similar to the Monk's, of both tragedy and comedy as the outcomes of movements of Fortune's wheel, appears in "The Prologue to *The Nun's Priest's Tale*" (ll. 2774–76). Comedy is the "contrarie" of tragedy, ending happily with "joye and greet solas, / As whan a man hath been in povre estaat, / And clymbeth up and wexeth fortunat" ("with joy and great solace, as when a man has been in a lowly condition and climbs up and grows fortunate," ll. 2774–76). It is in this very specific sense that "comic" figures in this book's title. *Chaucer's Comic Providence* does not intend a theory or history of comedy; "comic" is an adjective describing the narrative arc of the five tales, their common trajectory. The analyses of each tale intend to show how sexual difference and the absence of sexual relation are handled, leading to endings that bring about individual pleasure and social accord. My title's use of "Providence" is less straightforward. The meaning of Providence as cosmic law, a meaning drawn from Boethius, generally corresponds to

---

21 Translations are provided as needed by John M. Hill, with non-Chaucerians in mind.

the *Oxford English Dictionary* (*OED*) definition as "beneficent care or government of God (or of nature, etc.)."[22] The *OED* also lists the sense of "foresight, provision; *esp.* anticipation of and preparation for the future: 'timely care'," a sense implied by the conclusions' wit and their anticipated consequences. The *OED* definition also suggests the meaning "providential," denoting "opportune, lucky, fortunate," that is, what occurs as if by happy accident or chance, as in the archaic *hap*; in this sense, speech in the concluding scenes is providential, seeming to arise out of unanticipated chance. In the conclusions of the five tales I analyze, subjective space and unconscious law seem to appear providentially, as if emerging out of a timely accident. *Chaucer's Comic Providence* addresses the unexpected, surprising resolutions of these plots, the concomitant abeyance of sexual conflicts, and the links between emergence and abeyance, which issue in the hope of a beneficent future.

Chapter titles adapt film titles in a form of homage to Alain Renoir, the son of well-known French film director Jean Renoir, whose enthusiasm and infectious joy in teaching introduced me to a love of the inexhaustible resource that is Chaucer's poetry. The book is dedicated to his memory.

---

22 *Oxford English Dictionary* (*OED*), s.v. "providence." Hereinafter, *OED* references cited in the text.

CHAPTER 1

The Interminable Happiness of the Symptom: *The Merchant's Tale*

The five tales on which this book focuses are linked by the common problematic of arranging and testing the heterosexual relation between men and women; they are commonly included in "the marriage group."¹ These tales dramatize various strategies to rationalize and compensate for the lack of a "natural" heterosexual relation. The tales' marriages demonstrate what Lacan posits as the absence of relation between the sexes by showing that the accommodation of sexual division never quite works: men and women are at odds with one another; the difference between the sexes is asymmetrical and does not compose a unity.

Lacan formulates sexual division as a result of the logical demands of speech for the sexed subject "which finds itself in the position of inhabiting language."² Slavoj Žižek insists that for Lacan, "sexual difference is not a discursive, symbolic construc-

---

1 See George Lyman Kittredge, "Chaucer's Discussion of Marriage," *Modern Philology* 9, no. 4 (1912): 435–67.
2 Jacques Lacan, *The Seminar of Jacques Lacan, Book XX: On Feminine Sexuality, the Limits of Love and Knowledge, Encore 1972–1973*, ed. Jacques-Alain Miller, trans. Bruce Fink (New York: W.W. Norton, 1998), 80. The formulation of sexual division is developed in the seminar of March 13, 1973, "A Love Letter [une letter d'âmour]," Chapter VII, 73–89.

tion; instead, it emerges at the very point where symbolization fails: we are sexed beings because symbolization always comes up against its own inherent impossibility. What is at stake here is not that 'actual,' 'concrete,' sexual beings cannot fully fit the symbolic construction of 'man' or 'woman': the point is, rather, that this symbolic construction itself supplements a certain fundamental deadlock."[3] Formulations of sexual difference try to account for a real "deadlock" that in fact resists any account.

This means that sexual union is not possible: "Male and female are not two complementary parts of the Whole, they are two (failed) attempts to symbolize this Whole."[4] The division marks different ways of relating to the enjoyment of the Other who lacks something (e.g., the mother, the object of desire, etc.). The subject can never determine what she is for the Other or what the Other wants of her; she can never fill the lack of the Other. Understood one way, gender identifications are attempts to take on recognizable, socially validated modes of being. Lacan's formulation of sexual difference maps gender in terms of different modes of *unconscious* enjoyment that derive from different relations to the phallus, the signifier that installs signification as such, the operator of castration and of the enjoyment that castration limits. The child designated as male must accept limits to the use of his penis; he is the son, not the father, and while both have penises, the son accepts that he cannot use his in the same way his father does, i.e., with the mother. (The father is the person who has designated himself as the father *by means of language,* rather than by the "natural" emergence of the child from the body of the mother; the father is the man who symbolically accepts that he is the father). The son's "reward" is accession to the phallus, the signifier rather than the fleshy little organ. Hence the logic of the male side of sexual difference is that of the universal and the exception. Subjects who take up the male position form a universal group whose every member is subject to the phallic function. The group logically posits an exception in the real Father, not submitted to the phallic function, the leader of Freud's primal

---

3   Slavoj Žižek, *The Metastases of Enjoyment: Six Essays on Women and Causality* (London: Verso, 2005), 160.
4   Ibid.

horde who monopolizes all the women, for example; or the psychotic father who wants to be the real thing rather than taking on the symbolic position of the father; or else the exception is fantasized as the Woman who can enjoy, instantiated in the fantasy of the transsexual.[5] "All men are submitted to the phallic function, except one."[6] Desire for both men and women is determined in relation to an absent object that is its goal, but the male exception holds out the hope that castration can be escaped and complete enjoyment possessed.

On the female side of sexual difference, the logic is that of the necessary and the possible. It goes like this: "There is no woman who is not subject to the phallic function," but "not all of woman is subject to the phallic function." There is no exception in the form of the Woman, who does not exist, even if she is supposed in fantasy. Women do not form a group, and each is particular, but – and this is the most crucial point – something about a woman is impossible and escapes castration in an enjoyment that cannot be located or described. Each woman finds her singular way of becoming a woman, i.e., of accessing her enjoyment, in the absence of an exception that would provoke a forbidden excess. Each is the sole witness to her enjoyment; distrust of women is the result of an absence of sure, perceptual signs of feminine enjoyment. This, at least, is how things are "seen" (and not seen) from the standpoint of the phallus. Commenting on Lacan's formulations, Joan Copjec argues that sexual difference "does not positively describe the subject. We could put it this way: *male and female, like being, are not predicates, which means that rather than increasing our knowledge of the subject, they qualify the mode of the failure of our knowledge.*"[7] Lacan's logic schematizes a meaningless Real but keeps calling for meaning, while challenges to norms that loosen gender designations and

---

5   See Catherine Millot, *Horsexe: Essay on Transsexuality,* trans. Kenneth Hylton (New York: Autonomedia, 1990).
6   See Lacan, *Seminar XX*, 73–89.
7   Joan Copjec, *Read My Desire* (Cambridge: MIT Press, 1994), 212. Copjec's reading of Lacan's formulation of sexual division, "Sex and the Euthanasia of Reason," 201–36, is unsurpassed. My emphasis.

performative roles[8] answer to imaginary differences. The division between men and women remains fundamental for many Lacanian psychoanalysts – Moustafa Safoun comments that "it's a boy" or "it's a girl" is the first response to a child's birth – but a biological difference is not simply natural for the psychoanalytic subject who speaks.[9] It is always already captured by signification long before the subject's entry into language.

Uncertainty about woman as the Other sex and about a woman's desire issues in that eminently patriarchal question, "What do women want?" This is a question underlying *The Shipman's Tale*: women want money, clothing, sex, and more, in an insatiable metonymy. The Wife of Bath's response in her tale to the question of woman's desire, that women want governance over men, is the mirror image of the patriarchal demand; it confirms the need for both patriarchal domination of women and the fear of their power that fuels that need. *The Shipman's Tale* is true to desire in conceding that desire never grasps what it seeks, and the Wife of Bath personifies the persistence of desire. In both cases, the Woman is the symptom of man in the sense that she is constructed to serve men's desire to speculate on what remains radically Other, in sex and love or in nature and the cosmos. An object of speculation in psychoanalysis as well, woman is nev-

---

8 The term is Judith Butler's, theorized in *Gender Trouble: Feminism and the Subversion of Identity* (New York: Routledge, 1990).

9 See Moustafa Safouan, *The Seminar of Moustafa Safoun*, eds. Anna Shane and Janet Thormann (New York: Other Press, 2002), 19. Safoun elaborates: "At this moment [of birth], when you must say 'this is a boy' or 'this is a girl' as an attribute, the only marker used in all societies is the penis. This is almost compulsory for a gestaltic reason. This organ stands out as the immediate landmark to mark the difference. Why is this organ used as a signifier? You can't say this is a male invention or position; it's how things go in the universe" (20). That castration functions in the symbolic register and is not a biological condition defining an absence in women is further indicated by Safouan's comment that a woman "has no direct relation to castration" (ibid.) and hence tends less to perversion, a structure dependent on an imaginary presence/absence dialectic. Safouan also notes that birth provides the unique occasion for the unavoidable use of the terms "boy" and "girl," not as a subject but as an attribute.

ertheless an autonomous and singular subjectivity for Lacan. Arguably, she is so for the Chaucerian text as well.

In offering its own explanation of the absence of relation between the sexes, the Merchant's performance and *The Merchant's Tale* foreground the function of the *symptom* to explain the absence of relation between the sexes. As well, it gives an account of sexual difference by presenting an origin myth. Rather than providing a meaningful resolution for sexual division, however, the tale demonstrates that, in historical time, humans act out and reproduce the way things always are: difficult. The myth of origin proposes an imaginary solution to a real division by positing, as an ontological principle, that marriage is discord, a discordance caused by women's deceptiveness, a version of the mystery of their enjoyment, their elsewhere-ness vis-à-vis the phallic function. The narrator thereby justifies his characteristic subjective stance and the symptomatic misogyny in the story he tells. Over and above his cynicism, however, the tale exposes misogyny as an attempt to account for sexual dissatisfaction, and for sexual dissatisfaction as an expression of the impasse of the heterosexual relation.

The Real of the Symptom

The Merchant introduces his self-presentation with a complaint, drawing on an experience of unhappiness in marriage intended to authorize the narrative that follows. But however sincere his suffering, it is articulated as a stereotype:

> "Wepying and waylyng, care and oother sorwe
> I knowe ynogh, on even and a-morwe,"
> Quod the Marchant, "and so doon other mo
> That wedded been
> ....
> I have a wyf, the worste that may be;
> For thogh the feend to hire ycoupled were,
> She wolde hym overmacche, I dar wel swere. (ll. 1213–16, 1218–20)

> Weeping and wailing, care and other sorrow
> I know well enough, in the evening and in the morning,
> Said the Merchant, and so do many others who are married
> ....
> I have a wife, the worst that can be;
> For even if the fiend were coupled to her,
> She would out-match him, I dare well swear.

"Wepying and waylyng," with trochaic emphasis, resembles an alliterative formula; the antithesis of "on even and a-morwe" is a literary chiasmus that produces a perpetual cycle of duration; hyperbolic comparison – the Merchant's wife is "the worste that may be," worse than "the feend" – serves self-pity and self-regard. The Merchant presents himself as a victim, in the form of the stock type of the henpecked husband, a timeless joke binding him to other men. The host picks up the baton, greeting the Merchant's tale as a corroboration of his own formulaic convictions about women's "sleightes and subtilitees" ("sleights of hand and subtleties," l. 2421), and as further support of a shared identity in a class of "us sely men" ("we ignorant men," l. 2423).

The Merchant claims an extensive knowledge based on a limited experience of two months: "I have ywedded bee / Thise monthes two" (ll. 1233–34), the stop on "two" further undercutting his exaggerated claim that no unmarried man "ne koude in no manere [in no way] / Tellen so muchel sorwe as I now heere / Koude tellen" (ll. 1237–38). Yet the stereotype is also reinforced by the implication that it might only take two months to experience the nightmare all married men experience. In contrast, the Miller is a more sophisticated version of the type, and his is a more reasonable solution to sexual difference. He will not allow himself to adopt a stance of innocence: "Yet nolde I (I would not), for the oxen in my plogh (plow), / Take upon me moore than ynogh" (*The Miller's Prologue,* ll. 3159–60), choosing ("nolde I") not to be a victim under the yoke of marriage. The Miller refuses outright the fantasy of godlike seeing also satirized in *The Merchant's Tale,* preferring to *believe* he is not a cuckold – "I wol bileve wel that I am noon" (*The Miller's Prologue,* l. 3162)

In contrast, the Merchant himself, so to speak, is a stereotype, as is affirmed by the overstatement of his suffering and the repetitions of his speech. His pose is traditionally funny. As a type character, he is stuck in an identification; the commonality of the identification is the basis for the type. In Alenka Zupančič's theory of comedy,[10] the stock character is fixed in an ego ideal and held together by a trait – in the Merchant's case, by his position as *innocent* long-suffering husband. His subjective position as an object and innocent victim of the Other's malice, allows him to parade his misery in order to get sympathy, which establishes his fellowship with other unhappy husbands. The symptom (here in the form of complaint) gives consistency to his subjective structure, his denial of a willed participation in a chosen mode of handling the absence of sexual relation. But the structure of denial is repeated and made legible in his narrative: the debate between Januarie's counselors, Justinus and Placibo, personifies the Merchant's split ego, his simultaneous knowledge of limitation and demand for excessive enjoyment; the story of Januarie and May is intended to demonstrate the husband's victimization by his wife, but also demonstrates the similarity of their desires and discontents.

The Merchant's subjective position is thus revealed to be more than an ego trait, with which one might simply identify, for it betrays his desire, his unconscious decision to be the object of the Other's malicious enjoyment. The Merchant's self-characterization as aggrieved husband articulates his way of enjoying. Talking about his suffering in marriage is his symptom and his "sinthome."[11] As a symptom, his suffering is what Lacan understands to be a signifier, a message written on the flesh that is sent by and to the Other. A formation of the unconscious, the symptom condenses a conflict between a desire for enjoyment and the prohibition of that desire, so that it "functions as a replacement for a repressed wish that cannot express itself directly," in the words of Dany Nobus.[12] Whatever consistency the symptom attempts to impart to the subject's ego, then, the symptom nec-

---

10 See Alenka Zupančič, *The Odd One In: On Comedy* (Cambridge: MIT Press, 2008).
11 See below for discussion of the "sinthome."
12 Dany Nobus, *Jacques Lacan and the Freudian Practice of Psychoanalysis* (London: Routledge, 2000), 72.

essarily also registers a loss, a split, the impossibility of perfect enjoyment. In the form of a signifying metaphor, the symptom is a product of the oedipal transition that installs the symbolic law of the Father; the symptom condenses a subject's memories and ciphers a history that has structured desire in a fantasy.[13]

The signifying symptom is also what Lacan alternatively considered as the real sinthome, an organization of enjoyment lacking meaning but giving consistency to the subject's being by knotting together the unconscious registers of the Real, Symbolic, and Imaginary. The Merchant's sinthome of pleasurable suffering, then, is his way of enjoying *and* "being" (in the form of being divided). The sinthome responds to the sexual division, to the asymmetry between men and women that is a consequence of different ways of relating to the phallus. It is, according to Patricia Gherovici, "what helps one tolerate the absence of the sexual relation .... There is a rapport, but the lack of the sexual relation is maintained."[14] The sinthome is not to be dissolved in interpretation but lived; Lacan's example is the writing that kept James Joyce sane, and the writing of Jean Genet has also been described as installing a secure identity for a subject whose symptom was to be a thief.[15] The Merchant's sinthome of enjoying and parading suffering as victimized object of the Other's enjoyment signals a pain that can never remit, an itch he cannot not scratch, and his tale's various articulations of marital woe indulge an attachment to the disharmony supporting

---

13 Chaucer's characters are fictions, of course, existing within the discourse that produces them; they have no history, other than what the fiction allows, so that the psychoanalytic practice of determining a past of childhood sexuality is irrelevant. However, Lacan's technique centers on the structure of the subject (hysteric, obsessive, pervert, psychotic, all diagnoses of unconscious structure), which emerges in present, synchronic time, and that structure becomes apparent in the speech of the subject. The language of the tales is inflected by the rhetorical tropes that are unconscious activity, in the case of the Merchant, by a pattern of denial and disavowal.

14 Patricia Gherovici, *Please Select Your Gender* (New York: Routledge, 2010), 154, 231.

15 See Pierre-Gilles Guéguen, "The Extraordinary Case of Jean Genet," *lacanian ink 34* (2009): 94–105.

his mode of enjoyment.[16] His is one particular compromise any subject may construct, while it is also a conventional one, characteristic of the *fabliau* genre, a common way to enjoy and to make sense of sexual division.

The Merchant's suffering is, then, a signifier, a message sent by the body to the Other that is language. It is, as well, an address to the imaginary; the unconscious Other is the source and also the destination of desire. Suffering in marriage addresses the Other who victimizes him. As a real sinthome, suffering is a means to make up for the absence of sexual relation; as well, it is the excess of the *jouissance* that is a fusion of pleasure and pain. Suffering articulates the subject's obdurate refusal to give up on the fantasy of complete satisfaction, of a limitless enjoyment escaping restriction. His self-presentation as a victim of marriage allows him to keep pursuing the possibility of excessive gratification. Suffering is itself the form of the gratification he seeks.

The Merchant's demand for enjoyment and the inevitable disappointment of complete fulfillment in marriage are exaggerated in the tale's consistent repetition of *blisse* and *blissful*. Appearing on thirteen occasions, frequently in conjunction with *parfit* [perfect] and *joye*, *blisse* signifies Januarie's excessively egocentric and deluded demand that marriage provide perfect enjoyment, the source also of the Merchant-narrator's disillusion. That Januarie is a surrogate or mirror of the narrator is indicated by the description of the misery he suffers in being struck blind: "He wepeth and he wayleth pitously" (l. 2072), repeating the Merchant's opening complaint. The narrator's obvious irony in declaring a wife to be man's "paradys terrestre" ("earthly paradise," l. 1332) accounts not only for disappointment but also for the simultaneous, obdurate wish for a perfect happiness, understood in Christian terms as the perfect happiness that preceded knowledge of one's own participation in one's fall. The irony,

---

16 In "Marriage and the Question of Allegory in the *Merchant's Tale*," *The Chaucer Review* 24, no. 2 (1989): 115–31, Richard Neuse argues that "he is preoccupied with his personal unhappiness and eager to find its cause" (116), and that the tale thematizes the reading of allegory in its investigation of Biblical and Church treatments of marriage and allegorical interpretations in particular.

like negation generally, both denies the expectation and, at the same time, maintains a wish for more than what is delivered, a doubleness that keeps desire alive but also fixed to an immobile position. The negation put in play by irony functions to ignore unconscious knowledge; for example, the statement "I won't claim that marriage is bliss" (an example of the rhetorical strategy of apophasis) maintains that marriage is bliss in the very act of denying it, as do the narrator's hyperbolic expressions. Disavowal is another unconscious strategy to get around the prohibition of excessive enjoyment. Disavowal is exemplified in the cynical attitude, "I know very well, but nevertheless," evident in the narrator's attitude, "I know very well marriage is imperfect, but I want it to be bliss." Disavowal, like irony, opens a gap between what is enunciated as the statement and the act of speaking; the symptom of suffering fills up that gap. Objectifying his symptom in the delusions attributed to his character, Januarie, the Merchant displays an unconscious knowledge of his symptom, but maintains expectation with "but nevertheless," and thus sneaks enjoyment back in. The structure replicates the gap in the Merchant's subjectivity along with the split consciousness producing the narration's cynical affect and effects. Both the Merchant's and his character's expectations of bliss and the narrator's technique of disavowal signal their position as men in sexual division.

The Merchant's Tale tries to demonstrate that happiness in marriage is impossible because women emasculate men. This conviction recurs in the *fabliau* narrative of May and Januarie, in the narrator's characterizing symptom (suffering), in the tone of the narration marked by disavowal, in the lengthy debate on marriage that rehearses disavowal by dramatizing the antithetical positions of the allegorical spokesmen, and, finally, in the concluding origin myth. Every element of the tale's construction indulges the narrator's suffering. The tale, however, marks the limitations of its narrative position by manifesting the reasons for its cynicism, unmasking it as a strategy of disavowal, the unconscious position that "I know very well, but nevertheless," that chooses not to know. The *Tale*'s conclusion rises above its tale's limits to acknowledge the real obstacles that resist and continue to generate interpretation.

Speaking the Synthome

The Merchant attempts to account for the sexual division with a *fabliau* that takes off from a generic plot and generic characters. The old, wealthy Januarie decides on marrying young May, the surnames enforcing the predicate of other Canterbury tales where mismatches lead to male jealousy, and jealousy to inevitable betrayal. Thus, following the marriage, May agrees to love Damyan, a young squire in the household, despite obstacles to their desire. Januarie loses his sight. May and Damyan connive to meet in a garden Januarie has built. With May using the blind Januarie's back to climb into a tree, and with Proserpyne and Pluto watching on, they begin to have sex in the tree. Januarie's sight returns suddenly, and he berates his wife, and Pluto promises that men will forever have the ability to see women's treachery, a promise that intends to address the enigma of woman's enjoyment. May provides an alibi, for Proserpyne announces that women will always be able to excuse themselves. The epiphany of the gods transforms the *fabliau* into a fairy tale that gives a comic account of the origin of sexual discord in a real division that seems always to have always existed.

The narrative, however, is constantly interrupted and the action delayed, first by an extended commentary on marriage, then a debate that precedes Januarie's choice of mate, and throughout with narrative intrusions in the form of exempla, rhetorical encomia and epic apostrophes, descriptive dilations, literary allusions and biblical references. The structure of the symptom is repeated in the rhetorical features that characterize the narration: the commentary and debate on marriage, split between an insistence on an illusion of full enjoyment and a refusal of illusion; a recourse to the diction of high style undercut by coarse, low statement; and a slippage between metaphoric and literal levels of speech. Setting off and juxtaposing antithetical features of language, the rhetoric thereby reproduces the compromises of disavowal maintained by the symptom.

The debate on the wisdom of Januarie's wish to marry is bound to be ineffectual, since it merely dramatizes a forced choice meant to confirm his demand. It is a staging to support his will, like King Lear's demand for love. Speaking as embodied adjectives, each allegorical spokesman stands for an exaggeration of one side of the unconscious split that refuses the knowledge it knows; the debate acts out the symptom as a compromise formation, a synthesized conflict between enjoyment and obstacle: Placebo arguing in support of excess without limit, Justinus for distrust of women and the inevitable disappointment of excessive enjoyment. Attempting to flatter and to please, Placebo confirms a fantasy of sexual satisfaction; Justinus cites experience and stereotypes to warn of the evils of wives, and he appeals to Christian precepts to urge moderation. Clearly Justinus's is the more reasonable position, backed by doctrine and experience, while Placebo duly confirms the fantasy by presenting what Januarie wants to hear. But the conclusion is also predetermined by the conviction that men are victims of marriage, and Justinus is the voice of what the narrator thinks he knows. Hence, the supposed realism of Justinus perpetuates the misogyny that is a corollary of the symptom: alluding to the Wife of Bath with the warning that a wife "may be youre purgatorie!" (l. 1670), in an echo of the Wife's "By God! In erthe I was his purgatorie" (*The Wife of Bath's Prologue,* l. 489), he ends by enlisting her authority on marriage as one who succinctly "declared ful wel in litel space" (spoke economically, l. 1687) to confirm his bias. As Chaucer makes of his fictional Wife an authentic precedent for influencing judgment, the reference pulls back from the immediate dramatic context to put the advocacy of Justinus in suspense by reminding us that Justinus too is a fiction, one angle on the real that denies the intransigence of desire and of the sexual divide that does not in fact conform to reasonable constraints.

The debate demonstrates that this husband and his councilors understand marriage to be an arrangement intended for the satisfaction of the husband. That understanding is replicated in the commentary of the narrator that reflects on Januarie's initial decision to wed. The narrator's voice conveys a pose of innocence, reflecting Januarie's indulgent, forced, naïve tone, and his commentary insistently disavows with a knowing irony what is simultaneously asserted. For example, the narration simultaneously debunks the traditional expectations it hyperbolically cites:

If he be povre , she helpeth hym to swynke;
She kepeth his good, and wasteth never a deel;
Al that hire housbonde lust, hire liketh weel;
She seith nat ones 'nay,' whan he seith 'ye.'
'Do this,' seith he; 'Al redy, sire,' seith she." (ll. 1342–46)

If he is poor, she helps him work;
She keeps his goods and wastes not at all;
All that her husband desires, she well likes;
She not once says nay when he says yes.
Do this, says he; All ready, sir, says she.

The parody mocks an inexperienced anticipation of perfect wifely congruity with the husband's will in an impersonation whose exaggeration would be emphasized in oral delivery. The performance draws on commonplace instruction to wives and adopts the biblical declaration that a wife is a helpmate and of one flesh with man, notions validating the narrator's claim that a "wyf is mannes helpe and his confort, ... O flessh they been" ("they be one flesh," ll. 1331, 1335). The ideal is manipulated to dramatize the self-regard and selfish indulgence that allows Januarie his fantasy of limitless enjoyment and reflects the point of view of the male victim of marriage, and the narrator's overall cynicism disavows the disappointed demand for enjoyment to which it simultaneously caters. Obsessive talking over the ideals of marital satisfaction in order to contradict those ideals defends the enjoyment of the sinthome.

Swerving between high and low speech, the tale's language balances contradictory stylistic elements. The courtship between Damyan and May adopts conventions of sophisticated courtly romance. Damyan languishes and "So brenneth that he dyeth for desyr, / For which he putte his lyf in aventure" ("So burns that he dies from desire, because of which he puts his life in jeopardy," ll. 1876–77), his literal fever caused by Venus's metaphorical "fyr" (l. 1875), and he lies sick until "fully in his lady grace he stood" (l. 2018). May shows "pitee" (l. 1979) and grants "hire grace" (l. 1992), acting as physic to the lovesickness, "for to doon him ese" ("to ease him," l. 1981). The narrator approves, adopting the Knight's delicate phrasing and graceful rhythmic flow, "Lo, pitee renneth soone in gentil herte!" (l. 1986). The noble style of romance, however, is undercut by imagery, detail, and salacious diction. The rejuvenated Damyan cultivates the noble honor of narcissistic self-improvement, "He kembeth hym, he preyneth hym and pyketh" ("he combs himself, he preens himself and adorns himself, l. 2011), but to Januarie he fawns like an animal, "As evere dide a dogge" (l. 2014). May reads Damyan's letter and throws it, torn to little pieces, "al to cloutes" (l. 1953), into the privy, like waste. The coupling of May and Damyan in the tree is descried by the narrator's direct, colloquially monosyllabic "and in he throng" ("thrusts," l. 2353), while Januarie, his sight suddenly enabled, bluntly insists "in it wente!" (l. 2376).

Such juxtaposition of high and low style characterizes the elaborately detailed description of the wedding celebration, which, adorned with classical decoration, is introduced by a bare, perfunctory rite: "Forth comth the preest ... And seyde his orisons, as is usage, / And croucheth hem, and bad God sholde hem blesse, / And made al siker ynogh with hoolynesse" ("Forth comes the priest ... and said his prayers as is customary, and makes the sign of the cross over them and bade that God should bless them, and made all secure enough in holiness," ll. 1703, 1706–8). The haste imitated in a rapid-fire rhythm concluding the list of prescriptive acts is checked off with "and." The wedding ends with the company, "this lusty route" ("lusty company," l. 1800), leaving with suggestive, enigmatic purposes: "Hoom to hir houses lustily they ryde, / Where as they doon hir thynges as hem leste" ("home to their houses lustily they ride, where they are used to doing their things as they please," ll. 1802–3). Januarie himself can't get rid of the guests fast enough, stating "I wolde that al this peple were ago [gone]" (l. 1764) and indirectly tries to hurry the party from the banquet, "To haste hem fro the mete in subtil wyse" (l. 1767). The social rituals are no sooner finished than "this hastif Januarie / Wolde go to bedde" ("this hasty January would go to bed," ll. 1805–6). Ceremony is cynically enlisted as a pretext to legitimatize a demand for sex.

The narrator is especially cagey about the level of diction he employs, compensating for vulgarity with a coy concern for decorum, and with a salacious, tricky strategy of denial that permits a participation in just the coarse sexuality the decorum prohibits. The report that May, in order to read a love letter, "feyned hire as that she moste gon / Ther as ye woot that every wight moot neede" ("she pretended that she must go there where as you know every creature must," ll. 1950–51) at once alludes to and skirts what it more concretely designates with "pryvee" ("privy," l. 1954). An excuse for bad taste, "Laydes, I preye yow that ye be nat wroth; / I kan nat glose, I am a rude man" ("Ladies, I pray that you be not angry; I can not gloss over, I am a rude man," ll. 2350–51), prepares for what the narrator thereupon states directly, "this Damyan / Gan pullen up the smok, and in he throng" ("this Damyan pulled up the smock and in he thrust," ll. 2352–53). The address directed to "Ladyes" makes the diction the more smutty, and shames any women who may be listening and are thereby exposed to and potentially embarrassed by what should not be heard. The "rude," unglossed stab at bare speech is deliberately denied, retracted by the equivocation that "Damyan his wyf had dressed / In swich manere it may nat been expressed, / But if I wolde speke uncurteisly" ("unless I speak discourteously," ll. 2361–63), so that what has in fact been just so indecorously spoken is emphasized as it is refused. Description of sex on the wedding night likewise is avoided with a similar appeal to taste, "But lest that precious folk be with me wroth, / How that he wroghte, I dar nat to you telle" ("lest fastidious folk be angry with me, how he wrought, I dare not tell you," ll. 1962–63): avoidance is an invitation to further, voyeuristic speculation on what is already exposed when the husband "preyde hire strepen hire al naked" ("urged her to strip herself naked," l. 1958). The technique of denying what is stated builds up an implication that there is something to hide and so adds to the enjoyment of participation in the forbidden.

Such salacious decorum is a repeated technique, as is a related swerving between high and low diction, the literalization of metaphor, as criticism has noted frequently. More than "dissemination" – that is, the detachment or unmooring of the signifier from the signified that Peter Travis has studied in his reading of the semantic range and suggestiveness of Chaucer's diction, including slippage between trope and concrete language in this tale – all of that pushes language to a limit, to a confusion between figurative and literal levels, between the metaphoric and the concrete. Travis emphasizes this preoccupation of medieval thinking: "An issue of primary importance is the *transgressive* relationship metaphor creates between signifier and signified, that is, between *verba* (words) and *res* (physical objects and mental concepts)."[17] Repeatedly, a simile or metaphor for desire is made concrete in a physical object functioning in the narrative. For example, as has been noted frequently, Januarie's hope that he can control a young wife, "Right as men may warm wex with handes plye [bend]" (l. 1430), stated as a simile, becomes concrete when May manufactures a key to the garden gate for her lover: "[i]n warm wax" (l. 2117), the key is "emprented" in material much as May has taken "swich impression" (l. 1978) of Damyan in her heart. And May is likewise "depe enprented" ("imprinted deeply," l. 2178) in Januarie's thought. Januarie convinces himself that old and "hoor" ("hoary," ll. 1461, 1464) as he is, he yet remains full of vitality, "as dooth a tree / That blosmeth er that fruyt ywoxen bee" (ll. 1461–62), his own limbs "as grene / As laurer" ("laurel," ll. 1465–66), like the "laurer always grene" (l. 2037) in his garden—similes all materialized in an ultimate twist in the conclusion when the lovers meet in a pear tree.

Most obvious, and also well noted by critics, is the sliding of the adage "For love is blynd alday [always], and may nat see" (l. 1598), actualized in Januarie's blindness and then reshaped as an analogy in the narrator's comment, "For as good as blynd deceyved be / As to be deceyved whan a man may se" (ll. 2109–10). When Januarie regains vision, blindness is a metaphor for faulty judgment in May's exculpatory rationalization of his sight of her copulation, "Ye han som glymsyng, and no parfit sighte" ("you have some glimpse, and no perfect sight, l. 2383), to imply that in this world we see through a mirror darkly. And that association draws on an early association of the image of the mirror with vanity when Januarie's imagination reflects on women, "inwith his thogt" (l. 1586), his fantasy like a reflective surface in his mind, "As whoso tooke a mirour, polisshed bryght, / And sette it in a commune market-place, / Thanne sholde he se ful many a figure pace / By his mirour" (ll. 1582–85). Here the mirror figures the

---

17   Peter Travis, *Disseminal Chaucer* (Notre Dame: University of Notre Dame Press, 2010), 176.

distortion desire inflicts on perspective as Januarie compulsively calls up what "passeth thurgh his herte nyght by nyght" (l. 1581) to compose a fantastic conglomeration of the ideal features he wants in a wife (ll. 1589–93). The mirror image also calls up the narrator's warning of the insubstantiality of transient good, which passes "as a shadwe upon a wal" (l. 1315), noted again in "worldly joye may nat alwey dure [always endure]" (l. 2055) when Januarie is struck blind. This imagery, moreover, figures the anxiety of a mercantile economy, also developed in *The Shipman's Tale*. The comparison of imagination's mirror to the display of "a commune market-place" suggests a concern for mercantile interests and, in particular, the market in women. The comparison culminates with the narrator's sardonic claim,

> A wyf is Goddes yifte verraily;
> Alle othere mannere yiftes hardily,
> As londes, rentes, pasture, or commune,
> Or moebles – alle been yiftes of Fortune ...
> A wyf wol laste, and in thyn hous endure,
> Wel lenger than thee list, paraventure. (ll. 1311–14, 1317–18)
>
> A wife is God's gift verily;
> All other manner of gifts certainly,
> Such as lands, rents, pasture or the commons,
> Or personal property – all are gifts of Fortune ...
> A wife will last, and in thy house endure,
> Well longer than you wish perhaps.

The list of passing, worldly "yiftes of Fortune" (l. 1314) is appropriate to the commercial preoccupations of this Merchant who, the *General Prologue* reports, is engaged obsessively with "Sownynge alwey th'encrees of his wynnyng" ("making known the increase in his profits," l. 275), although less appropriate for the patrician Januarie in Padua, a minor commercial center better known for its prestigious university. In the setting of *The Shipman's Tale*, the assertion that worldly goods "Passen as dooth a shadwe upon the wal" (l. 9) carries a more developed commercial anxiety; in the context of the Merchant's narrative about an aging husband, the admonition responds to a greater anxiety over mortality.

Slippage in the narration between literal and metaphoric levels of speech goes to the very nature of language, every signifier of which is a metaphor: a substitution for a concrete object, or a means to condense a thought process in an abstraction, or an approximation of what cannot be said, such as a feeling or an unconscious real, but always by means of the substitution of another signifier. As if in an effort to reach a Real of sex, the narrator's diction comes as close as it ever does to concrete literalism in describing the arborial copulation with the brutal recoil from decorum, "and in he throng" (l. 2353). But the "it," in Januarie's insistence, "in it wente!" (l. 2376), is a deictic pronoun, capable of pointing to anything; literal as "it" may seem, it is not. Much of the narrator's language cannot easily be classified as either literal or metaphoric. For example, the paradoxical character of the trope, that is, its being both literal and metaphoric, is best illustrated with the exquisite phrase "bely-naked" (l. 1326), signifying the newly created Adam: while seeming to state the thing itself, the bare fragility of corporal being, in concrete terms, "bely-naked" is actually a synecdoche, the belly substituting for the entire, exposed body. Unpacking metaphor to approximate the object and to arrive at bare, literal signification continually runs up against what cannot be spoken, an obstacle motivating the perpetual innovation of language. Language is metaphor, according to Lacan, the substitution of the word for a real that cannot be spoken;[18] in the words of Travis, "metaphor is the defining feature both of human kind and of the knowable world."[19] What seems "literal," then, in language, is perhaps more appropriately described as "unmarked" and context-dependent, easily capable of functioning in marked (noticeable) and metaphoric fashion in a different utterance.

---

18 Lacan's formula for metaphor is developed in "Agency of the Letter in the Unconscious," in *Écrits* (Paris: Éditions de Seuil, 1966), 166.
19 Travis, *Disseminal Chaucer,* 189. Travis gives a cogent summary of medieval and modern treatments of the "oddity of linguistic tropes" (171), focusing on metaphor's "denotive functions, truth-value, ontological character, and epistemic powers" (169–200).

Perhaps the nearest the approach to an absolutely concrete, zero-degree of language[20] that would literally correspond to truth by yoking signifier to reference and avoiding rhetorical structure is the series of signs May and Damyan use to communicate.[21] The lovers' letters and "privee signes" ("private signs," l. 2105) convey feelings and intentions, "what she mente" (l. 2105) and "his entente" (l. 2106). Similarly, May signals to direct Damyan in the garden. The body physically makes meaning – "On Damyan a signe made she" (l. 2150), "And with hir finger signes made she" (l. 2209), "And every signe that she koude make / Wel bet than Januarie, hir owne make" (ll. 2213–14); however, the make here, signifying "make" and "mate" – not really a rhyme but a repetition of a single word with differing significations – demonstrates that language will go on sliding no matter how hard we try to control what can and can't be seen and understood. All of the metonymic chains of key signifiers / images in the *Tale* are condensed and literalized in the final scene in the garden. May gives Damyan a key to open its gate and gestures with her hand to direct him to the pear tree. Kneeling on the back of the old, blind Januarie, she climbs into the branches to have sex with the young lover. Januarie regains his eyesight, while allowing himself to remain blind to her deception. Yet both husband and wife are subject to the gaze, unaware of the gods watching on as they act out the discords and illusions of the absence of the sexual relation, and literal "seeing" is also shown to guarantee nothing in the way of access to the Real.

The urge to approximate a zero-degree language, performed by the tendency of metaphor to approach the literal in the *Tale*'s narration and by the characters' efforts to communicate with gesture, is a desire to get at the Real, to so extend language to bring forth what is unspeakable or to bypass language altogether in

---

20 The term is adapted from Roland Barthes, *Writing Degree Zero*, trans. Annette Lavers and Colin Smith (New York: Hill and Wang, 1968), who develops an ideal of an opaque, written language that refers only to itself.

21 Elain Tuttle Hansen, *Chaucer and the Fictions of Gender* (Berkeley: University of California Press, 1992), discusses the lovers' gestures as a form of communication in her treatment of the tale (245–66).

order to access an imagined essence or original condition posited as preceding language.[22] Such an urge is also enacted in Lacan's notion of lalangue, described by Dylan Evans as "the ... chaotic substrate of polysemy out of which language is constructed."[23] The inscriptions of letters, sounds, morphemes, and semantic condensations of lalangue compose an enigmatic, unconscious real knowledge, with effects that "go well beyond anything the being who speaks is capable of enunciating."[24] Lalangue suffuses the body, with no meaning but the non-sense of enjoyment, but it lays out the template for unconscious meaning. The nonsense of lalangue demonstrates for Lacan "that language is not simply communication"[25] and that speech is permeated with a surplus of meaningless enjoyment that makes it an object of pleasure. Enjoyment likewise suffuses the symptom that uses the material body to signify and to structure unconscious knowledge.

Bringing in May

The various techniques composing the narrative and the several discourses that contribute to the narration invariably present marriage according to the demands of men. The Merchant narrator's cynical disillusion and the doctrine he calls upon leads to a misogyny that conveys a troubling, pervasive tone of snide, narratorial sarcasm. Medieval theology and exegetical interpretation contribute to a patriarchal discourse on sex and marriage to begin with, and their deployment by the narrator and his character betrays its bias; distortions in both the narrator's and Januarie's speech bring into relief what is in any case

---

22 Julia Kristeva redirects Lacanian theory of the imaginary and the mirror stage to develop a "semiotic" level of language, expressing drives, affects, and abjection, that precedes the symbolic law and would be closer to a maternal body and to the real. See especially Julia Kristeva, *Desire in Language: A Semiotic Approach to Literature and Art,* ed. Léon Roudiez, trans. Thomas Gora and Alice Jardine (New York: Columbia University Press, 1980).
23 Dylan Evans, *An Introductory Dictionary of Lacanian Psychoanalysis* (London: Routledge, 1996), 97.
24 Lacan, *Seminar XX,* 139.
25 Ibid.

latent in the discourse.[26] So too the outlines of the Woman who emerges from the discourse is an effect of the limits of the narratorial perspective, as Sheila Delany argues when referring to the Wife of Bath's question, "Who peynted the leon [lion], tel me who?" (*The Wife of Bath's Prologue*, l. 692).[27] The cumulative effect of *The Merchant's Tale* is to foreground the misogyny of patriarchal ideology, which, like any other ideology, seeks to repress its work. As Slavoj Žižek explains ideological discourse, "the figures of 'sexuality' it portrays as the threat to be controlled – such as the figure of the Woman, whose uncontrolled sexuality is a threat to the masculine order – are themselves phantasmical mystifications. Rather, what this discourse 'represses' is (among other things) its own contamination by what it tries to control—say, the way the sacrifice of sexuality sexualizes sacrifice itself" (as in ascetic practices that eroticize self-discipline and self-punishment), and "the manner in which the effort to control sexuality sexualizes this controlling activity itself" (the homosocial relation).[28] Responding to the biases of the ideology and to its consequent bitter misogyny, critical responses seem to be inflected by those same limitations. Elaine Tuttle Hansen summarizes the prevailing judgment of *The Merchant's Tale*,

26 Robert R. Edwards, "Narration and Doctrine in the *Merchant's Tale*," *Speculum* 66, no. 2 (1991): 342–67, examines the biblical, classical and medieval sources that contribute to the encomium and debate on marriage to show that the characterization of both the Merchant as narrator and Januarie's motives bend those sources to their own purposes to offer "a contested domain of values" questioning the pervasive cynicism. Roberts argues, "Though the Merchant's telling colors much of what we see, the sources he enlists remains something other than expressions of his intentions; the play of ideas set in motion offers perspectives that retain some measure of their own coherence." The result is that "elements of his storytelling suggest alternatives to his vision" (343). Edwards's investigation confirms the reading that the tale opens alternative perspectives showing the limitations of self-interested misogyny.
27 See Sheila Delany, *Medieval Literary Politics: Shapes of Ideology* (Manchester: Manchester University Press, 1990), 112–29.
28 Slavoj Žižek, *First as Tragedy, Then as Farce* (London: Verso, 2009), 102.

emphasizing the emotional inflections of its criticism: "most often it is noted for its darkness, its 'unrelieved acidity'; it is said to offer a 'perversion' of the courtly code." Especially she emphasizes the common condemnation of May, "deemed 'a completely unfeeling wife'," a condemnation that sees what happens to May in the tree" as "a 'culminating outrage,' [a] 'high and horrible fantasy'."[29] The longstanding consensus on May is itself blind to the workings of misogynistic ideology, from Tatlock's references to her "simpering blandness" as bride and to the marriage as her "filthy bargain," along with his summation that "so blooming a girl can be so unscrupulous,"[30] to Lee Patterson's comments on "her depravity" and "grossly duplicitous" speech.[31]

Characterization is vital to narrative, but because characters are founded on the imaginary, on the representation of figures that resemble actual human beings and on imaginary attachments based on audience identification with those figures, it necessarily invites investment in the fiction it constructs. *The Merchant's Tale,* however, works to break down identifications in its audience as well as in its characters. Techniques of characterization, point of view and focalization, and the effects of realism that create the illusion of verisimilitude are the grounds of narrative fiction, and while in *The Merchant's Tale* the cumulative result of these techniques is to undercut misogynistic ideology, they also inevitably encourage readers' unconscious identifications. But the tale ultimately blocks emotional identification; it works to dislodge its audiences' ego investments. The narrator indirectly appeals to the audience's judgment when the collocation "bitwixe ernest and game" ("between earnest and play," l. 1594), used in the context of Januarie deciding upon a mate, echoes the instruction of Chaucer's surrogate Geoffrey to treat comedy according to its spirit, "And eek [also] men shul nat maken ernest of game" (*The Miller's Prologue,* l. 3185). The

---

29 Hansen, *Chaucer and the Fictions of Gender,* 245–46.
30 J.S.P. Tatlock, "Chaucer's *Merchant's Tale,*" *Modern Philology* 33, no. 4 (May 1936): 370.
31 Lee Patterson, *Chaucer and the Subject of History* (Madison: University of Wisconsin Press, 1991), 337, 338.

Merchant's repetition points back to the start of the collection of tales, reminding us that this tale too is a fiction.

Precedents in the Canterbury *fabliaux* showing that the mismatch of old and young is socially inappropriate, that prohibition spurs transgression, that jealousy is ineffectual, that sex is a source of humor, and that stories about uncontained sex bring pleasure – these load the Merchant's *fabliau* with expectations. The marriage of Januarie to May is characterized by the *Tale*'s allegorical designations to stand for a generic type of mismatch, and Januarie is an especially egregious example of a lecherous, aging husband. Not only his unseemly physicality, but also his lack of judgment, excessive appetite, vanity, and exclusive selfishness provide motivation for the wife's infidelity. A fool invites gulling; Januarie is set up to be betrayed.[32] His loss of vision, however fittingly motivated and pitiful, presents him with an occasion for even greater selfish possessiveness, as affliction adds to "the fyr" (l. 2073) of avid jealousy already consuming him and augments a consuming passion: "So brente [burned] his herte that he wolde fayn / That … neither after his deeth, nor in his lyf, / Ne wolde [would not] he that she were love ne wyf, / But evere lyve as wydwe in clothes blake" (ll. 2075–76, 2077–79). Here his thoughts anticipate May's symbolic death, along with his own, to deny her any life of her own. Any sympathy for the deceived husband is further mitigated by the same foolishness that enables the union of the lovers, first when Januarie encourages May to visit Damyan pining away, lovesick, and then when he offers his back for May to climb up into the pear tree: his indulgence of her pretended taste for pears is not just an extension of his overwhelming self-indulgence but a sign of his heedless want of judgment, since her longing for "smale peres" (l. 2333) is a common metaphor for testicles, implicitly conveying a warning of what is about to occur.

The marriage is defined as entirely his choice. Januarie's expectations are entirely selfish; his lust is salacious and grotesque. He

---

32 Peggy Knapp, *Chaucer and the Social Contest* (New York: Routledge, 1990), emphasizes that Januarie's pretensions, "blind arrogance," "limited point of view" (110), and commanding power "cry out for some sort of 'trickster tricked' denouement" (109).

may call on the need for "leveful procreacioun / Of children" ("lawful procreation," ll. 1448–49) as a motive for marrying, and he is concerned that his patrimony be secured, preferring that "me were levere houndes had me eten" than that "myn heritage sholde falle / In straunge hand" ("I would rather that hounds had eaten me," 1438–40). The macabre, spiteful force of his avarice and fear fuels his jealousy and misogyny. The image of being consumed by dogs – similar to the imagery of dogs relating to sex and finance in *The Shipman's Tale* – conveys Januarie's anxiety to secure his heritage, that is, both his wealth and his paternity. He reveals the preoccupation of noble families to maintain control of wealth in marriage, rather than a submission to sanctioned, "leveful" procreation. As well, Januarie's age and suggested impotence make any begetting of an heir improbable.

May appears suddenly, following his decision, as an object of male dealings, of the counselors who "wroghten [arranged] so, by sly and wys tretee" ("sly and wise negotiation," l. 1692). In the marriage arrangements, she is an object of a passive grammar: "she, this mayden, which that Mayus highte, / As hastily as ever that she myghte / Shal wedded be" (1693–95). Introduced as only a name, without qualities, she lacks class identification. While May is endowed by the commercial transaction to be securely "feffed in his lond" ("endowed with," l. 1698), women in medieval urban Italy did not have much say in marriages that were arranged to serve family interests. May certainly gains by marrying the patrician Januarie, and she shows that she is acutely aware of her acquired status when she asserts, accurately, "I am a gentil womman and no wenche" (l. 2202). Aware of Damyan's lower status as a squire, she is indifferent to it and willing to give her love though "he namoore hadde than his sherte" (l. 1985). May manages to take advantage of the marriage market and follows her desire within the economy that situates her.

Nevertheless, May is also the locus of an autonomous point of view that produces a subjectivity effect; this perspective escapes the limits of the narrator's misogyny and thereby introduces an unlocated voice. Sex on the wedding night is anticipated by the husband's self-sided and gross warning during the celebrations, "Now wolde God ye myghte wel endure / Al my corage [ardor], it is so sharp and keene! / I am agast ye shul it nat susteene" (ll. 1758–60), repeated in bed by "Allas! I moot trespace / To yow, my spouse, and yow greetly offende / Er tyme come that I wil doun descende" (ll. 1828–30). It is for him completely a phallic triumph, distasteful and unpleasant: "He lulleth hire, he kisseth hire ful ofte; / With thikke brustles of his berd unsofte, / Lyk to the skyn of houndfyssh [dogfish], sharp as brere [briar]" (ll. 1825–28). The simile repeats Januarie's rejection of an old woman as an unsuitable mate: "Oold fissh and yong flessh wolde I have fayne. / Bet is ... a pyk than a pykerel, / And bet than old boef is the tendre veel" (ll. 1418–20). The woman is an object of appetite, for consumption. The detail of "brustles," the residue of shaving – "For he was shave al new in his manere" (l. 1826) – and his actions – "He rubbeth hire aboute hir tendre face" (l. 1827) – invoke May's sense of touch. "The slakke skyn aboute his nekke shaketh" (l. 1849) is focalized up close from her spatial location, and her hearing is evoked by "Whil that he sang, so chaunteth he and craketh" ("while he sang, he chanted and croaked," l. 1850). The narrator's speculation, "But God woot what that May thoughte in hir herte" (l. 1851), albeit a suggestively salacious intrusion into her privacy, also has the effect of attributing a private subjectivity to her. If only God knows what she thought, she must have her own thoughts. The scene is seen, finally, from May's perspective – "she hym saugh [saw] up sittynge in his sherte, / In his nyght-cappe, and with his nekke lene" (ll. 1852–53) – and is judged by May's impression: "She preyseth nat his pleyyng worth a bene" ("not worth a bean," l. 1854), nor is there anything here to impress a larger audience. That the whole is enabled by the medieval version of pharmaceutical performance enhancements – "He drynketh ypocras, clarree, and vernage / Of spices hoote t'encreessen his corage; / And many a letuarie hath he ful fyn" ("he drinks sweetened, spiced wines, and many a medical preparation," ll. 1807–9) – implies Januarie's impotence.

The scene of the wedding night, prolonged by consistently unpleasant detail, is the only hint given of May's subjectivity; her internal reality is otherwise inaccessible in the narration. (An analogue would be Emelye's prayer to Diana in *The Knight's Tale*, Chaucer's invention and another private moment, overheard by a god, clarifying the difference made by a woman's desire.) Like the other Canterbury *fabliau* wives, the Miller's Alison and the Shipman's wife, May suffers no consequence for adultery and is not punished for her desire. She is an object of men's desire, and she acts autonomously. In Elaine Tuttle Hansen's succinct words, she "has a subjectivity and a sexuality that is something more than a projection of male fantasy and can therefore never be fully known or controlled."[33] And it is precisely the autonomy of an unknown desire that provokes the husband's jealousy. Sequestered in a wealthy household, May is denied privacy. She is accompanied by "alle hir wommen" (l. 1933) when she visits Damyan's quarters and, presumably, wherever she goes without the guidance of her husband. The force of his surveillance only increases after he becomes blind: "He nolde suffre hire for to ryde or go, / But if that he had hond on hire alway" (ll. 2090–91) – adding another obstacle for Damyan, frustrated that Januarie "hadde an hand upon hire everemo" (l. 2103). May's resorting to the privy to read Damyan's letter further indicates the limits of her freedom. Sarah Stanbury points out, "That she reads Damian's letter and throws it down the privy points, however scatologically, to her annexation of mental or we might even say literary privacy as a territorial right," although she concedes that, "yet in the same passage it also defines her 'privetee' as the privy,"[34] less a judgment on May, it would seem, than on the conditions of her enclosure and lack of privacy. Moreover, should *The Miller's Tale* echo in our minds at this point, we might also be reminded of the dangers of trespassing on God's own privacy.

The concluding scene is set in Januarie's version of a garden of love, whose splendor surpasses the medieval romance para-

---

33 Hansen, *Chaucer and the Fictions of Gender,* 258. However, this characterization is introduced by the suggestion that it may "presuppose another disturbing possibility inherent in medieval misogyny." The point here is not that May confirms misogyny but that precisely through her ascribed subjectivity she escapes the status as unruly object; put otherwise, the tale's characterization of woman as the Other sex demonstrates that misogyny is an ultimately ineffective attempt to control what cannot be known by men.

34 Sarah Stanbury, "Women's Letters and Private Space in Chaucer," *Exemplaria* 6, no. 2 (Fall 1994): 283.

digm: "he that wroot the Romance of the Rose / Ne koude of it the beautee wel devyse" (ll. 2032–33). If the garden, furnished with its tree of sexual knowledge, is read allegorically, as critics frequently do, it suggests that Woman is the cause of the Fall, full of guile, the source of man's deception. References early in the narration to the creation in Eden, to a wife as man's "paradys terrestre" (l. 1332), and to the biblical ideal of married union – "O flesh they been, and o fleesh" (l. 1335) – as well as references to the "Song of Songs" (ll. 2138–42) in January's invitation to enter the garden: these all support the analogies to the sacred history embedded in the narrative. The *Tale*'s reprise of the Fall may even mimic the notion of the *felix culpa*, the "fortunate fall," with May performing as both Eve and Mary to requite the fault she introduced.[35] But if it does so, it does so in the *Tale's* customarily cynical fashion, and further, exposes its template's ideological underpinnings. If knowledge of sex and mortality is the fruit of the tree, it is the aging male who first introduces a lascivious sexuality in choosing his mate, not May as Eve. Nor did May cause her already self-deceived mate's fall into blindness. Further, redemption is merely the restoration of the fantasy that covers over the fault in the sexual relation.

May's unlikely excuse upon being seen fornicating in the tree – "Up peril of my soule, I shal nat lyen, / As me was taught, to heele with youre eyen, / Was no thing bet, to make yow to see, / Than struggle with a man upon a tree" ("Upon peril of my soul,

---

35 See D.W. Robertson, "The Doctrine of Charity in Medieval Literary Gardens: A Topical Approach through Symbolism and Allegory," *Speculum*, 26, no. 1 (January 1951): 44, which initiates this reading. Kenneth Bleeth, "The Image of Paradise in the *Merchant's Tale*," in *The Learned and the Lewed*, ed. Larry D. Benson (Cambridge: Harvard University Press, 1974), 45–60, studies the scene in the context of the tale's references to paradise to expose a "scriptural parody" (46) that does not map onto salvation history. His conclusion is that "In the larger world of Christian history, the love of a woman offers the possibility of redemption for fallen man; in the Merchant's parody of the world, the hero, believing only what he wants to believe, continues to live in his fool's paradise" (60). See also Lawrence Besserman, *Chaucer's Biblical Poetics* (Norman: University of Oklahoma Press, 1995) for the use of biblical references throughout the tale.

I shall not lie; it was taught to me that to heal your eyes, there was no way better to make you see, than to struggle with a man upon a tree," ll. 2371–74) – gives her credit for the divinely motivated contingency that restored Januarie's sight. The excuse condenses a striking array of signifiers: ministering courtly physic, "my medicyne" (l. 2380), she claims that she provides the cure of suffering, which is to say that she continues to deceive, suggesting as much by warning "Til that youre sighte ysatled [settled] be a while, / Ther may ful many a sighte yow bigile" (ll. 2405–6). The alibi for her action, that she was taught to struggle with a man in a tree, is outlandish, a less than heroic parody of Jacob wrestling with the angel. Along with May's courtly-medical language, this parody stages, in the *Tale's* cynical fashion, the intertext of the "inhuman partner," another means of evading the impossibility of the sexual relation, as does the evocation of the sign of Gemini, as V.A. Kolve has noted.[36] Moreover, her excuse is also an joke, one that January doesn't "get," and hence leads to a further occasion for May's and Damien's enjoyment insofar as it summons but excludes the old man who intrudes on their equally fantasmatic twinship.[37] January plays his part by failing to insist on what he saw, more than ready to indulge himself and to follow her opportunistic appeal to his bad judgment: "ye may wene [think] as yow lest [like]" (l. 2396). He chooses again to believe what serves him, that he is like "a man that waketh out of his sleep, / He may nat sodeynly wel taken keep [notice] /

---

36 V.A. Kolve, *Telling Images: Chaucer and the Imagery of Narrative II* (Stanford: Stanford University Press, 2009), 123–70, who traces the image of copulation in a tree to illustrations in calendars showing Caster and Pollux, the twins who rule the sign of the Gemini under which the scene takes place, as they wrestle or caress, between or among trees. On the "inhuman partner," see Jacques Lacan, "Courtly Love as Anamorphosis," in *The Seminar of Jacques Lacan, Book VII: The Ethics of Psychoanalysis, 1959–1960,* ed. Jacques-Alain Miller, trans. Dennis Porter (New York: W.W. Norton, 1992), 139–54, and L.O. Aranye Fradenburg, "Introduction: Sacrifice in Theory," in *Sacrifice Your Love: Psychoanalysis, Historicism, Chaucer* (Minneapolis: University of Minnesota Press, 2002), 1–41.

37 See Sigmund Freud, *Jokes and Their Relation to the Unconscious* (1905), ed. and trans. James Strachey (New York: W.W. Norton, 1960), 197–223.

Upon a thyyng, ne seen it parfitly" (ll. 2397–99). They exit with a variation on his nuptial advances: "He kisseth hire, and clippeth [embraces] hire ful ofte / And on hire wombe he stroketh hire ful softe" (ll. 2413–14), which is an echo of "He lulleth hire, he kisseth hire ful ofte" (l. 1823). The repetition indicates that nothing has been learned since that time, despite even divine intervention. If stroking his wife's belly may imply that she is pregnant, or that he wishes she were, his gestures also suggest further lust and further enclosing control. Januarie remains in metaphorical blindness, and the absence of sexual relation remains as it is, which is just what the gods are called in to explain.

The Last Laugh

The unlikely, surprising appearance of Pluto and Proserpina arguing in a tree provides a conclusion to the narrative action. Their intervention introduces a punctuation that blocks the tale's ideological work, its cynical treatment of marriage and of women. If the gods' epiphany is a sudden and unexpected intrusion, it has been prepared for by prior narratorial references to pagan gods presiding over the wedding feast and to the description of these very fairies playing in the garden. But the epiphany, literally a showing of the presence of the fairy king and queen, has the force of a revelation because the gods come to life here when they speak. Their speech is a transcendent performative, the fiat that in the fiction of the narrative time establishes for one spring afternoon in medieval Padua the ahistorical, sexual non-relation once and for all time.

The logic of that same fiction is, nevertheless, contained again in the time it is supposed to institute, for the gods' own behavior and their knowledge of history show that the sexual divide has long preceded their inaugural act. As in any origin myth – like the story of the Fall, for example – their act is supposed to inaugurate what is the case anyway; the myth is introduced by the Merchant retroactively to provide a cause, a reason for what he would like to believe is an ahistorical necessity. The gods act as representatives of sexual difference, the lack of relation that persists across time, but they enter into history under the particular, contingent arrangements that are the tale's setting. The inadequacy of the explanation, the myth's incapacity to posit a timeless origin in a historical moment for what has no origin, turns back on the Merchant narrator's humorless cynicism and misogyny. In the concluding section, the voice of the Merchant narrator is subsumed by another agency, an anonymous subjectivity that critiques the teller's limited perspective by containing it within a greater insight into time and space.

The gods' interruption perpetuates the sexual divide and reconfirms the absence of sexual rapport that has already always been happening, to them and to humans as well. The gods are introduced by the narrator as an unknown cause: May and Januarie have no access to them, and they are seen and heard only by the tale's audience. The gods are supposed to give an explanation for an unchanging condition. But what they enact is the unconscious sexual divide as a kind of fatality, determining the rules governing desire. The revelation of an inveterate, obdurate obstacle to enjoyment makes known what we already know about what cannot be changed but may at least be mediated. The gods' mutual acceptance of division and disharmony models a way of gaining access, not to full and perfect jouissance, but to such enjoyments as an acceptance of limits permits. The tale then ends with the assurance established by the gods' recognition and acceptance of unconscious truth: this is their means of handling what cannot be changed, their form of *savoir-faire*. The gods show only that the supposed origin is a repetition, or a retroactive positing, of what always continues to happen – which is, in any case, one definition of an unconscious that is posited by ideology to be what is "natural."

The statements of each god support the position of enunciation each is subject to within the narrator's misogynistic ideology. Squabbling like human spouses in support of their differing interests, the divinities are personified projections of the impulses of thought, the condensed mental work that springs into the language of the man and woman each inspires. Pluto's determination to cure the mortal man – "Now wol I graunten, of my magestee, / Unto this olde, blynde, worthy knyght" (ll. 2258–59) – performs the insight that determines the precedent for all male knowledge of women's future perfidy by allowing that, "Thanne shal he knowen al hire harlotrye [wickedness], / Bothe in repreve [reproof] of hire and othere mo [more]" (ll. 2262–63). Pluto's masculinist bias is obvious, and his elevation of Januarie as an "honorable" (l. 2254) and "worthy" (l. 2259) knight frees the husband from responsibility and is thoroughly discordant with Januarie's character. Proserpina's protection establishes May as the model for women's independence:

> Now by my moodres sires soul I swere
> That I shal yeven hire suffisant answere,
> And alle wommen after, for hir sake,
> That, though they be in any gilt ytake,
> With face boold they shulle hemself excuse,
> And bere hem doun that wolden hem accuse. (ll. 2265–70)

> Now by my mother's sire's soul I swear
> That I shall give her sufficient answer,
> And to all women after, for her sake,
> That, though they be taken in their guilt,
> With bold face they shall excuse themselves
> And bear them down that would accuse them.

Prosperina ensures women's power to brazenly nag, lie, pretend, and dominate, to boldly face it, "visage it hardily / And wepe, and swere, and chyde subtilly" (ll. 2273–74). On the one hand, the gods confirm misogyny, and their intervention corresponds to the narrator's will to fall back on an omnipotent Other that knows in order to justify his cynicism. On the other hand, the narrator introduces the couple with a reminder of old Pluto's rape of the young Proserpina and of his imprisonment of her in the underworld.

Their history demonstrates that violence against women founds the misogyny that supports patriarchal power. Prosperina speaks from within the conditions of that history, and she is further contained by her recital of an original patriarchal genealogy in her appeal to the soul of Cronos, the father of her mother, Demeter, which established the beginning of time as timeless. At the same time, as Laura Kendrick points out, Prosperina undoes enclosure and control, for she "regularly reverses the patriarchal order of things, ... bringing spring with each of her rebellions against his constraint"; in Kendrick's reading, "the tale inverts the paternalistic hierarchy of both earth and heaven."[38] Prosperina, in her history and her action in the narrative, demonstrates that the supposed institution of men's knowledge of women's perfidy as well as women's concomitant deception are consequences of just the ideology that already produces these gods. This is to say that by calling up the violent precedents supporting patriarchal power, the tale "unrepresses" the sources of the power of the ideological system supporting male dominance whose workings it dramatizes. What remains, once the ideology is shown to be merely an ideology, is the real sexual division the ideology doesn't succeed in explaining.

The Greek divinities open up an infinite regress, from the historical present, to biblical time, to the eternity the Greeks invented for their gods. They inhabit a history purportedly timeless, and they can range through tradition; they have apparently read scripture, with Pluto citing "Jhesus, *filius Syrak*" (l. 2250), reputed author of "Ecclesiastes," and Proserpina appealing to Solomon, each to support a side in the division they are supposed to inaugurate. The gods don't cause or really give a reason for anything, for they merely repeat in their own conflict the lack of harmony between the sexes throughout the history they are supposed to be initiating. In this sense, the story of origins they present differs from other origin myths: their improbable timeliness functions as an admission that their story cannot serve as an origin, that their myth cannot achieve the purpose it is supposed to serve. The tale thereby critiques the ideology the narrator sponsors.

The tale's solution to the problem at its source – that is, the "woe in marriage" the gods are enlisted to explain – shows itself unable to account for the real of sexual division. It describes the division, but the misogyny supposed to explain it is demonstrated to be a rationalization supported by power. The meaning the gods ostensibly institute is that there is no meaning to the condition of sexual division. How that condition is handled is not inevitable, however. The climactic epiphany brings about

---

38 Laura Kendrick, *Chaucerian Play: Comedy and Control in the Canterbury Tales* (Berkeley: University of California Press, 1988), 116.

the "happy" ending of a compromise between the mortals. May and Januarie end in an agreement not to know, he to remain in the blindness of being "in love," she to follow her desire. The gods, more able to address knowledge and power, come to a reconciliation: he to surrender to the inevitable, to "yeve [give] it up" (l. 3212), she proposing, "Lat us namoore wordes hereof make" (l. 2318), each accepting the desire of the other and living on in peace. They enact a means of dealing with the absence of rapport without explaining it, accepting it with a graceful adjustment.

Admitting to the inevitability of sexual division, the gods also present themselves as establishing the origin of the *fabliau* within the *fabliau* in which they participate, or at least of the conventional *fabliau* of sexual gratification and irrepressible desire the Merchant delivers. The ending extends beyond the limitations of the narrator's consciousness. The tale thereby reflectively achieves a self-consciousness of its literary genre, solidifying its other intratextual references to Chaucer's work. The reflexive gesture also situates this tale as one example within the medieval *querelles des femmes* and alludes coyly to Chaucer's participation in that tradition in *The Legend of Good Women,* with Proserpina's argument that she can cite plenty of good women, "ful trewe, ful goode, and virtuous" (l. 2281), as did Chaucer. It follows that the tale is one more treatment of the sexual nonrelation that keeps generating tales, one more attempt to explain it with a literary fiction.

The gods' active presence introjects a widened space and an illogical break in time into the narrative's contemporary setting and into the logic of chronology to open up a perspective on the history it recontains. They introduce the literal dimension of cosmic extension into the garden and the transcendence of time into history. The breakdown of temporal and spatial logic produces a kind of anamorphic effect, uncovering the tale's blind spots and displaying what the narration has blocked out. The tale would not be comic if the audience believed the narrator or took the fairy tale seriously, but the limitations of the Merchant's authority and of the gods are apparent, and their authority undermined by the larger perspective of the tale's acceptance of sexual discord and asymmetry. As Robert R. Edwards argues, "Chaucer's artistry opens what the Merchant tries to close and preserves the possibilities of meaning that he intends to reduce or eliminate."[39] The effect of a widened perspective is exhilarating. The epiphany is evidence of resources and potential perspectives beyond the limits of any given reality.

The gods intrude as the representatives of unconscious knowledge. They remind us that sexual division and the absence of sexual relation amount to a timeless condition, or at least an irreducible limitation. The narrator blames Woman for what in any case cannot be changed in order to maintain his symptomatic enjoyment; making it her fault makes up for the lack constitutive of subjectivity. The joke would not work if that reasoning did not collapse before the simultaneous eruption of unconscious knowledge, punctuated by the tale's acceptance of contradiction and limitation when imaginary identities, meanings, and relations collapse. Such a perspective is an ethical response to a lack of ultimate knowledge and enjoyment, the temporal absence of what Chaucer and his culture imagined as the fulfillment of true pleasure and knowledge in "the blisse ther Christ eterne on lyve ys" (l. 1652).

---

[39] Edwards, "Narration and Doctrine in the *Merchant's Tale*," 351.

CHAPTER 2

The Magician, the Squire, the Knight, and His Wife: *The Franklin's Tale*

Initially, *The Franklin's Tale* presents a smooth surface, an image of harmony between the sexes in marriage and of mutual support and honorable dealing between men. Black rocks are made to disappear; the obstacles to satisfaction and pleasure that emerge in its elegant plot, contradictions inherent in the agreements that anchor that plot, fissures to collective wellbeing dependent on the social system it pictures – indeed all threats to the tale's graceful performance disappear by the end. The narration apparently shows that rapport between the sexes is possible, that women need and support male domination, that masculine identification can be assured within the collective good, and that social tension can be resolved. The harmony is only apparent, however: beyond its surface, what the tale demonstrates is the ideological construction of social harmony and the enduring power of the Real.[1]

---

1   Stuart Hall studies ideology through discursive representations in "The Problem of Ideology: Marxism without Guarantees," in *Critical Dialogues in Cultural Studies,* eds. David Morley and Kuan-Hsing Chen (London: Routledge, 1996), 25–46: "By ideology I mean the mental frameworks – the languages, the concepts, categories, imagery of thought, and the systems of representation which different classes and social groups deploy in order to make sense of, define, figure

The narrative is based on the operation of separate but interlocking forms of exchange: exchanges of promises, of money, and of a woman. These separate exchange systems compose the narrative function within the symbolic register, that aspect of the unconscious that forms the human subject within social relations. The structures that name, place, and construct the individual subject – the ego and ego ideal, kinship, geographical maps, the relation to the object of desire – are formed in a dialectic with the symbolic O/ther (Ø), so that subjectivity is always located within language and the signifiers of specific structures of exchange. The systems of exchange remain unconscious for the subjects who participate in them, as they do for the Franklin's characters. Likewise, they remain unaware of underlying unresolved social and historical contradictions and conflicts; characters respond to social incoherence and tensions as if they were individual problems, issues troubling private, separate agents. As well, latent social conflicts are effectively concealed in the Franklin's construction of an ideal image of social inclusion that validates the interests of his own emergent class. And Brittany's status as a colony of refugees fleeing the Anglo-Saxon invasions of Britain is almost completely occluded, however well-known to the cultures that produced the genre to which *The Franklin's Tale* belongs, the *lai*.

The idealization the tale achieves is due in the first place to its generic provenances. It is a courtly romance, if a troubled one. The enlistment of the ancient romance form contributes to the teller's efforts to present ideology as sempiternal, as what has been transmitted from the past. It is presented as a narration transmitting a short Breton narrative, the work of an unnamed origin, one of "[t]hise olde gentel [noble] Britouns" (l. 709)[2] the

---

out and render intelligible the way society works" (26). The study of ideology has to do with "the concepts and languages of practical thought which stabilize a particular form of power and domination" so that ideas "become a 'material force'" and consequently through those "categories and discourses we 'live out' and 'experience' our objective positioning in social relations" (27). For Lacan, the Real is what escapes signification and hence representation.

2 All quotations from Chaucer are from Larry D. Benson, ed., *The*

Franklin says he remembers; like a dream, it transforms material from memory to represent the narrator and his interests. Breton lays, like romances generally, traditionally told of the marvelous and the supernatural, although *in The Franklin's Tale* the marvel is cut down to size: an illusion produced by a magician, perhaps by his use of rational procedures, so that if the illusion is accomplished, it is accompanied by a nagging worry about its authenticity. This is perhaps a comment on the type's general reliance on the marvelous.

The remote and archaic source in noble ancestors offers the melancholic patina of a lost past and place while lending security, or perhaps fatality, to the narrative progress, because the tale is supposed to be a repetition of what has already been. Perhaps it would be better to say that it is supposed to repeat what has already been repeated in past tellings, since the history of Brittany is in part a history of leaving Britain. The impression of inevitability, stemming from the tale's ascription to an ancient source, has ideological force. The tensions disturbing the plot – within the oxymoronic courtly marriage, about the nature and power of magic, arising from the intrusion of money and social fluidity into its idealized aristocratic setting – undercut the idealization of its proposed origin, like unconscious currents surfacing, and they are soothed and relieved by the efforts of the narration. The tale seeks to contain conflict and to preserve social stability. Still, those who have heard or read the tale are not likely to forget those rocks, which also had to be negotiated by every refugee arriving from Great Britain to the shores of Little Britain, just as no amount of ideological sleight-of-hand can do away with the Real entirely.

The narrative action works a little like the old Bissell commercial: "Life's messy. Clean it up." A series of reciprocal verbal acts motivate it, each involving an agreement and a promise, a commitment to a return and so a debt, and therefore invoking future consequence. The discourse of courtly love idealizes the exchange of women, the master signifier *trouthe* validates promising, and the financial transaction is obscured by inexact and vague expressions. A knight and his lady, Arveragus and Dorigen, agree to a

Riverside Chaucer, 3rd edn. (Boston: Houghton Mifflin, 1987).

marriage allowing each to act with equality and to maintain status. The marriage is an agreement between subjects performing as independent agents. After Arveragus departs to return to old Britain to "seke in armes worship and honour" (l. 811), Dorigen is wooed by a squire, Aurelius, who eventually obtains Dorigen's promise of love on the impossible condition that he remove from the coastline the rocks that would endanger her husband's return. This is the old trope of impossibility ("tell her to find me an acre of land / between salt water and the sea strand") in European courtship literature, refigured here as disenchanting and disenchanted exchange of service for access to the woman's body: Aurelius finds a magician who contracts to make the rocks appear to disappear, for a fee. Riddle-solving is replaced by different kinds of "cunning" that cannot finally rise to the occasion. Each promise incurs an obligation of repayment, and each commitment is not fully met, proof that each was flawed from the start. However canny or skilled the participants in this exchange, they cannot subject the Real to their wishes; as Lacan reminds us, business, "the goods," only "screen" the Real, and at some distance of mediation.[3] Transitions from one form of exchange to the next are accomplished as an agent from one participates in the next, leaving the magician in the end to cover over inherent problems. The plot design follows an elegant logic that only serves to make overreaching more obvious.

The narrative structure supports the ideological purposes of the narration: to cover up the inevitable conflicts of interests that interfere with social stability. Especially, it contributes to the preservation of the fiction of accord in the institution of marriage. Each of the agents in the tale works to cover over, or heal, or compensate for the absence of sexual rapport the institution is supposed to avoid. The subordination of woman to male power, the dependence of masculine honor on female chastity, the primacy of social relationships between men – these effectively perpetuate the refusal to acknowledge the instabilities of marriage. Superficially, at least, the absence of sexual relation is thereby

---

3 Jacques Lacan, *The Seminar of Jacques Lacan, Book VII: The Ethics of Psychoanalysis, 1959–1960,* ed. Jacques-Alain Miller, trans. Dennis Porter (New York: W.W. Norton, 1997), 33–34.

avoided. But the problems impinging on the tale's social relations remain unresolved. Critical readings of the tale, notably those of Alan T. Gaylord, Susan Crane, and Cara Hersh[4] have recently focused on the ways commercial interests enter into its archaic, feudal setting, without emphasizing the potential tensions they introduce or the tale's efforts to subdue those potentials. In contrast, I want to show how the narrator works to construct a new ideology of marriage, "screening" (showing *and* hiding) the unconscious sources of the conflicts and incoherencies the Franklin represses; under the master signifier *trouthe* (truth, troth, fidelity), tensions and competition are resolved, marriage is preserved, and men maintain a social fiction that subdues potentially destabilizing forces, but loss is never fully adequate.

The Appropriation of Courtly Love

In his studies of the elemental structures of early societies, Claude Lévi-Strauss postulated, "Although they belong to another order of reality, kinship phenomena are of the same type as linguistic phenomena."[5] Social groups and languages are regulated and function systematically; anthropology, like linguistics, "does not treat terms as independent entities," but rather analyzes "relations between terms" within "the concept of system" with the goal of arriving at general laws "to discover an unconscious

---

4 Alan T. Gaylord, "From Dorigen to the Vavasour: Reading Backwards," in *The Olde Daunce: Love, Friendship, Sex and Marriage in the Medieval World,* eds. Robert R. Edwards and Stephen Spector (Albany: State University of New York Press, 1991), 177–200; Susan Crane, "The Franklin as Dorigen," *The Chaucer Review* 24, no. 3 (1990): 236–52; and Cara Hersh, "'Knowledge of the Files': Subverting Bureaucratic Legibility in the *Franklin's Tale,*" *The Chaucer Review* 43, no. 4 (2009): 428–51.

5 Claude Lévi-Strauss, *Structural Anthropology,* trans. Claire Jacobson and Brooke Grundfest Schoepf (Garden City: Doubleday, 1967), 32. Anthropologists following Lévi-Strauss analyze communities as texts. See, for example, Clifford Geertz, "Deep Play: Notes on the Balinese Cockfight," in *The Interpretation of Cultures* (New York: Basic Books, 1973), 412–53.

infrastructure."[6] The axiom orienting Lacan's theory of psychoanalysis, "the unconscious is structured like a language," also orients Lévi-Strauss in his approach to "infrastructure" in structural anthropology. As with language systems, social relations and practices, like cooking, myths, and arrangements of residential space, are governed by rules combining single units defined by difference, laws that remain largely unknown to participants who nevertheless carry out, transmit, and are positioned by them within a social field. The knowledge of social structure thereby operates independently of the consciousness of social agents, as an unconscious knowledge functions, unknown to the subject. For both Lacan and Lévi-Strauss, structure is a set of rules with no content, like the individual unconscious that is operated by the common laws of a grammar to be filled with contingent signifiers. As Dany Nubus and Malcom Quinn argue, the symbolic "constitutes the very fabric of the human mind, without this mind being fully aware of its exact remit and its precise ramifications. It provides the rational building blocks of human experience, pervading the subject's knowledge and actions, and situating him in relation to others."[7]

The regulation of marriage and kinship relations constitutes "a kind of language" allowing communication "between individuals and groups." The "mediating factor" in this exchange is "the women of the group, who are circulated between clans, lineages, or families, in place of the words of the groups, which are circulated between individuals."[8] Women are the mediating factor that allows the substitution of "the mechanism of a sociologically determined affinity for that of a biologically determined consanguinity."[9] Culture for Lévi-Strauss is the displacement of nature, and for Lacan biological being, "the organism," is recast as "the body" in the human subject constituted by language. Lacan refers to the structural model when discussing the function of woman in courtly love literature: "She is strictly speak-

6 Ibid., 31.
7 Dany Nobus and Malcolm Quinn, *Knowing Nothing, Staying Stupid* (London: Routledge, 2005), 53.
8 Lévi-Strauss, *Structural Anthropology*, 60.
9 Ibid., 59.

ing, what is indicated by the elementary structures of kinship, i.e., nothing more than a correlative of the functions of social exchange, the support of a certain number of goods and symbols of power."[10] However, Lacan's description applies more readily to the realities of aristocratic marriage than it does to most medieval courtly love literature, which is typically not a "marriage plot," a plot aimed at marital repurposing of the absence of the sexual relation, but rather a plot that values freedom in love outside the social link. Moreover, as Lévi-Strauss acknowledges, but Lacan in this instance does not, women, unlike goods and symbols, speak: "For words do not speak, while women do; as producers of signs, women can never be reduced to the status of symbols or tokens."[11] Is Lacan's image of the courtly lady as an "inhuman partner" spewing out arbitrary demands a critique of the notion that anything spoken by a woman *character* in courtly love discourse might have some connection with things women might have said in non-literary life, like "show me those accounts," or "I want to be a *femme seule*," or "gather the warriors – I see our neighbors are riding here to take advantage of my husband's absence," or "roll that brewing vat over to me, you good-for-nothing bastard!" Or does Lacan's image underscore the absence of the sexual relation, in the sense that a woman's desires are never intelligible to men in the patriarchal social link? Either way, a good deal of trouble in *The Franklin's Tale* arises from the complicating factor of women's ability to exchange words and not simply be exchanged, since women, while functioning as a value in marriage, have value in themselves because they talk – and the Franklin's Dorigen does talk, talks too much to her suitor and so jeopardizes her marriage, vilifies the rocks at length – everything is their fault – and talks to her own self in

10 Jacques Lacan, *The Seminar of Jacques Lacan, Book VII: The Ethics of Psychoanalysis,* ed. Jacques-Alain Miller, trans. Dennis Porter (New York: Norton, 1992), 147. For a critique of the patriarchal bias of the model of kinship developed in structural anthropology, see Gayle Rubin, "The Traffic of Women: Notes on the 'Political Economy' of Sex" in *Toward an Anthropology of Women,* ed. Rayna R. Reiter (New York: Monthly Review, 1975), 157–210.
11 Lévi-Strauss, *Structural Anthropology,* 60.

order to avoid responsibility for her impetuousness and so save her marriage. Her fondness for signifying, I suggest, is a sign of change, of modified expectations about power dynamics within marriage. While no system makes use of every unit available to it, during transitional periods in complex societies marriage exchange may admit new units of circulation or transform existing patterns, so that it is modified diachronically in time. A man's "gentleness" – The notion that a man "ought" to treat his gentle, noble wife gently, nobly, and/or as an equal, or should "serve" her (in the courtly sense) as she does him, is one such (in this case) hypereconomic unit, linked to the late medieval repurposing of courtly love *for* the marriage plot. How to combine these? Only the magic of gift, magnanimity, versus commerce, can do it; but the extended temporality of the gift, however effective in concealing crass exchange, also has the potential to throw everything into confusion; almost anything can happen.

Courtly love, as discussed by L.O. Aranye Fradenburg in *Sacrifice Your Love: Chaucer, Psychoanalysis, Historicism,* is defined by Lacan as "a highly refined way of making up for ... the absence of the sexual relationship, by feigning that we are the ones who erect an obstacle" to it.[12] Courtly love pretends that the sexual relation's failures are not inevitable; we're just messing it up by asking the wrong questions or being too clumsy or balking at crossing sword-bridges. The dissatisfactions and limitations of desire in the social link are further idealized to become the very goal of love: "the point of departure of courtly love is its quality as a scholastics of unhappy love."[13] Courtly love is narcissistically focused on an inaccessible woman whose very inaccessibility furthers male self-awareness. It must be kept secret. The woman imposes tests on the man who serves her and her will, although she ultimately serves his will by accepting his love. The lover's

---

12 Jacques Lacan, *The Seminar of Jacques Lacan, Book XX: On Feminine Sexuality, the Limits of Love and Knowledge, Encore 1972–1973,* ed. Jacques-Alain Milller, trans. Bruce Fink (New York: Norton, 1998), 69, and L.O. Aranye Fradenburg, *Sacrifice Your Love: Chaucer, Psychoanalysis, Historicism* (Minneapolis: University of Minnesota Press, 2001), passim.

13 Lacan, *Seminar VII,* 146.

lengthy courtship, his endurance of prolonged frustration, and his subordination make her the occasion for a *jouissance,* or perhaps more properly a remainder thereof, wrung out of the absence of the sexual relation. It is this downstream enjoyment that is the goal of courtly love, "the pleasure of desiring or, more precisely, the pleasure of experiencing unpleasure."[14]

The Franklin's Tale puts the conventions of courtly love to work in the setting of upper- class marriage. The tale is framed as a courtly romance, a triangle of noble knight, lady, and rival lover, and superficially it follows the conventional assumption that only aristocratic persons can love properly. The knight's courtship is a service – Arveragus engages to "serve a lady" (l. 730) – of exalted martial effort, of "many a labour, many a greet emprise" (a great, chivalric enterprise, l. 732). The woman is of high status and superlatively lovely: "For she was oon the fairest under soone, / And eek therto comen of so heigh kynrede" (she was one of the fairest under the sun and also came from a noble kindred, ll. 734–35). Conventional signifiers compose the description of the knight's behavior. The lover in distress suffers in pain and constant anxiety: "wel unnethes dorste this knight, for drede / Tell hire his wo, his peyne, and his distresse" (hardly dared this knight, out of dread, tell her his woe, his pain, and his distress, ll. 736–37); his honorable action and subordination to her will merit her acquiescence: "But atte laste, she, for his worthynesse, / And namely for his meke obeysaunce, / Hath swich a pitee caught of his penaunce / That pryvely she fil of his accord" (but at the last, she, because of his worthiness and especially for his humble obedience, developed such pity for his suffering, that privately she fell into accord with him, ll. 738–41); courtly diction adapted from Marian devotion – pitee, penaunce – carries, and legalizes, sexual passion,[15] though the pledge to fulfill passion is a

14 Ibid., 152.
15 J.D. Burnley, *Chaucer's Language and the Philosophers' Tradition* (Cambridge: D.S. Brewer, 1979), shows how "the borders between philosophical, religious, and courtly works are rarely very well marked in fourteenth-century writing, and linguistic terminology easily moves from one sphere to another" (89) His study illustrates the varied sources and contexts of the diction of courtly romance in political

private agreement, following courtly tradition's agreement that *jouissance* can only suffer from the social link. In stark contrast, the marital contract, however workaday, becomes *un*conventional and problematic, for, as noted, aristocratic lovers in most courtly romances do not marry. The lady in Provencal poetry for the most part remains exalted and unavailable, her exaltation dependent on her unavailability. From the start of narrative romance with Tristan and Iseult, courtly love is adulterous, and to whatever degree it reflected contemporary social practices, the poetics of courtly love remained outside of the symbolic practices of aristocratic marriage arrangements based on the exchange of women intended to secure political alliances, to increase wealth through the consolidation of estates, and to ensure the integrity of estates transmitted in inheritance, especially in northwestern Europe where primogeniture was instituted – in short, the kinds of benefits that also had likely assisted the social mobility of the Franklin, householder *extraordinaire*.

Arveragus and Dorigen try to bridge this *aporia* by behaving like courtly lovers even as they marry. The contract negotiates between the conventional diction of aristocratic romance and a new discourse of companionate marriage.[16] The contradictions between its terms articulate the difficulty of the balance:

> Of his free wyl he swoor hire as a knight
> That nevere in all his lyf he, day ne nyght,
> Ne sholde upon hym take no maistrie
> Agayn hir wyl, ne kithe hire jalousie,
> But hire obeye, and folwe hir wyl in al,

and juridical, philosophic, religious, and affective psychology. I thank John Hill for leading me to Burnley's work. See also Louise Olga Fradenburg's discussion of Julia Kristeva's concept of "legalized passion" in *City, Marriage, Tournament: Arts of Rule in Late Medieval Scotland* (Madison: University of Wisconsin Press, 1991).

16 C.S. Lewis, *The Allegory of Love: A Study in Medieval Tradition* (Oxford: Oxford University Press, 1958), follows the transition from "the old romance of adultery to the very frontiers of the modern ... romance of marriage" and specifically relates the "lawful loves of Dorigen and her husband" to this problematic (197).

As any lovere to his lady shal,
Save that the name of soveraynetee,
That woulde he have for shame of his degree. (ll. 745–52)

Of his free will he swore to her as a knight.
That never in all his life, neither in day nor night
would he take mastery to himself
against her will nor show her any jealousy,
But obey, and follow her will in everything,
As any lover to his lady would,
Except for the name of sovereignty,
That he would keep because of his rank, to avoid shame.

This is a particularly fraught compromise that follows the model of courtly love, with the husband promising, as would "any lovere to his lady," to establish the wife as sovereign over the subordinate husband. As a husband, however, he takes the formal *name* of the Master, refusing to subordinate his position of power, his "degree." The narrator's defense of the contract's incompatible terms registers his unease in making that defense and emphasizes its difficulty:

Thus hath she take hir servant and hir lord, –
Servant in love, and lord in marriage.
Thanne was he bothe in lordshipe and servage.
Servage? Nay, but in lordshipe above,
Sith he hath bothe his lady and his love;
His lady, certes, and his wyf also,
The which that lawe of love acordeth to. (ll. 792–98)

Thus has she taken her servant and her lord, –
Servant in love, and lord in marriage.
Then was he both in lordship and service.
Service? Nay, but in lordship above,
Since he has both his lady and his love;
His lady, certainly, and his wife also,
Both of which the law of love accorded to each other.

Yoking antinomies together – servant and lord, lady and wife – he repeats them in various combinations. Manifesting the tortured process at work here is the questioning, denial, and redefinition of "service" as the sequence tracks back and undoes itself. Its conclusion is punctuated by an appeal to "the law of love," at the very moment that said "law" is being repurposed to make the roles of wife and lover "accord."[17] The force of law substitutes for reason in the rhetorical equivalent of a performative statement that asserts the truth of a statement by means of the power that upholds it, even though the agreement is based on "free wyl" and despite the assertion that love must be free, "nat constreyned by maistrye" (l. 764) and that constraint does away with love: "Whan maistrie comth, the God of Love anon / Beteth [beats] his wynges, and farewel, he is gon!" (ll. 765–66). But the contract asserts the male domination of the historical society in which the marriage is instituted.

The contract joins oxymoronic aristocratic married lovers and moreover resignifies them as friends to rationalize the unequal burden of obedience, "That freendes everych oother moot obeye, / If they wol longe holden compaignye" ("that friends each other must obey, if they would long hold company with each other," ll. 762–63). The incompatibility of bourgeois and aristocratic economies coexisting in England during the late fourteenth century determines the competing, incompatible claims in this agreement: an aristocratic marriage, a private relation founded on the demands of family interests, attempts to merge with a new institution, the form of companionate, consensual marriage that was beginning to penetrate the upper middle classes. Lee Patterson argues that evidence suggests "the practices and values that typify modern marriage found their nearest late medieval analogues within the gentry and wealthy urban classes."[18] Dorigen and Arveragus are ahead of their time,

---

17 The god of Love in the *Prologue* to *The Legend of Good Women* (F version, l. 330, G version, l. 256) castigates the narrator for writings that constitute "an heresye ayeins my lawe," without expanding the reference.

18 Lee Patterson, *Chaucer and the Subject of History* (Madison: University of Wisconsin Press, 1991), 345. Patterson continues: "While

for it will be the achieved hegemony of the middle class in later centuries that sponsored the merger of courtship and marriage in the diluted, less dramatic passion of the everyday marital arrangement appearing to serve the interests of autonomous agents rather than those of extended families. The couple anticipates this future in what Robert R. Edwards describes as a "contract negotiated between them and known only to themselves." A demand for the secrecy of illicit passion was a characteristic of courtly love, while it is unnecessary for these married lovers. The *Tale* tries to repurpose secrecy for the marriage contract itself and for the growing culture of contracts and secrecy in the economic practices of the later Middle Ages; Chaucer's Merchant is also weighed down by his many secrets. Edwards points out that secrecy allows the couple to "create a form of subjectivity out of isolation and concealment that stands at the heart of their marriage. They are joined in reciprocity, mutuality, and subterfuge," and he argues that such an arrangement expresses the consciousness of middle class agents, "the freedom of the interiorized, mercantile subject to negotiate and act in his best interests."[19] Theirs is a marriage between agents who use the tropes of courtly love to enact their own mixture of old nobility and new economic temptations, as is witnessed by the fact that they make their contract between themselves, without intermediaries; no father or family hands Dorigen over to Arveragus, but the husband maintains the position of power in place of the father. The inconsistencies built

> the evidence is not extensive, what there is does indeed suggest that for the literate urban middle class the affectional relations between the spouses had become by the late middle ages an important topic of discussion .... The effect of this bourgeois attention to marital relations was to make glaringly visible ... the contradiction between the traditional supremacy of patriarchy and the equally traditional desire for mutuality and love between the spouses" (346). The primary audience for *The Canterbury Tales* may well have been members of this urban class Patterson identifies.

19 Robert R. Edwards, "Rewriting Mendon's Story: *Decameron* 10.5 and the *Franklin's Tale,*" in *The* Decameron *and the* Canterbury Tales*: New Essays on an Old Question,* eds. Leonard Michael Koff and Brenda Deen Shildgen (Madison: Fairleigh Dickinson University Press, 2000), 233.

into the marriage demonstrate the discordance between specific, historical arrangements of the sexes practiced by the superior, aristocratic class, in contrast to, but also, increasingly, in rapprochement with, the bourgeoisie, and concomitantly between public and private spheres[20] and gender roles. The contract tries to honor the claims of love, marriage, friendship, and romance; but, again, no sleight of hand can finally reconcile the law, in the Lacanian sense, with full *jouissance*. The cost of the accord is a certain hypocrisy.

Dorigen does not fulfill her end of the bargain, because she cannot; it is impossible. Her desire then is represented as the source of trouble, not the marriage agreement itself. Arverargus's decision to depart Brittany to fight in arms at the expense of his marriage provides the reason for the frustration of Dorigen's desire, the necessary "obstacle" that masks the impossibility of lasting and perfect *jouissance*. His leaving inscribes a lack in Dorigen, and she experiences the absence of the object as a frustration: something is keeping her from having what she wants.[21] Obsessing over her husband's safety and transferring her complaint to the rocks as agent of the lack, she avoids confronting his decision to leave, nor need she acknowledge his autonomous and different subjectivity, as a source of the obstacle to desire. But

---

20 In an analysis of troubadour lyric in *Ermengard of Narbonne and the World of the Troubadours* (Ithaca: Cornell University Press, 2001), 233–47, Frederic L. Cheyette shows that courtly love poetry expressed political relations from the start: "When we see the language of power relations – of loyalty and faith, of treason and deceit – used in what are clearly erotic contexts, we have, to be sure, a projection of those relations of power and status into the world of intimacy" (247). Courtly discourse could also express longings for native territories or for conquest of the Holy Land. Lee Manion, "The Loss of the Holy Lang and *Sir Isumbas:* Literary Contributions to Fourteenth-Century Crusade Discourse," *Speculum* 85, no. 1 (2010): 65–90, notes that troubadours' "audiences learned to understand traditional love lyrics expressing longing for a distant love object as an allusion to, or allegory of, crusade doctrine or practice" (89).

21 In *Le séminaire, livre IV: La relation d'objet,* ed. Jacques-Alain Miller (Paris: Seuil, 1994), Lacan distinguishes between privation in the real, castration in the symbolic, and imaginary frustration.

obstacles just motivate further desire; Arverargus's absence fuels the narrative by allowing a further displacement of frustrated desire onto Aurelius, who poses as an alternative means to fulfillment. Dorigen's desire is hysteric insofar as it is addressed to a supposed master who can fill her lack with an imagined enjoyment that is nonetheless denied her. Her attempt to save married love by bargaining with a lover manifests a hysterical structure that cannot be satisfied.

In the event, Dorigen further displaces her desire to her husband's control; her collapse confirms the need for male control of marriage. As Sheila Delany puts it, "she tries to create a new social form (the egalitarian marriage) only to abandon the effort in crisis and return, humbly, to the protective authority of an old-fashioned man, her husband," and, in so doing, she has "accepted the premise that a woman is a possession on a par with money, an object without will or moral responsibility."[22] The actual prospect of freedom, presented as a choice whether or not to fulfill her promise to Aurelius, is paralyzing, leading to a theatrical, rhetorical performance that enacts the ideal of the ego in a series of virtuous models she imitates by contemplating suicide. The performance remains self-enclosed and ineffectual, and it falls flat, because it only leads to her putting herself in the hands of her husband, relinquishing her will to his power, with the expectation that he will solve her dilemma.

Her paralysis reduces her to exchange value, as Arveragus orders her to be true to her word – "Ye shul youre *trouthe* holden, by my fay!" (You shall hold to your pledge, by my faith, l. 1474) – and to submit to Aurelius;[23] Dorigen would thereby privately

[22] Sheila Delany, *Medieval Literary Politics: Shapes of Identity* (Manchester: Manchester University Press, 1990), 126. Elaine Tuttle Hansen offers an astute analysis of Dorigen's submission, emphasizing the undoing of any power she may have had initially, in *Chaucer and the Fictions of Gender* (Berkeley: University of California Press, 1992), 270–83. That women in Chaucer's *fabliaux* behave with greater agency than does Dorigen may be explained by R. Howard Bloch's discussions in *Medieval Misogyny* (Chicago: University of Chicago Press, 1991) relating misogyny in courtly literature to sources in classical philosophy and medieval theology, traditions that have little influence on *fabliaux*.

[23] Elaine Tuttle Hansen nicely describes this surrender of freedom: "she

serve in the role of an object mediating public relations between men.[24] Unable to maintain her autonomy, Dorigen continually acts out the desire of the hysteric: she wants a master, all the while challenging his mastery. Her paralysis is, then, also an effect of the contradictory structure of hysteria that attempts to keep alive desire for the subject who will not allow her to have what she wants; Dorigen's submission to Aurelius and his rejection maintain this contradictory dynamic. The absence of the sexual relationship, of "fredom" and frankness, in traditional marriage is screened once again by rhetoric; they cannot be harmonized by complaint. We cannot always talk our way out of the binding power of certain words. The ease with which Arveragus arrives at the resolution commanding that Dorigen, in speech and in bodily expression, "contenance," keep hidden the deal she has pledged to complete is another symptom of disavowal: "I yow forbede, up peyne of deeth, / That nevere, whil thee lasteth lyf ne breeth, / To no wight telle thou of this aventure / ... Ne make no contenance of hevynesse" (I forbid you, upon pain of death, that never while your life and breath lasts, to tell no one of this development, ll. 1481–83, 1485), where "aventure" denotes not the heroic deed or quest, but a woman's debasement by her husband, who exchanges his rights over her body for the chance to keep "*Trouthe*," but in secret, by hiding the deal from public view, so "That folk of yow may [not] demen harm or gesse" (that folk won't deem or guess harm, l. 1486), even the servants accompanying her. Taking charge of her desire presents an opportunity for Arverargus to cover his own lack and to fill the master's role. The prospective harm to her virtue, or reputation, or to the vow of fidelity, is glossed over, while the arrangement makes clear the entanglement of ostensibly distinct public and private spheres in a bourgeois economy. The husband controls action in public, the wife indulges in emotion in private, and the compromising of

---

is to be chivalrously rescued from humiliation and abasement by the proper intervention of her husband and the chain reaction of male virtue he sets in motion" (*Chaucer and the Fictions of Gender*, 273).

24 Eve Kosofsky Sedgwick, *Between Men: English Literature and Male Homosocial Desire* (New York: Columbia University Press, 1985) initiates the analysis of homosocial relations mediated by women.

their relationship remains invisible, except to Aurelius, who then disavows the knowledge; but the rocks never really disappear.

The tensions motivating the characters' hypocrisy are untangled in the action as the narrative progressively plays out the conflicts of the initial marital agreement. That the husband's solution is unsavory, or an embarrassment, is both admitted and finessed in the narrator's comment to the audience, "Paraventure an heep of yow, ywis, / Wol holden hym a lewed man in this / That he wol putte his wyf in jupartie" (Perhaps a heap of you, I know, will hold him an ignorant man to put his wife in such jeopardy, ll. 1493–95). His willingness to hand over his wife does not uphold the sanctity of Christian marriage; and lots of people will think that Arverargus has pimped her even if everything works out on the level of appearances. The solution that dissolves nothing Real also shows how patriarchal power carries over to govern the bourgeois model of marriage: Aurelius's readiness to surrender his claim only reinstates the husband's rights over the woman's body. The Franklin's narration ends by magnifying the contradictions the marriage are intended to contain, by showing us the sketchiness of the maneuvers we must undertake to hide them.

The narrative action demonstrates that symbolic structure functions as an unconscious, hidden relation, since the men who participate in it need not meet with or know one another: Arveragus has no contact with Aurelius and knows nothing of the magician, although the magician's service affects the marriage from a distance, and each participates with seeming autonomy in a social structure that nonetheless implicates them all. Each improvises, each acts independently as an individual making choices, and yet each is ultimately caught up in the operations of interlocking systems of exchanges. In the end, each props up the institution of marriage by conspiring to conceal the absence of sexual relation, whatever guise that absence takes, old-fashioned or new.

Words That Bind

The marriage between Dorigen and Arveragus is confirmed by their promises: he "swoor hire" to its terms, supporting his words with his public honor as a "knyght" (l. 745), and she vows by her "*trouthe*" (l. 759) to be "youre humble, trewe wif" (l. 758). *Trouthe* functions as a master signifier in the tale, governing a chain of signifiers, to take on several meanings as the narrative develops, and it operates to join the separate strands of the exchanges of women, words, and money. For Dorigen, *trouthe* is a private ideal trait, determined by her role as a faithful, subordinate wife, signifying chastity and loyalty and a commitment to her word. For both lovers, speech acts produce the marriage. George Duby traces the fraught process during the medieval period by which the church gained control of marriage as a sacred rite, at the expense of the power of aristocratic families,[25] but agreement remained sufficient to establish the legal status of a couple's agreement, whether in a promise to marry that preceded a sexual engagement or in a more formal pledge before wit-

25 Georges Duby studies the competition between patriarchal power over aristocratic marriage alliance and the consensual model sponsored by the church in *The Knight, the Lady, and the Priest* (New York: Pantheon, 1983), based on data largely from France. See also Georges Duby *Medieval Marriage: Two Models from Twelfth Century France* (Baltimore: Johns Hopkins University Press, 1978) for the influential argument that a model of indissoluble, Christian marriage resulting from the consent of the partners replaces aristocratic marriages arranged for short term political and economic advantage. For the long arc of the transition to a consensual model in England, see Lawrence Stone, *The Family, Sex and Marriage: In England 1500–1800* (New York: Harper, 1977), showing that parents' control of marriage remained powerful up to the nineteenth century, although his survey begins after Chaucer's period. For a general review of marriage in medieval rural and urban communities in England, see Stephanie Coontz, *Marriage, a History: From Obedience to Intimacy or How Love Conquered Marriage* (New York: Penguin Books, 2005), 104–22, whose discussions of women's rights indicate the range of choices available to women. Claudia Opitz, "Life in the Late Middle Ages," in *A History of Women: Silences of the Middle Ages*, ed. Christiane Klapisch-Zuber (Cambridge: Harvard University Press, 1992) 267–316, provides a thorough review of women's status in medieval Europe under the regulation of families and husbands; according to Opitz, any greater freedom in choice afforded by the Church was "limited to the rural population and the lower classes in urban areas" (273).

nesses; even in church the spoken consent of the couple was the condition for the priest's pronouncement.

Marriage is a confirmation of the law; however, the language of marrying resituates subjects in new social relations, and hence is always vulnerable to breakdown. The Franklin, in his role as narrator, resists submission to symbolic authority. Lacan distinguishes the register of speech, the symbolic Other that enables exchange, from the imaginary register of the ego, a formation given shape by the outline of the body in the mirror phase and identified by means of traits attributed by a speaker, the mother or caretaker addressing the subject-to-be, to confirm the mirror form as a "you" who is loveable and a "this" that is "you." The ego, however, is a misrecognition, merely an image reflected at a distance, reversed from left to right, and perceived as an other. The ego's form is filled out by identifications with symbolic, ideal traits, producing an ideal ego, and it is propped up by identifications with others who may stand in "my" place. Language may itself be used by the subject to continue imaginary aggression against others. The rhetoric of the Franklin, both as character and as narrator, seeks consolidation of the form of the ego and a "gentle" identity that is tied to an ego ideal. As Alan Gaylord points out, his rhetoric operates to establish mastery: "the Franklin plays to win ... under rules he invents. His aim is total control. His behavior seems deferential and permissive, but the tale is an absolutely authoritarian structure."[26] A manifestation of individuality and a claim to upper class membership, his rhetoric is supposed to demonstrate the credentials of the courtly speaker who can "wel speke of love,"[27] recreating and adapting romance convention. His manipulation of language is his approximation to nobility, and his performance of the tale fulfills an egoistic wish to achieve status.

The portrait in the *General Prologue* of the Franklin as bourgeois – he is a civil servant and wealthy landholder and so a gen-

---

26 Alan T. Gaylord's reading, "From Dorigen to the Vavasour," points to the Franklin's control: "the Franklin plays to win and under rules he invents. His aim is total control. His behavior seems deferential and permissive, but the tale is an absolutely authoritarian structure" (196).
27 *Troilus and Criseyde*, Book II, l. 503.

tleman, but not a member of the aristocracy – likewise points to a self-conscious pretense of courtliness.[28] As Susan Crane shows, the Franklin's "access to gentility" is based on "his rank's restricted claim to gentility, a claim based almost solely on behavior."[29] His

28 But see John M. Flyer, "Love and Degree in the *Franklin's Tale*," *The Chaucer Review 21,* no. 3 (1987): 321–37, for the view that the tale "seems to reflect the fluidity of fourteenth-century English society" (329). While Flyer argues that the Franklin's narrative attempts to level or entirely eliminate status, "it gestures from within a world of hierarchies to a world before degree, or alternatively ... to a world after degree has withered away" (330), the tale does mark status and the prologue is clearly concerned to finesse rank in its archaic setting. Leonard Michael Koff, *Chaucer and the Art of Storytelling* (Berkeley: University of California Press, 1998), describes the Franklin as a feudal landowner, rather than a bourgeois; perhaps at stake here is the larger issue of the point at which "aristocracy" takes on a new meaning when self-made men infiltrate landowners' inherited status. Koff cites Anne Middleton to support his contention that the tale is "not even an example of bourgeois nostalgia for a heroic ideal. Rather, the tale imagines medieval life as the extravagant spectacle of personal magic" (198). However, the narrator does not so much express nostalgia as enlist it in support of a bourgeois bid for inclusion; moreover, to describe magic operating in the tale as "the prerogative of princes that neither changes reality nor dominates it" and as "the exercise of absolute self-sufficiency that belongs to the Franklin's grandiose imagination" (199), is to deny the magician's self-ascribed status as a clerk and to neglect the effects of magic on the action.
29 Susan Crane, "The Franklin as Dorigen," 238. Crane is concerned to draw parallels between the Franklin and Dorigen's subordination and to their similar lack of power in the fiction: "Both vavasour and lady can inhabit romance but do not control its events" (246), but she offers a full review of the Franklin's social position (238–43), arguing that "in Chaucer's milieu his status would not have seemed high" (240), and that "Chaucer's first audience would have perceived this pilgrim as worthy enough to be gentle, but not chivalric enough to be unequivocally of the second estate" (241). Crane does insist, however, that the Franklin is not a bourgeois: "His orientation is not bourgeois, however. He is a rural figure not an urban one; he seeks to hold property, not to engage in trade" (242). It is certainly the case that "bourgeois" refers to town dwellers, that the term's etymology is "bourg," although the members of the middle class, those who earned money rather than

hospitable generosity is a flamboyant presentation of food constantly at the ready – "His table dormant in his halle always / Stood redy covered al the longe day" (*General Prologue*, l. 353) – and it is subtly ridiculed: "It snewed in his hous of mete and drynke" (*General Prologue*, l. 345), preparations of meat and drink pouring down like a natural phenomenon, but insubstantial as snow. His hospitality, however liberal, is not an exchange, nor an offer of charity to others, but a display imitating aristocratic magnanimity, the generosity that is one of the identifying traits of the nobility he endeavors to claim through the imitation. It is a gesture of expenditure for the sake of excess or waste. Unlike the competition of the pilgrims, regulated by the Host, or in fact any game or exchange that necessarily follows commonly accepted regulations, the generosity of the Franklin's table follows his own rules within his own, enclosed space, as could in truth be said of most aristocratic households of the period.

The Franklin's competitive ego is apparent in the pretense of humility he performs in the bridge to the tale. Simultaneously offering a compliment to praise the Squire's skillful speaking –

> inheriting wealth in estates, often invested in land, and rural crafts workers were not peasants.
>
> Sylvia Thrupp describes the "middle division" to be "conceived of as including the lesser types of gentry, the merchant class, country yeomanry cherishing a tradition of free ancestry and perhaps the more substantial semi-mercantile elements in London and other cities." *The Merchant Glass of Medieval London 1300–1500* (Chicago: University of Chicago Press, 1948), 299. Thrupp presents aspirations of such men that correspond to the Franklin's self-presentation: "as many of the wealthier men are known to have done, he then assumed the role of a gentleman in his county serving on public commissions, arguing private hunting rights ... and preparing at least one of his sons for one of the careers that were associated with gentility" (280). Jenna Mead even more pointedly identifies Chaucer as a bureaucrat in civil service in "Chaucer and the Subject of Bureaucracy," *Exemplaria 19*, no. 1 (2007): 39–66. Cara Hersh, "'Knowledge,'" adds to Mead's research to develop the Franklin's bureaucratic responsibilities, as a contour checking revenues reported to administrative offices, as a sheriff "calculating and reporting the worth of landowner in his county in response to writs of distraint," 433, responsible as well for "analyzing his neighbor's possessions for the king" (435).

"For of thy speche I have greet deyntee" (l. 681) – he also sets up a rivalry – "I have a sone, and by the Trinitee, / I hadde levere ... He were a man of swich discrecioun / As that ye been!" (ll. 682–83, 685–86). And he slanders his son for being profligate, ironically his own defining trait, and ends by insinuating family connections with courtly personnel: "he hath levere talken with a page / Than to comune with any gentil wight / Where he myghte lerne gentillesse aright" (ll. 693–94). The comments work to establish a relation with the Knight through their shared status as fathers of sons who "lese" (l. 691) and "despende" (l. 690), the Knight's son on showy clothing, the Franklin's on gambling, and thereby a relationship to men of high status. As well, his comments offer an introduction to a tale that will teach the "gentillesse" noble behavior, framing what follows as a version of advice for princes or a handbook of household management. That the Franklin's noble posture is self-serving is emphasized by the Host's intrusion, the interruption "Straw for youre gentillesse!" (l. 695), which is his rejection of the pretense and a defense against a potential slight against his own inferior class standing.

The tale's *Prologue* contains an even stronger example of the Franklin's ambitions in his manipulation of the modesty topos:[30] "by cause I am a burel [unlearned] man ... Have me excused of my rude speche. / I lerned nevere rethorik, certeyn; / Thyng that I speke, it moot be bare and pleyn" (ll. 716, 718–20) is a disclaimer at odds with his rhetorical authority. The pose of humility and self-presentation as a rude or coarse man resembles Chaucer's self-effacing posture in Geoffrey and his assumption of verbal incompetence and social subordination, as well as those of Chaucer's early narrators. In social standing, the Franklin resembles the poet Chaucer, bourgeois servant of aristocrats, whose birth limits social mobility, whatever his achievements. The Franklin's rhetorical display suggests a class anxiety that likely affected Chaucer as well.[31]

---

30 See Ernst Robert Curtius, *European Literature and the Latin Middle Ages* (New York: Harper & Row, 1963), 83–85.
31 See Paul Strohm, *Social Chaucer* (Cambridge: Harvard University Press, 1989), for a full discussion of Chaucer's place in the changing social relationships of the period. Strohm convincingly argues that

The rhetoric of the narration is another means towards a self-conscious self-presentation, a bid for attention and for the recognition of the ego's exalted identity. For example, the narrator describes the magician's learning in astronomy and astrology, amassing a list of esoteric terms to illustrate both his and the character's specialized knowledge, only emphasized by his humble disavowal, "I ne kan no termes of astrologye" ("I know no terms of astrology," l. 1266), although astrological terms are sprinkled throughout. He demystifies the art of the magician as "apparence or jogelrye [conjuring]" (l. 1265) and "swiche illusiouns and swiche meschaunces" ("dark practices," l. 1292), what "heathen folk useden in thilke [those] dayes" (l. 1293). The rhetorical display is at the character's expense. Likewise, the narrator trivializes Dorigen's sorrow at her husband's absence, describing an exaggerated expression of banal emotion:" For his absence wepeth she and siketh [sighs], / As doon thise noble wyves whan hem liketh. / She moorneth, waketh, wayleth, fasteth, pleyneth" (as do these noble wives when they like. She morns, wakes, wails, fasts, complains, ll. 817–19). Here he undercuts feeling with a list of unhappy verbs and further reduces her speech to that of the stereotypic "thise," women. Her complaint is congruent with the ineffectual rhetoric with which she determines on suicide before her surrender to her husband's will. We are invited to consider that the narrator's rhetoric, no less than the character's, is silly, by means of the dilation, "Til that the brighte sonne lost his hewe; / For th'orisonte [horizon] hath reft [deprived] the sonne his light – / This is as much to seye as it was nyght" (ll. 1016–18); the concession, "This is as much to seye," is self-consciously redundant. Does this perhaps indicate that the Franklin has seen quite enough of the flummery ongoing not only in social mobility but

---

Chaucer's primary audience was composed of bourgeois civil servants, like himself. Strohm's research bears out Burnley's claim that "the large immigration into London in the first decades of the fourteenth century consisted of a disproportionately high number of men with legal and clerical training .... It is among men of this class, among their fellow civil servants and lawyers, among the educate gentlemen on the fringes of the court, and perhaps merchants who had been to school that we should look for the audience" of Chaucer (*Chaucer's Language*, 8–9).

also in the performances of sensibility and artfulness so flattering to the aristocratic ego itself? Is his *Tale* as much critique of the emptiness of rhetoric as it is an admired mode of Imaginary display?

Despite the rhetorical manipulation that exhibits the ideal of an imaginary ego, in his role as narrator the Franklin emphasizes the obligations incurred by promising and the ways promises are entangled in and limited by the discourses they employ. The promises propelling narrative action effectively link the characters in a relay that connects them all, no less than the Franklin's promise to engage with the Canterbury pilgrims in the promise to tell tales involves him in exchange with others. Not only is the marriage founded on mutual oaths, but each character engages another in a promise: Dorigen promises Aurelius that she will love him if he can make the rocks disappear (however much her sincerity is in question); Aurelius swears to pay the magician for the labor he promises to accomplish (in spite of his lack of cash). The design is elegant, establishing a reciprocity on which the well being of each hangs.

A promise is a commitment to the future, as much as to a person, and in a sense it takes place in the future perfect tense, like an anticipation of what will have been accomplished. It is founded on the unstated assurance that the speaker will keep his or her word that an action will be accomplished; it is a kind of exchange of trust, and accepting it is a bet. Each of the tale's characters makes good on the necessary assumptions of promising, precisely as a result of their good will, although the promise establishing the marriage is compromised by what might but does not happen and Aurelius's promise by the absence of resources. Social processes are oiled by good will, with generosity and leeway allowing for a little slack. The most significant idealism in the tale is the picture of a generous functioning of the exchange of promises made possible by the *trouthe* of each actor.

The *signifier trouthe* is the support of the speech acts of promising, and it also functions as the exchanges' quilting point. In the position of a master signifier, it crosses between the several forms of exchange to make them compatible within a coherent, if conflicted system. It thereby operates what Stuart Hall explains as the articulation of an ideology: "the so-called 'unity' of a discourse is really the articulation of different, distinct elements which can be rearticulated in different ways because they have no necessary 'belongingness.' ... ideological elements come, under certain conditions, to cohere together within a discourse."[32] The primary signified of *trouthe* is "keeping one's word," an accord between what is spoken and the act of speaking that hinges on *entente*, illustrated by Aurelius's avowal that the magician will "be payed trewely, by my *trouthe!*" (l. 1231). Consequently, *trouthe* also signifies "keeping one's commitments." As the mentions of *trouthe* accelerate over the tale's concluding section, and everyone proceeds to act according to *trouthe* in order to demonstrate noble status, it is invested with both personal and ideological senses to become what Ernesto Laclau defines as a "nodal point" which fixes meaning.[33]

For the men, the many references to *trouthe* also connote "acting in order to demonstrate nobility" – in the case of Arveragus and Aurelius, by honoring a promise and paying a debt, and for the magician, by forgiving a debt owed for the promise he kept. How each sees the self is the primary motive of the men. Each tries to live up to an ideal of the self, imitating the other's generosity and seeing his own goodness in the other; sympathy for the other is an opportunity for self-regard. Each sacrifices in order to perform a social role and maintains a fiction to keep up appearances. In this sense, while they strive to behave in accord

32 Stuart Hall in Lawrence Grossberg, "On Postmodernism and Articulation: An Interview with Stuart Hall," *Journal of Communication Inquiry* 10, no. 2 (2016): 53.

33 See Ernesto Laclau and Chantal Mouffe, *Hegemony and Socialist Strategy: Towards a Radical Democratic Politics* (London: Verso, 1996) for the notion of hegemony accomplished by the operation of discursive "articulation" that unites social differences under a master signifier, "the construction of nodal points which partially fix meaning" (113). In *On Populist Reason* (London: Verso, 2005), Laclau studies populist movements, but his discussion of the construction of hegemony (67–166), under a "tendentially empty signifier" (96) describes the process by which *trouthe* in the tale expresses the "cathexis of a singular element" in "a performative operation constituting the chain as such" (97) to fill in the empty space of a lack in discourse and thereby to represent an emergent class.

with noble virtue, each of the men acts like a bourgeois. Lacan's discussion of charity is relevant here, insofar as charity always prefers that the objects of largesse resemble the givers (but don't get any ideas). The fantasy depends at least on the hope that the image of the receiver will come to resemble that of the giver through the transformative power of generosity, or being "fre."[34] The bourgeois takes up a role and watches himself acting, not fully sure of his place, insecure that the ego matches the ideal ego, and so keeps a distance between himself acting and his performance. If his nobility is not granted by birth and inheritance, the bourgeois must be extra alert to the system's changes and potentials and adjust his performance accordingly, following models. Honor and status, the rewards of a kind of game or struggle for rank, are based on imitative behavior, and since the behavior is an imitation, it puts at risk the supposed integrity and solidity of the ego in a relation of potential rivalry. At the same time, keeping *trouthe* assures that individuals will subdue aggression in a mutual agreement.[35]

In addition, for Aurelius and the magician, who are not upper-class men, *trouthe* successfully performs an ideological interpolation that "hails" the subject to recognize himself in a model of behavior he is to identify with. Louis Althusser, it will be remembered, explains that the subject of ideology is called to identify within an ideological regime by an address coming from an apparatus that offers the subject a point of identification with the position of addressee and so, on an unconscious level, to consent to the dominant regime.[36] The subject is thereby drawn

---

34 Jacques Lacan, *Seminar VII*.
35 See L.O. Fradenburg's chapter "Tournament" in *City, Marriage, Tournament,* for a similar argument about aristocratic performativity. Aristocratic culture has its own endless work: proving that aristocrats are morally noble – that they have "true gentilesse."
36 See Louis Althusser, "Ideology and the Ideological State Apparatuses," in *Lenin and Philosophy and Other Essays* (London: New Left Books, 1971), 170–77, for the operation of interpellation. See also Slavoj Žižek's critique of Althusser in the chapter "Why Is Woman a Symptom of Man?," in *Enjoy Your Symptom! Jacques Lacan in Hollywood and Out* (London: Routledge, 1992), 31–67: The "big Other," or "ideology," for Althusser, "is retroactively posited, i.e., presupposed, by the subject

into a system that will authenticate the ideal ego, and the adaptation of the trait of the ideal other is supposed to be evidence that status has already been achieved. The Franklin characteristically tries to pass as an aristocrat. Under the signifier *trouthe*, then, bourgeois interests are "articulated" with established interests to stake out the membership of an emerging class in a cohesive system. Aurelius gives up the offer of Dorigen to imitate his rival's generosity as an equal: "Thus kan a squire doon a gentil dede / As well as kan a knyght, withouten drede" (thus can a squire do a noble deed as well as can a knight, without doubt, ll. 1543–44). The exhibit of his title to belonging among the "gentils" fulfills his class aspiration. The intersection of class and putative sexuality serves to dissipate the power of the latter rather than insisting on it as an insistent black rock in the water of paradise.

Moreover, the magician puts Dorigen and Arveragus in his debt, enabling the fairy-tale conclusion that they "In sovereyn blisse leden forth hir lyf" (l. 1552) – an unlikely future, given their inability to sustain the terms of their contract and, moreover, the unresolved tensions remaining in the marriage. The happy ending is tempered as well by the suspect generosity of both husband and lover, not only because each treats the woman as a piece of goods to be possessed or given away, but also because each responds to a narcissistic desire to look good. Yet despite the persisting tensions, the marriage generally functions as a way of handling the absence of sexual relation, and this marriage offers

> in the very act by means of which he is caught in the cobweb of an ideology. The subject, for example, (presup)poses the big Other ... in the very moment and gesture of conceiving himself as its executor, as its unconscious tool. This act of (presup)position which makes the big Other exist is perhaps the elementary gesture of ideology" (59). Of course, none of the men in the "Franklin's Tale" are aware of presupposing an ideology – each behaves as if making a free choice – although with the Franklin, Chaucer is consciously fashioning an ideology and simultaneously sponsoring one. In any case, every subject is either caught up in the symbolic or is psychotic; perhaps Žižek needs to distinguish between the big Other as speech and as ideology; one can choose to adopt a different ideology than the prevailing one and may reject a given regime, but only the psychotic chooses not to be alienated in language.

one, historically emergent form of marriage. At the end of the tale, Dorigen and Arveragus are not in the same position they were at the beginning: whatever equality the marriage contract originally agreed to, they have demonstrated they are unequal to it in practice. Male control over feminine subordination will order their relation, Dorigen having shown she is incapable of a freedom she does not in fact desire. Yet the weakness at the heart of male control is entirely indicated by the same narrative.

The unnamed magician, no less than the other men, acts to approximate an ego ideal that calls upon him through Aurelius's speech to demonstrate that he is as generous and hence noble as the others. His refusal of the offer of future payment for the debt due for service includes the magician in the circle of approbation: "But God forbede, for his blisful myght, / But if a clerk koude doon a gentil dede / As well as any of yow, it is no drede" (ll. 1609–11). This implies that the approbation is a reward in a contest between male egos to outdo one another in generosity. The statement both anticipates the contest invited by the Franklin's concluding question to the pilgrims, "Which was the mooste fre [generous], as thynketh yow?" (l. 1622), and it advances the competition for status: if a squire can act as well as a knight, the magician, a "clerk" and a businessman, can act as well as any. And having pardoned the debt, in a curious moment the magician takes off on his horse and exits, "took his hors, and forth he goth his way" (l. 1620), as if he rides out of the tale to join the frame of the Canterbury pilgrims on their horses. The Franklin has prepared for this move by establishing an identification with the character through a shared feature of aristocratic gentility: when he welcomes Aurelius, the magician is reported to lay out a superlative table: "Hem lakked no vitaille [victuals] that myghte hem plese. / So wel arryed hous as there was oon / Aurelius in his lyf saugh nevere noon" (ll. 1186–88). And makes a fuss ordering the service of the dinner (ll. 1209–18). The diegetic character spills over into the person of the narrator in a trait that exemplifies an assumed status.

Having established a fictional community in which individual worth modeled on aristocratic traits allows the inclusion of new claimants, the Franklin ultimately subordinates his ego to social community, in spite of the ego's resistant defense of autonomy. His is a willed subordination to the symbolic, that is, to his necessary acceptance of the autonomy and efficacy of language and an immersion in social being greater than self-interest. Uncharacteristic of the Franklin's prior performance, then, the conclusion is a surprise transcending the limitations of his ego. He is, of course, lured by the promise that identification with aristocratic traits will in fact serve his self-interest quite well.

The invitation to his audience to reflect on his performance, "Lordynges, this question, thane, wol I aske now" (l. 1621), following immediately upon the magician taking to horse, is a bridge between the competition between the men in the tale and the competition of the pilgrims to tell the best tale in a contest that diverts and sublimates rivalry into language production. The question, "Which was the moste fre, as thynketh yow?" (l. 1622), is a kind of *demande d'amour,* the courtly convention according to which the delivery of a narrative should end with a question or instigate a debate. Romances delivered in medieval courts often concluded with a request to the audience to deliberate, whether to discuss a fictional dilemma, to judge characters' behavior, or to weigh competing claims and ethics at stake in the narrative. The Franklin's question encloses the pilgrim audience in an aristocratic circle, or, at the least, it situates its members in an analogous position and thereby flatters them as *lordynges*. Even while *lordynges* is frequently employed in the tales as a general form of address, here it serves the Franklin's purposes by trying to ingratiate him with his distinctively non-noble audience. It flatters and calls attention to the Franklin as well, since if "fre" signifies "noble," "generous," "gracious," his liberality and mastery of rhetoric have put on display his title to the virtue. As well, in the context of the characters' behavior, "fre" signifies the subject's capacity for affective, responsive sensibility. Sympathy pacifies the dialectic of imaginary identification and rivalry by putting the ego in the other's situation: "I" may feel like the other without needing to destroy or to take over something of the other's place.

The concluding address extends further to Chaucer's audiences, past and present, to include them in the relay of nobility and thereby embrace them in the fictional reality.

With this question to the audience, the tale shifts perspective. The shift asserts itself not as an opening or crease in the narration but, rather, as a sudden jump from the tale to the frame, and further on to a future of anticipated audience inclusion. The question attempts to nail down the tensions the tale works to contain, interpolating the audience under the signifier *fre* by implying that the pilgrims are as capable of judging noble character as the narrative is of embodying it, and by attempting to coerce acquiescence in the assurance of a happy ending. It identifies the pilgrim audience as an audience for fiction that, despite its apparent diversity, depends on shared assumptions and on common values and standards enabling judgment of behavior. The conclusion thereby resignifies, extends, and reinforces, in the register of audience response, the tale's work of molding social consensus.

Veiling Money

Medieval economies are complex. Notwithstanding its provenance in a mythical Brittany, and its courtly marriage, cocooned and protected from the finances that still affect it, the Franklin's courtly tale demonstrates that an economy of cash, a bourgeois exchange form, is penetrating the feudal, aristocratic economy founded in land ownership. The promise between Aurelius and the magician to exchange work for money is not of the same order as the other promises: money is an object, an abstract equivalent to rate the value of goods, but a woman is a subject, although she may be treated or treat herself as an object to be rated by what should be equivalent goods or money. Nor does money function in all market exchange, while language is universally shared. Yet the idealism of the tale shows that commercial transactions, like language, run on good will and trust, and that gifts also participate in exchange and self-interest. The necessary assumption of speech, that people mean what they say and will keep their word, is matched by its corollary in the market that actors will take responsibility for their financial transactions, that debtors will be willing to repay debts and sellers to provide worthy goods. In both cases, a just system provides for the cancellation of the payment of debts that would cause hardship. In both cases, justice, like "*trouthe*," is hard to come by.

The Franklin's Tale constructs the ideology of a beneficent bourgeois society to validate the new economy emerging in late fourteenth century England. It works to submerge class tensions in demonstrations of idealized behavior by all its characters acting according to honor: the move to equalize the distribution of a noble attribute is already a move to displace power. The title of *trouthe* consolidates a new hegemony based on cash earnings, one founded on an already established attribute, the nobility of character that can be shared by members of an emergent class, signifying the worth of the person without the privilege of inheritance.[37] The standard of *trouthe* accommodates claimants to status under the fit of an already sanctioned master signifier, allowing the displacement of power while making change effectively invisible. The new system of exchange is naturalized, seemingly a continuation of the past.

Every social formation, because speakers of language institute them, depends upon illusion, on trust or credit in subjects' words, even on what may be pretense, on subjects' willingness to act better than they might be. In the end, of course, any symbolic system – the conglomerate of persons, institutions, and systems of governance – is a fiction, since ultimately it is backed up by the law. The force of the law remains in the performative language establishing the rules of the system, in a constitution or a legal code that could be otherwise, according to different assumptions or a different code. This is to say that any individual symbolic is

---

37 In the chapter "Base and Superstructure in Marxist Cultural Theory," in *Culture and Materialism* (London: Verso, 1980), 31–49, Raymond Williams distinguishes residual, dominant, and emergent cultures in a social system, separating "oppositional forms" from "something we can call alternative to the effective dominant culture," and he considers the inclusion of "those practices, experiences, meanings, values which are not part of the effective dominant culture" (40). "The Franklin's Tale" appropriates "dominant culture" conventions in an effort to include an "emergent" group. As Williams argues, "It is an important fact about any particular culture, how far it reaches into the whole range of human practices and experiences in an attempt at incorporation" (41).

unfounded.[38] Every system adopts an ideology that covers over the insecurity of its origins and the contingency of its particular arrangements. Ideology is the imaginary rationalization of the symbolic fiction.

Illusion then is a necessity for social being. Ideology may be illusory, but it is no less generative and active for that; in Žižek's formulation, ideologies have a "symbolic efficiency" because "they regulate activity which generates social reality."[39] Ideologies are also in artifacts as well as artifice, in the buildings we design, the environments we destroy, the animals we "domesticate." *The Franklin's Tale* constructs the ideology of a beneficent bourgeois society to validate the new market forces emerging in fourteenth-century England. Like Chaucer's portraits of the Parson and the Plowman, the tale works to submerge class tensions in demonstrations of an idealized behavior by all its characters acting according to honor. The tale's archaic source in a Breton lay assures that the social system it represents is natural, that it comes from the past and so is the way things have always been. The myth that culture is natural, not the product of the rule of a superior force mastering the symbolic (insofar as that is possible), is the constant of ideology generally.[40] The tale does not admit that its appropriation of aristocratic values to picture a gracious, satisfying exchange is a means of denying class conflict and change, and indeed its idealization is itself a form of denial. In its happy fictional world, toleration and accommodation mutes conflict. Social actors do not lie or renege on promises, and if they cheat – Aurelius employing the magician, the magician illusion – they merely bend the rules. Competition is a benign

---

38 See Willy Apollon, "A Lasting Heresy, the Failure of Political Desire," in *Psychoanalysis, Politics, Aesthetics,* eds. Willy Apollon and Richard Feldstein (New York: State University of New York Press, 1996), 31–44, esp. 32–37, for a discussion of the violence that is the origin and support of the symbolic.

39 Slavoj Žižek. *First as Tragedy, Then as Farce* (London: Verso, 2009), 78.

40 See Roland Barthes, *Mythologies,* trans. Annette Lavers (New York: Hill and Wang, 1972) for the process by which culture may be transformed into the natural.

means for demonstrating one's worth, and exceptions can and will be made.

The articulation of the "feudal social vision" with the emerging "mercantile culture" depends upon a degree of trust, one meaning of "credit." Consent to the symbolic of language is a forced choice, a necessity the subject assumes unconsciously simply by being born into it.[41] The giving of conscious consent to a particular arrangement of a society and to the ideology that rationalizes can be said to be voluntary, but is always underpinned by subjects' unavoidable immersion in the symbolic, long before they are themselves capable of speech. *The Franklin's Tale* puts into play this necessitated choice by means of actors' commitments to their speech, and also demonstrates the willed choice to support an ideology. As well, its articulation of competing economies that function seamlessly within a single structure appeases potential conflict, to the satisfaction of all participants.

In an only apparently different way, dramatizing public interests in the form of private transactions also naturalizes the new economy and disguises change. The private relations, whether between men or within marriage, cover over invading public relations and already express the ideology of commercial exchange; as Edwards claims, the tale's "private and domestic spheres … register the internal tensions of a feudal social vision and the conflicts of moving toward relations governed by promises and contracts, the foundations of mercantile culture."[42] It is not only the marriage that demonstrates those tensions and transformations, for the cash economy also contaminates the courtly model governing Aurelius's formulaic courtship of the

---

41 Jacques Lacan discusses the forced choice in the process of alienation as one between meaning and being in *The Seminar of Jacques Lacan, Book XI: The Four Fundamental Concepts of Psychoanalysis*, ed. Jacques-Alain Miller, trans. Alan Sheridan (New York: W.W. Norton, 1978), 203–15. Psychosis is understood to be a refusal of that choice in a foreclosure rejecting the Name-of-the-Father. See Jacques Lacan, *The Seminar of Jacques Lacan, Book III: The Psychoses 1955–1956*, ed. Jacques-Alain Miller, trans. Russell Grigg (New York: W.W. Norton, 1993), 143–57.
42 Edwards, "Rewriting Mendon's Story," 343.

married lady:[43] like any "servant to Venus" (l. 937), in protracted "sorwe" (l. 949) the lover "langwissheth" (l. 950), keeping secret his quasi-sacramental "penaunce" (l. 942) and his "grevaunce" (l. 941), a signifier deriving from juridical process, earning a characteristic "worshipe and honour" (l. 962) while he, in anxiety, "nevere dorste"(l. 941) approach her by speaking his sorrow; his "aventure" (l. 940), however, rather than the hazard of battle, is a service delegated to a professional who is enlisted for the promise of a fee. Financial dealings may enter the courtly genre, but their presence needs to remain hidden in order to perpetuate conventional manners in a hybrid form. In this respect too, the marriage of Dorigen and Arveragus are ahead of their time: increasingly, marriage will function as the institutional support of the cash economy. Whether as a unit of production or capital accumulation or a unit of consumption, the nuclear, bourgeois marriage – dominated by male power – supports, manages, and furthers the expansion of capital.

Aurelius's cavalier gesture of prodigality while lacking resources diminishes the importance of financial transactions to the enactment of graceful, risky, courteous behavior. Indeed, in sealing the bargain with the magician, he dismisses the expense as incidental, exclaiming "Fy on a thousand pound!" (l. 1227). Cara Hersh's discussion of the responsibilities of bureaucrats shows how several mentions of *certein* in Aurelius's speech manage to keep secret exact sums of cash with equivocations and circumlocutions.[44] Aurelius treats money as if incidental, its weighty matter glossed over. The basis for social stability in money, as well as the source of what he understands to be masculine virtue, or *trouthe,* remains repressed. The squire's improvident posture and the magician's beneficence thus contribute to the concealment of the mediating function of finances. The strategy of the desire of Aurelius has been to disavow lack by gambling with money he doesn't have. He knows very well that he can't

---

43 D. Vance Smith shows how features of economic exchange enter into fourteenth-century romance and appear as well in "The Franklin's Tale," in *Arts of Possession: The Middle English Household Imaginary* (Minneapolis: University of Minnesota Press, 2003).

44 Hersch, "'The Knowledge of the Files'," 445–49.

afford to pay what he promises, but he carries on in spite of that knowledge. Absolved of debt, he really doesn't give up anything. He is reinforced in an hysterical desire to play with an imaginary absence. The magician alone gives up what is his due. He accepts lack in the form of castration, that is, the inevitable failure of the demand for complete satisfaction.

At the end point of exchange, the magician's closure of the relay of social dependence ensures the smooth operation of the economy and the integrity of the system. It may be that the accomplishment attributed to him, the disappearance of the coastal rocks, was marvelous, or it was a sleight, a natural movement of the tides his astrological knowledge could foretell and takes credit for. Also, no explanation is provided for the marvelous visions with which the magician entertains Aurelius. He introduces the uncanny supernatural, congruent with the tale's setting in a mythical "Britayne," known as a locus of marvels. But perhaps this puts "Britayne's" reputation for marvels into question. Perhaps the ambiguity or lack of explanation of the marvels is the point, since the appearance of illusion opens up uncertainty while suspending disbelief at the same time.

His ability to produce magic is an analogue to his function of ensuring the operation of the ideology. His generosity puts everyone in his debt and sutures the cracks in the appearance of a desirable reality of gracious reciprocity among moral equals. By refusing his earnings, he maintains the ideal that actors in the market behave by following an innate virtue rather than crass profit. Simultaneously, he strips the fiction of its natural foundation to show that it is enabled by a necessary illusion and that it rests upon both consent and good will. The magician's loss installs a lack at the center of the articulated symbolic system that the tale constructs. The symbolic, as noted elsewhere, is itself founded upon a lack. In the individual subject, lack takes the shape of the loss of the object of desire, the real object which that desire attempts to retrieve in contingent objects, and in ideology it takes the shape of the phantasm of a "sublime object" whose absence is filled in with master signifiers.[45] The lack of the object

---

45 For a Lacanian theory of ideology, see Slavoj Žižek, *The Sublime Object of Ideology* (London: Verso, 1989).

maintains the movement of desire and also of the continual combinations and substitutions in the symbolic. In miniature, the symbolic works like the children's game known as the slider box puzzle, in which fifteen numbered tiles in sixteen places are manipulated so that the numbers are sequentially aligned; the possibility of moving the inscribed tiles depends upon the opening of an empty space. The magician's act retrospectively establishes the lack necessary at the origin of unconscious structure, a vacancy subsequently filled by the object of desire and by the law protecting against the inertia of the real that threatens to overwhelm meaning and action.[46]

The magician's acceptance of debt exemplifies ethical action. By ensuring the continuing movement of the system he participates in, the magician displaces and thereby keeps its instabilities and tensions, its unconscious incoherencies, going, by allowing them to remain unconscious. "In the ethical act, one always proceeds by a strategy of discursive refusal and withdrawal of agency, in order to reveal the disequilibrium of a discourse .... It ensures that two orders of signification, conscious and unconscious, appear within knowledge and discourse, whereas before there seemed to be only a single order of communication."[47] Representing the structures of its several systems of exchange and unmasking the fissures between the discourses it simultaneous stitches together, *The Franklin's Tale* confronts the unconscious processes that support social discourses. It reveals what remains hidden by ideology. In the end, however, the magician's generosity enables the married lovers' continuing refusal of knowledge, so that the unconscious knowledge of sexual division and the absence of sexual relation that was supposed to be handled by the marriage contract of Dorigen and Arveragus is not acknowledged. They do not handle that knowledge so much as follow its social figuration in and as a form of marriage dominated by the commercial interests of men.

---

46 See Apollon, "A Lasting Heresy," 32–37 for the foundation of symbolic law in the gap of the real.
47 Nobus and Quinn, *Knowing Nothing*, 166, 167.

CHAPTER 3

That Elusive Object of Desire: *The Shipman's Tale*

The Franklin's Tale demonstrates that a larger, more complex structure of exchange emerges from the interlocking of distinct forms of exchange like language, marriage, and money. The bourgeois ideology thus created purportedly ensures trust, or mutual good will, among men, whose homosocial bonds are cemented by the exclusion of women from negotiations. The performance of an ideal of reciprocity advances masculine honor, while subordinating women's value to the roles of token, object, intercessor, obstacle. Partly by inviting the affective participation of the audience in a suspenseful narrative of subordination, the romance form perpetuates this social ideal, as does the gratification of the happy ending: subjects' desires are fulfilled. If desire is frustrated, it is redirected to the satisfaction of a larger, social purpose. The decorum of the tale's narration, its ideological purpose, and the literary conventions of the romance form prohibit any direct confrontation with sexual division even while perpetuating male dominance as a response to the absence of sexual relation.

The narrative of *The Shipman's Tale* is structured by the operations of many overlapping systems of social exchange, but in this *fabliau* narrative the exchange of money is paramount. Money is the metonymic means to, or cause of, sex. Here, however, rather than being decorously managed and cancelled, as in *The Franklin's Tale,* debt is plainly transmitted through separate exchanges, obviously present as an absence of money that is temporarily filled by a loan. A desire for money ostensibly motivates the characters, since money gives access to their objects and thinking about money itself brings enjoyment, but the loan, or rather the lack of money covered by the loan, performs as an independent presence determining the action. Transmission of this lack subordinates to profit any ideal of social reciprocity between men or honorable masculine behavior. It simultaneously bares the absence of sexual relation, as debt exaggerates an absence of accord in heterosexual marriage, and husband and wife pursue different interests, each manipulated by the monk who intervenes between them.

In contrast to the Franklin's narrative, structured like a metonymic chain in which a transaction in one register leads sequentially to the next, in *The Shipman's Tale* lack moves through a metaphoric circuit in which one form of exchange substitutes for another while the lack that motivates the circulation returns to its starting point in the original form of debt. The wife is in debt for a hundred francs she has paid for a dress, and she agrees to have sex with a family friend, the monk daun John, in exchange for the money. The monk borrows the sum from the husband, a merchant; when the husband asks for repayment, daun John, the monk, claims he has returned the loan to the wife, who is not aware that he borrowed from her husband the money he gave her. The husband then confronts the wife and asks for the money she is supposed to have, and the wife explains that she accepted it as a gift and spent it on clothing, promising to repay with her body the hundred francs the husband has lost. The loan completes a circuit and returns to the creditor as missing, coming back to its origin like a message in an inverted form.[1]

[1] The circulation of debt structuring the narrative follows the contours of the circulation of the letter in Edgar Alan Poe's short story, "The Purloined Letter," as Lacan explains in his essay devoted to it. See "Seminar on 'The Purloined Letter'," trans. Jeffrey Mehlman, in *The Purloined Poe: Lacan, Derrida and Psychoanalytic Reading*, eds. John P. Muller and William J. Richardson (Baltimore: Johns Hopkins University Press, 1987), 28–54. Lacan shows how the letter, the tale's representative of the signifier, defines characters' positions. Although money circulates as an object, in *The Shipman's Tale* it functions also as a signifier. Indeed, a main point of Alenka Zupančič's Lacanian theory of comedy, in *The Odd One In: On Comedy* (Cambridge: MIT

Exchange in this tale operates as a metaphor, the substitution of one form of value and one object of desire for another. Its circuit complete, exchanging money becomes an equivalent of exchanging speech and engaging in sex, as all three forms of exchange are condensed in the single signifier, *taillynge* (credit, tallying), that punctuates the tale's conclusion. While sexual exchange acts as an equivalent of financial exchange in the tale, the lack of money is simultaneously a metaphoric substitution for the lack that founds desire and the absence of sexual accord.

The Lack of the Object

The characters' manipulations of ostensibly separate forms of exchange subject them to the unintended consequences of their location in exchange systems that engage them beyond their control. The merchant arranges exchanges of money and goods, but coincidentally allows for the circulation of his wife's body precisely because his desire is fixed on calculating his accounts and little else. The monk exchanges the husband's money for the use of the wife's body and gets away without paying his debt, but it is his very evasion that makes him the instrument of the couple's further exchanges. The wife, as subject of exchange, trades the use of her body for money to pay a debt for clothing, but to act as a subject she uses her body as an object of exchange, moving from the merchant's possession, to the monk's, and returning to the husband's. Each separate exchange takes place in the absence of one of the three characters; these absences allow the circulation to continue operating. Because one piece of the puzzle is always missing, the other two can move, and all three remain in play.

The debt that motivates exchange is itself a consequence of the lack that motivates (the wife's) desire. What is circulated is lack as such, and that lack ensures the perpetuation of both debt and desire. Lee Patterson shows that in highlighting the problematic of profit, the narrative at the same time demonstrates the fundamental character of desire: "Somehow, by a process we can only

> Press, 2008), is that the object and the signifier are two sides of the same coin and that comedy shows each transforming into the other.

with difficulty specify, the very fact of exchange has produced a surplus value: something has come from nothing .... What is the founding premise of a system of exchange that enables it to produce, by its very workings, a surplus value? How can something come from nothing?"[2] From the Lacanian point of view, the "nothing" that is the lack that produces desire is the result of the transformations that produce the human subject, which needs must, for the sake of surviving and thriving, respond to the demands (and desires) of others and the Other. "Need" in turn is an experience of the lack, dependency, vulnerability common to all creatures. The "something" that emerges, for the human subject, is in fact the social link.[3]

The wife is unsatisfied; she can't get what she wants (nobody can, because of our constitutive and ongoing dependence on the desire of, hence the lack in, the Other), so she continually wants more. The husband is anxious; he can't be sure that he has what he wants, for merchants and financiers like him "moote stonde in drede" (l. 237), subject to chance and to fortune (the whims of the Other, the lashings of the Real). The monk means to make himself a master of the lack in the Other. He thinks he knows how the fill the lack of the Other, disavowing his lack while showing others what they don't have. But all along his agency is merely instrumental with respect to lack; his machinations depends on it absolutely. So, while wife, husband, and monk each pursue money as they follow ostensibly separate trajectories of desire, all are captured by the process of circulation itself.

To clarify: lack places the subject in relation to an other/the Other (to a "lender" and to the (economic) symbolic order). To be in debt means that the subject seeks beyond itself for an object that will cover over and take the place of the constitutive lack that determines desire. The object lacked by the subject is the primal object that founds desire, a consequence for Lacan of the fact that the human subject does not have and cannot obtain

2 Lee Patterson, *Chaucer and the Subject of History* (Madison: University of Wisconsin Press, 1991), 349–50.
3 On the social link, see Françoise Davoine and Jean-Max Gaudillière, *History Beyond Trauma,* trans. Susan Fairfield (New York: Other Press, 2004).

what it needs on its own and is, for an extended period of time, entirely dependent on an Other that will provide for its needs. The object that would bring satisfaction is, at first, experienced as a body part rather than a person, or rather a detached body part: the breast or the voice of the Other, the anal object, the phallus of the subject-to-be. This *objet a,* this detachable "object is what is cut from the subject of desire, it is ... what is missing from him."[4] The subject will first appeal to the Other for the missing object, and then speak an unconditional demand for it; however, because the object is also lacking in the Other, which means that the Other has its own demands and desires, the Other cannot satisfy the subject. One consequence is the subject's attempt to be, to replace, the object for the Other. As desire emerges out of this exchange of demands, the subject seeks out contingent objects that will take the place, however fleetingly, of what is supposed to have been lost – money, lovers, rights to power. Freud, claims Lacan, does not affirm "that this object was really lost. The object is by nature a refound object. That it was lost is a consequence of that – but after the fact. It is thus refound without our knowing, except through the refinding, that it was ever lost."[5] This is, again, the means by which the social link is founded; it is how new subjects are created, by means of links with others/the Other that promise to replace the "lost" object but never fully can. It is worth noting that a great deal of meaningful thriving can happen along the way, provided the subject learns from the vicissitudes of desire that perfect, lasting *jouissance* is impossible for him/her/them. This is not quite the outcome of *The Shipman's Tale,* however; its snick-snack ending is hauntingly and, in critical tradition, legendarily unappealing because it functions only to redistribute lack.

We must underscore that the object of desire can only be a substitute for the first object-cause of desire, which is supposed to replace the lack in the subject or the Other. Desire is articulated

---

4   Lorenzo Chiesa, *Subjectivity and Otherness: A Philosophical Reading of Lacan* (Cambridge: MIT Press, 2007), 130–31.
5   Jacques Lacan, *The Seminar of Jacques Lacan, Book VII: The Ethics of Psychoanalysis 1959–1960,* ed. Jacques-Alain Miller, trans. Dennis Porter (New York: W.W. Norton, 1992), 118.

through the dialectics of need, demand, and desire: as Lorenzo Chiesa explains, "what is at stake for Lacan is a passage from the *'unconditionality'* of demand to the *'absoluteness'* of desire: such a change basically involves a *'positivization of lack'* on the part of the subject. The child manages to 'positivize' the lack that surfaced with the unconditionality of the demand for love, and in so doing he subjectivizes himself and emerges as a desiring lack-of-being."[6] The object is what is in you that is more than you, meaning that the object of desire is merely a filler for what never belonged to the subject in the first place. Displacements between subject and Other, and substitutions of contingent objects for the *objet a,* account for the elusiveness and illusions of desire acted out in narratives, but also for the atmosphere of necessity that accompanies these twists and turns.

The object of the desire of the self-conscious subject of language is like the *agalma* that, according to Socrates, is presumed to be incarnated in the loved one.[7] It is attributed to and displaced onto the Other as an *extimate* object, a part of the subject transferred to the possession or the being of the loved one that the lover desires to possess (again), so as to attain a missing wholeness, and that the loved one attempts to incarnate, so as to cover the lover's lack. There is, therefore, no "real" sexual relation in large part because the object of desire is a stand-in, a so sup-

6   Chiesa, *Subjectivity and Otherness,* 153–54.
7   Lacan discusses the place of the object in transference in *Le séminaire, livre VIII: Le transfert,* ed. Jacques-Alain Miller (Paris: Seuil, 1991) and specifically as *agalma* in chapter 10, 163–78. Moustafa Safouan provides further clarification of object and *agalma* in *The Seminar of Moustafa Safouan,* eds. Anna Shane and Janet Thormann (New York: Other Press, 2002), 1–12. Lacan's first full treatment of the object is *Le séminaire, livre IV: La relation d'objet,* ed. Jacques-Alain Miller (Paris: Seuil, 1994). *The Seminar of Jacques Lacan, Book XI: The Four Fundamental Concepts of Psychoanalysis,* ed. Jacques-Alain Miller, trans. Alan Sheridan (New York: W.W. Norton, 1978) discusses the gaze as object (67–105) and the object in the drive (123–200). Slavoj Žižek, *The Sublime Object of Ideology* (London: Verso, 1989), focuses on the place of the object in ideology, but his definitions of concepts, explanations of Lacan's theories, and illustrative jokes are informative in themselves.

posed re-incarnation of an original lost object. What is sought is not really an "other" but a substitute for a part of the subject experienced as lost. More specifically, what the subject seeks is the gratification the object brings: the pleasure of sucking at the breast, the sound of a voice, the Other's look of recognition or admiration. Over and above the satisfaction of need (for food, for emergency alerts, etc.), drive is directed at a surplus of enjoyment, and it is this enjoyment, extracted from circling the object, that is the goal. As Slavoj Žižek points out, the "elementary matrix of drive" is that "of our libido getting stuck onto a particular object, condemned to circulate around it forever."[8] Desire aims at an object that might deliver an impossible, full enjoyment fantasized to have been originally available; the object is valuable not in itself but as a materialization of the subject's enjoyment, something like rapture, ecstasy, or *jouissance* for Lacan. The overwhelming and deathly, excessive enjoyment of the drive is counter to well being, in contrast to its modulation in the pleasures of desire that are attained, e.g., through language. How can we eat breakfast, take a child to school, read a paper, fix a car, in a state of ecstatic self-loss? Desire for the speaking being is a compromise, satisfied by less than the "real" Thing and less than full enjoyment. The unconscious does not accept compromise, and urges us always on: the demand for enjoyment and the retrieval of the lost object is always supposed in expectations of sexual harmony. Our fate is accordingly to succumb to repetitions of the search for full enjoyment or to acknowledge the workings of this engine and the fictional status of its productions, and welcome the transient joys of living creatures. The *fabliaux* often leave us

8 Slavoj Žižek, *The Parallax View* (Cambridge: MIT Press, 2006), 25. The distinction between instinct and drive emerges here: "The basic paradox" is that "drive as opposed to instinct ... emerges precisely when what was originally a mere by-product is elevated into an autonomous aim: ... man perceives as a direct goal what ... has no intrinsic value ... we get caught into a closed, self-propelling loop of repeating the same gesture and finding satisfaction in it" (62–63). A fixation on enjoyment, the outcome of the return of the drive to the same place, accounts for repetition. Such an account of drive demonstrates how conservative, in the sense of "conserving," unconscious processes can be.

with this wisdom: take responsibility for your own part, for your own enjoyment, Everything is not within your purview. But sometimes they leave us cold.

The object of desire brings a pleasure that makes up for a loss of what the subject never fully had, but approaching too close to the object carries a disturbing anxiety. Just because it circulates as a debt, that is, as lack, money as an object of desire in *The Shipman's Tale* provokes anxiety. According to Freud, money is an anal object, a substitute for excrement, and the subject who is fixed on the anal stage is characterized as retentive; this theorization was simplified in popular psychology, especially during the fifties in the United States,[9] and the anal character has become a contemporary stereotype. But the anal stage is importantly the inculcation of a discipline that shapes us all; it introduces the control of letting go and holding on to the object at "appropriate" times (the time of the Other), so that the anal object may relate to the Other as a gift, when it is given in accord with a demand, or is withheld in an act of aggression. However, money is a peculiar object of desire. Shit is largely regarded as an epitome of worthlessness despite its potential value as manure, but money in Chaucer's time was regarded as valuable material, composed of metals and weighed scrupulously, while at the same time functioning more and more as a universal equivalent, a measure of value. In this sense, the anal object may serve as a signifier. The anal object that is money performs both as a material object of desire and as a signifier in exchange.

If, in the imaginary, narcissistic relation, to love is to give what one does not have so as to cover the lack of the other, then the other is itself an object. The subject is separated from itself by the object of drive and lacks the object of desire, and it is alienated in an image of the body form that is the narcissistic object of love and rivalry. Without a clear distinction between itself and the surrounding world, stimulated by internal drives and external stimulation, the would-be subject grasps itself in an image in the mirror and see the other in its place, so that the reflection

---

9 See especially Norman O. Brown, *Life against Death: The Psychoanalytic Meaning of History* (Middleton: Wesleyan University Press, 1986).

is both the ego's image and an other who may be the object of comic recognition or aggression, for example, in the rivalry between Nicholas and Absolon in *The Miller's Tale* or in the Reeve's anxious identification with the Miller's carpenter. Hence the subject is split in several registers: misrecognized in an image; divided by a real object that carries enjoyment; and also alienated in the symbolic by language, through identification with a name, by master signifiers standing for the ego's ideal traits, and by letters marking the sources of enjoyment on the body's openings. The object is desirable insofar as it figures the original, lost object and is hence supposed to be capable of suturing the subject: "you complete me."

Enactments of this fundamental relation of the subjectified human to lack are as various as the day is long. The object of desire that covers over lack operates in relation to the subject in an unconscious structure that determines a particular, characteristic mode of relation to the object in a specific mode of enjoyment. The characters in *The Shipman's Tale* all desire money as their object, but each gains enjoyment in a specific structure. There is, at the same time, a typicality, a driven stereotypy, to their actions that reflects the hopeless effort to *derive* substance from their object. The husband is an obsessive who enjoys by calculating profit and loss; the obsessive disavows lack and so works to deny the desire of the Other. The monk performs as a pervert who makes of himself an object for the enjoyment of the Other; he enjoys not merely the wife's body but also being an instrument mediating the married couple's enjoyment. The pervert acts to break the law in order to force the law to declare itself, just as the monk avoids repayment but engineers the discovery of his evasion. The wife is a hysteric whose desire is for the perpetuation of desire; she wants to maintain lack so that she may keep on desiring. The hysteric seeks out a master in order to show that the master is lacking and thereby attempts to perpetuate dissatisfaction. Moving the debt from character to character, and so keeping lack in motion, the narrative as a whole is motivated by the desire of the hysteric, by the wife's original lack of money, as a productive, if anxious, source of object enjoyment and pleasure.

Signifying Exchange

As lack circulates between speakers in the Shipman's narrative, the systematic exchange of money, functioning as the object that is supposed to replace debt, increasingly becomes a means towards the exchange of sex and speech. Repetitions of several master signifiers in the narration and in the characters' speech condense the signifieds of the several, imbricated, metonymic chains of money, sex, and language, suggesting that objects may become interchangeable and substitute for one another. *Bisy* and *bisynesse* signify both the obsessive mental calculations and accountings of the merchant and the movement of money through public space. The merchant warns his wife that she cannot comprehend his esoteric business – "litel kanstow devyne / The curious bisynesse that we have" (ll. 224–25). He leaves home quickly and busily – "Now gooth this marchant faste and bisily (l. 302) – to pursue his financial transactions. Then, when the adulterous lovers pursue their transactions, *bisy* also describes sexual activity: "In myrthe al nyght a bisy lyf they lede" (l. 318). The tale is in fact busy with the merchant's and the monk's comings and goings, and the identifications of specific cities, such as Bruges, Paris, and Seint-Denys, which locate the men's movements in a large and contemporary, recognizable, commercial world of trade and finance. The pulsations of the drive, shaped by rapidity, formal intricacy, the geography of trade, serve as a kind of compensation for substance and lasting *jouissance*.

The adverbs *up* and *doun* and their associated synonyms denoting standing and rising up describe bodies' activities in space and in sex. The married couple is as happy with daun John's coming to their home "As fowel is fayn whan that the sonne upriseth" (l. 51). The merchant "up ariseth" (l. 75) to go to work on his accounts; the wife goes to his counting house, "Up to hir housbonde" (l. 212), to urge him to come down to dinner – "Com doun to-day, and lat youre bagges stonde" (l. 220), with "bagges" as an implied reference to testicles, an indication that finances have displaced sexual pleasures for him. The husband complies by going down – "And doun he gooth" (l. 250) – to a hasty meal that unites the three in a parody of the domestic social exchange of eating together. The monk also gets up in the morning – "was rysen in the morwe" (l. 89) – and the wife questions what bothers him that he arises so early: "What eyleth yow so rathe for to ryse" (l. 99)? She then proceeds to indulge in complaints about her marriage: her husband has not kept her awake all night, for "it stant nat so with me" (l. 114), to hint at his inadequacy, and while she is miserable, she must not reveal how it stands with her: "Dar I nat telle how that it stant with me" (l. 120). The phallus is veiled. The repetition of *stant* in the context of talk about sex suggests that for the husband to leave off his accounting and let his "bagges stonde" would be to engage in sex. Explicitly concealing meaning by means of indirection allows her to indicate what she wants: the wife desires sex, but the husband isn't interested. Still: would that satisfy her? Because she also wants clothes.

The suggestion throughout the narrative is that the merchant either makes money or makes love and that these activities are linked in their mutual exclusion. Anxiety about money interferes with his desire, substituting for anxiety about sex and his marriage. He is too preoccupied with his accounting, his reckoning, to attend to the body, thereby putting in danger his wife's body by extending its circulation: He goes upstairs "To rekene with hymself ... / how that it with hym stood" (ll. 78–79). The language implies there is something masturbatory about his business and busy-ness, and before he can "come adoun" (l. 156), the monk arranges to have the wife "in his armes bolt upright" (l. 316). The merchant explains that men of finance always "moote stonde in drede" (l. 237), anxious about money. As the narrative concludes, he completes his commerce and, with a very large profit, returns to attend to his wife: "this marchant gan embrace / His wyf al newe, and kiste hire on hir face, / And up he gooth and maketh it ful tough" (ll. 377–79), so that in the final scene the connotations of up and doun become explicitly sexualized denotations.

As it does in *The Miller's Tale*, the signifier *pryvetee* likewise accumulates ambivalent meanings as it is repeated in differing contexts. *Pryvetee* or *privitee* generally denotes "secretly" or "in secret." The wife "cam walkynge pryvely" (l. 92) as she enters a garden to make arrangements with the monk. She offers a pretense of feminine modesty – "But sith I am a wyf, it sit nat me / To tellen no wight of oure privetee, / Neither abedde, ne in noon other place" (ll. 163–65) – before going ahead to reveal the sexual frustration she has refused to reveal, with *privetee* referring to the marital relation and obliquely to the private parts she is planning to trade on. The pun here recalls the Miller's advice to the Reeve in *The Miller's Prologue*: "An housbonde shal nat been inquisityf / Of Goddes pryvetee, nor of his wyf. / So he may fynde Goddes foyson [God's plenty] there, / Of the remenant nedeth nat enquere" (ll. 3163–66), where pryvetee outrageously couples God's hidden wisdom with the woman's body part, "there," and the weighing of "plenty" with "what's left"; the remainder also conjoins sex with economic judgment. As well, the relation between money and sex in *The Shipman's Tale* links *pryvetee* to finances. The merchant explains to the wife the necessity to "kepen oure estaat in pryvetee" (l. 232), but allows himself to be duped secretly by the monk when in he conveys the hundred francs "prively ... to daun John" (l. 294) and thereby allows access to the wife. Privacy is a space for mental calculation, as well as for closeness in relationship, as in *cosynage,* and for cunning calculation, as in the *cosynage* of taking advantage of or cheating another. It is for intimacy but also exclusion, secrecy, and sharing.

External physical space, bodily space, and internal consciousness are ambivalently related throughout the narration and in conversations through the signifier *pryvetee,* while transactions of money and sex take place in the several private places the narrative inhabits. These spaces, as they provide room for privacy, come to enable and to figure an effect of subjectivity, that is, the impression that characters are engaged in autonomous, inner processes of thought.[10] The domestic enclave is at the same time

10 In a complex article that focuses on women writing and reading letters, Sarah Stanbury, "Women's Letters and Private Space in Chaucer," *Exemplaria* 6, no. 2 (Fall 1994): 271–86, points out that the divide between public and private domains and the attachment of rights to the private person vary greatly in times and cultures. In relating internal to architectural and spatial privacy, she investigates the "spatial taxonomy of the self" (277, 299) and in especial "physical seclusion and mental autonomy, privacy as a territory" (282), showing that the autonomy of Chaucer's women in space raises tensions and complex "questions about control ... [and] protections and vulnerabilities in a patriarchal domestic empire" (279). The Miller's pun on "privetee" is

both private and public, filled with a *meyne,* the company of attending servants, and the visiting presence of the monk; notably, a surplus young girl, a "mayde child" (l. 95), accompanies the wife to the secret conversation with the monk in a garden. The monk takes the merchant husband apart in privacy to arrange the loan: "sobrely / This chapman took apart, and prively / He said hym thus" (ll. 255–56). The husband spends inordinate amounts of time in his *countour,* the study or counting room in which he figures his accounts, as the wife complains, "How longe tyme wol ye rekene and caste / Youre sommes, and youre bookes, and youre thynges?/ The devel have part on alle swiche rekenynges!" (ll. 216–18). Mental calculations are not animated but synonymous with physical objects, "books" and "things," in a parallel structure separating each noun with "and" so that each carries a discrete weight.

His professional role in an economy of money demands of the merchant a privacy and secrecy in his calculations. The narrator's detailed, exact reports, that "chaffare is so deere / That nedes moste he make a chevyssaunce, / For he was bounden in a reconyssaunce / To paye twenty thousand sheeld anon" ("the merchandise is so dear that he must borrow money, for he owed

> a key locus for the nexus of feminine desire, subjectivity, and physical space, for it "acknowledges that both God and women share certain kinds of privacy in common – that there are things men cannot know …. [and] suggests that women in Chaucer's fictions could indeed claim privacy as a territory of the person" (279). Stanbury cites Charles de la Roncière's chapter "Tuscan Notables on the Eve of the Renaissance," in *A History of Private Life, vol. II: Revelations of the Medieval World,* ed. Georges Duby, trans. Arthur Goldhammer (Cambridge: Harvard University Press, 1988) 157–309, for its treatment of women's private spaces, and studies of later periods that also indicate the coincidence of subjectivity, privacy, interior architectural spaces, and various aesthetic objects, e.g., Patricia Fumerton, *Cultural Aesthetics: Renaissance Literature and the Practice of Social Ornament* (Chicago: University of Chicago Press, 1991), 69. The merchant husband's *countour* is an early example of personal, private space; likewise the enclosed domestic garden allows for secret conversation and for the wife's revelation of privacy that itself indicates inner processes of calculation.

by formal pledge twenty thousand sheelds," ll. 328–31), and "wel he knew he stood in swich array / That nedes moste he wynne in that viage [trip] / A thousand frankes aboven al his costage [expenditure]" (ll. 370–72), though presented in indirect diction, point to a mental accounting and thereby imply a private consciousness at work, but to a consciousness, no matter how private, that is vulnerable to the world.[11] The merchant must take advantage of opportunity, "Of hap and fortune in oure chapmanhede" (l. 238), and respond to chance. The wife and monk, as well as the merchant husband, are characterized with a similarly calculating mentality in their sexual relations. As Cathy Hume points out, the wife manipulates her roles in the domestic economy "as hostess, social networker, housekeeper, business assistant, and status symbol" to get what she wants, particularly with the monk: she "uses her role as hostess to provide a pretext for her interaction with the monk that her husband thoroughly approves, and, indeed, requires of her."[12] The monk insinuates his way into the household, taking advantage of social networking between contemporary monastic societies and merchants, by bringing gifts "of money, food, and drink" and offering a "satisfying, high-status connection,"[13] all for his own benefit.

The tale also achieves its remarkable subjectivity effect by managing what the characters do *not* say. In their encounter in the garden, lines 98–208, the wife and monk engage in a kind of delicate song and dance,[14] each teasing out the other, wait-

---

[11] Thomas Hahn spells out the complex nature of the dealings of the merchant, who he explains is "a financial entrepreneur" in "the newly flourishing fourteenth-century money market" (238), in "Money, Sexuality, Wordplay, and Context in the *Shipman's Tale*," in *Chaucer in the Eighties,* eds. Julian N. Wasserman and Robert J. Blanch (Syracuse: Syracuse University Press, 1986), 235–49, esp. 237–39. See also John M. Ganim, "Double Entry in Chaucer's *Shipman's Tale:* Chaucer and Bookkeeping Before Pacioli," *The Chaucer Review* 30, no. 3 (1996): 294–305.

[12] Kathy Hume, "Domestic Opportunities: the Social Comedy of *the Shipman's Tale,*" *The Chaucer Review* 41, no. 2 (2006): 138–62, at 139, 141.

[13] Ibid., 143.

[14] Derek Pearsall, *"The Canterbury Tales* II: Comedy," in *The Cambridge*

ing on time to pick up on what each implies to attain what each wants, so that what remains unspoken leads directly to the verbal agreement, sealed indirectly by the wife, "For at a certeyn day I wol yow paye, / And doon to yow what plesance and service / That I may doon, right as yow list devise" (ll. 190–92), and by the monk's implicit understanding of her desire, suggested in his promise, "For I wol delyvere yow out of this care" (l. 200). His explicit commitment to give her money, "I wol brynge yow an hundred frankes" (l. 201), temporarily veils that sexual bargain with the fig leaf of a gift of money, while the consequent action, "And with that word he caughte hire by the flankes, / And hire embraceth harde, and kiste her ofte" (ll. 202–3), conveys both familiarity and ownership, marking their mutual understanding that sex is exchanged for money. As with the *Manciple's Prologue and Tale,* elaborate circumlocution points to the absent presence of the object-cause of desire and to the full subjectivity that could never be.

Especially in the concluding, bedtime reckoning, the silences between husband and wife lie thick, because of the focalization on the couple in bed; in the absence of a described setting, their speech, and lack of speech, fill up the space of the tale's visual screen. When the husband admonishes her for not reporting the supposed return of his loan, the wife understands that the monk has cheated them both by using the husband's money to pay her and that she must account for what has happened to the money. She comes up with an alibi and a compromise that has to involve complex and quick thinking: first, she must comprehend that the monk has cheated the husband of the loan, for the money the monk gave her was payment for sex, not a repayment to the

---

Chaucer Companion, eds. Piero Boitani and Jill Mann (Cambridge: Cambridge University Press, 1986), 125–42, somewhat disturbingly discusses the scene in detail, studying it as "a beautifully decorous comedy of manners, with each delicate advance towards mutual understanding carefully planned and signaled" (135). He sums it up, stating that "It is like making love over the counter, and in some strange way the exchange of money seems to legitimize rather than corrupt the encounter. Nothing comes out in the open, of course" (136), diminishing what is perhaps a more predatory confrontation.

husband; second, she must swallow whatever indignation she harbors, for the monk has indirectly revealed to the husband that she has been paid for sex; third, she must give a false explanation of what happened to the missing money to account for the lie without explaining what actually happened; and finally she must resolve the debt.

The husband "sees," understands, he has lost his money – "This marchant saugh ther was no remedie / And for to chide it nere but folie, / Sith that the thing may nat amended be" (ll. 427–29) – and he accepts the outcome silently in compromise, since, *sith,* nothing can be done. What *the thing* signifies is ambiguous: in a different context, daun John has "his thynges seyd" (l. 91), perhaps said his prayers perfunctorily or greeted the household; for the husband here, however, certainly *thing* is the situation, the loss of his money, but suggests also the wife and specifically her sex: he cannot control what she does with herself. However, while he does not directly confront her with her adultery, his silence produces a subjectivity effect, the impression that he is considering what she says, that unspoken mental work accompanies listening to another. What he does not say is an acceptance of an absence of relation; his silence is the outcome of a choice, leaving her to her desire and acknowledging her difference. The choice acknowledges, without saying so, the indissolubility of the lack that drives the human subject and its sociality.

The ambiguity of the terms negotiating the couple's ultimate settlement further builds on the lack-imbued subjective space of each character. Throughout the tale, conversation – between the monk and the wife, as well as the wife and the husband – has depended on ambiguous signifiers and on what has not been said. The couple's concluding exchange is a radical example of such getting at the truth by half-truths. The wife's ready and testy explanation plays on the husband's honor – "for I have bistowed it so weel / For youre honour, for Goddes sake, I seye" (ll. 420–21) – that is, the honor he displays by showing off a well dressed wife; implicitly, however, she is reminding him that publicizing adultery or calling in the debt will cause the husband to lose further honor by risking public exposure.[15] Taking vengeance

---

15 In a study of jurisdiction concerning adultery in fifteenth-century

will amend nothing, but rather expose him to ridicule. His reconciliation may then be a covert warning: "Now wyf," he seyde, "and I foryeve it thee; / But, by thy lyf, ne be namoore so large. / Keep bet thy good, this yeve I thee in charge" (ll. 430–32). His is an admonition, "take better care of your money," or a threat, "don't betray me again," with *thy good,* which he should control. The husband falls back on the good husbandry that is his virtue. Lack can be managed in the future, he hopes, by means of better keeping.

Nevertheless, in spite of and in part due to the compromise they achieve, personal relations in the tale are revealed to be a species of *cosynage:* the familiar friendship between husband and monk that the monk denies and manipulates, the monk's deception of both husband and wife, and the domestic deception, all conveyed in silence and in the silent awareness of verbal implication. In this sometimes cynical representation of marriage in a mercantile environment of calculation and risk, lies are efficacious and compromise necessary to keep desire, and business, rolling along.[16]

Toulouse, Leah Otis-Cour, *"De juro novo:* Dealing with Adultery in the Fifteenth-Century Toulousain," *Speculum* 84, no. 2 (2002): 347–92, while admitting "that female adultery could sometimes provoke violent reactions in the late Middle Ages," argues that "the very emphasis on Christian, monogamous, indissoluble marriage and the quality of the marital relationship led, generally speaking, not to harsh repression but to the opposite, a decline of repressive responses to female adultery" (347–48). She accumulates examples of cases from a region of France from a period later than Chaucer's, but her discussion reveals the many reasons adultery might be handled to avoid risking public exposure. Her argument is perhaps limited by a failure to discuss more fully what "repressive responses" might entail.

16 Cathy Hume's discussion of *The Shipman's Tale,* in "Domestic Opportunities," does not focus on the manipulation and exploitative potential of the interactions between the husband, wife, and monk. Her discussions of *The Franklin's Tale* and *The Merchant's Tale,* as well as *The Shipman's Tale* draw on expected norms of marriage to provide a context for female responsibilities and behaviors in marriage. I was not able to consider her arguments, since her book was published after my manuscript was completed.

Anxieties of Exchange

Duplicity is a sort of relation, but an anxious relation lacking trust. *The Shipman's Tale* is permeated by anxiety, despite and even because of its witty ending, punctuated by *taillynge,* the signifier drawing together all the circuits of exchange. Some of that anxiety surely arises from the duplicitous relationships the narrative tracks and from the concomitant self-deception that maintains relations; if each knows that the other is lying, each must act in spite of that knowledge, as if without knowledge, thus essentially lying to oneself. A certain cynicism is thereby produced, underlined by the repeated epithets characterizing proper names and nouns: the merchant is *noble,* generous, and forbearing, despite his loss of honor; the wife is "this goode wyf" and "this faire wyf," despite her petulant impatience and cunning; the scheming monk is "this noble monk," "this gentil monk," *daun,* that is, noble, John. The monk is himself a source of anxiety, positioned as he is in an intimate exclusion in the marriage. A monk's place is in the monastery, but daun John continually intrudes into the domestic household, taking advantage of friendship with the husband, and he travels on commercial business for his abbot. He functions within symbolic exchange, but at the same time he escapes its reciprocity, making use of the loan while disavowing his debt. The monk acts in the position of the pervert, the subject who acknowledges the law in order to avoid it, exploiting that acknowledgement just to play with the law. His effort is to prove the law's existence by transgressing it. Violating not only the regulations of his order against fornication, he also puts sexual difference in question, for he is characterized by an ambiguous gender identification: he is described as *fair,* "a fair man" (l. 25), "so fair of face" (l. 28), a conventionally feminizing epithet he shares with the wife. In his disavowal of the law, he acts like a shifter, performing in varying positions – friend, needy applicant, sympathetic confidante, adulterous lover – to insert himself as a substitution to take a role in an exchange while remaining outside it. For example, he avoids repaying his debt by adapting the potential of language for duplication, uncertainty, and ambiguity: "I took unto oure dame, / Youre wyf, at hom, the same gold ageyn, / Upon youre bench; she woot it wel, certeyn, /

By certeyn tokenes that I kan hire telle./ ... Grete wel oure dame, myn owne nece sweete" ("greet well our dame, my own sweet niece," ll. 356–59, 363). The polite address to the husband masks a cynical exploitation of intimacy and sociability. What security can the ambiguous "certeyn tokenes" offer, when the wife and the loan have changed places by entering into exchange, so that neither remains stable? Whom do the pronouns contain and exclude, and in what capacity is possession indicated? *Myn, youre,* and *oure* as shifters inherently destabilize both possession and identity, both indicating and moving between enunciative positions. Since possessives are available to identify any speaker, the pronouns suggest that a man may not be sure in his property. The monk's speech acts as blackmail, his pronouns and *tokenes* positioning him between, even as they identify him alternately with, the husband and the wife's possible positions.

The monk's perverse disavowal of the law holds the marriage hostage by coercing others into silence, for he anticipates that the wife will have to comply with and support his deception, especially since he claims to have *tokenes* with which to betray her. He knows that the wife will know he has tricked her. What is curious is that, as he speaks here, he is revealing himself to the husband in the process of sharing pronouns that allow them to be identified; he wants his deception to be recognized at the same time that he wants to get away with it. The question remains what the husband's following silence signifies: this merchant, who was ironically so cautious and wise, "This marchant, which that was ful war and wys" (wary and wise, l. 365), does not respond to the monk's speech, either having noted its implications or falling for the excuse, for immediately he is said to have finished his business and returns home pleased, in which case he is also the dupe of the narrator's cynical description. The audience, however, does not *know* for certain what the husband is thinking; something is held in reserve or "pryvete," putting the audience on the same uncertain footing as the gulled, which helps to generate *The Shipman's Tale's* anxiogenic and ambiguous affective effects. The cynicism of duplicitous speech becomes a perverse dramatic irony when the monk hints at his intentions by justifying the loan with the explanation that he must buy "certein beestes ... To store with a place that is oures" (ll. 272–73). The beasts are legible as his own animal parts, which he will keep in the secure place he shares with the husband, as his own admission indicates: "God helpe me so, I wolde it were youres!" (l. 274). He offers sly regret for what he is about to do, exposing his exploitation of what is not his. At this point in the narrative, if the husband does not know what is up, the audience does, so that his suggestive diction might encourage sympathy for his naiveté and spontaneous generosity or a cynical disdain for the gulled who enables the guller. As noted above, however, the audience's knowledge with respect to the "minds of others" is neither secure nor complete.[17]

Shiftiness has dangerous associations in *The Shipman's Tale*. The imagery suggested by "certain beestes" is linked to several other references to bodies torn apart. The monk compares sexually inactive husbands to a hare in a warren threatened by dogs: "thise wedded men, that lye and dare / As in a fourme sit a wery hare / Were al forstraught with houndes grete and smale" (ll. 103–5). The wife vows to the monk to keep their affair a secret, on pain of punishment "As foul as evere hadde Genylon of France" (l. 194); Ganylon was torn apart by horses in punishment for his betrayal in the *Song of Roland*. The two allusions to bodies torn by beasts is linked to a third in the wife's promise to maintain the monk's confidence, "I swere / Though men me wolde al into pieces tere" (ll. 135–36). The imagery expresses the anxiety associated with what Lacan describes as the body in bits and pieces, *morcellé*, the French more literally signifying "bitten off" or "chewed up," an anxiety about bodily integrity that is mastered by the sight of the mirrored form but aroused and repeated with every threat of castration or danger to ego integrity. The fear of bodily dismemberment is also attached to male fears of the demands of women's sexuality, and the monk's innuendo that that wife is not sufficiently "laboured" (l. 108) confirms and underscores her unsatisfied appetite.

Female sexuality is at stake here, but in a certain historical form: the female sexual Thing looked at from the standpoint

---

17 See Mark Solms on "the problem of other minds," in *The Hidden Spring: A Journey to the Source of Consciousness* (New York: W.W. Norton, 2021), 9.

of the socio-economic link in later medieval Europe.[18] The overriding source of anxiety in the tale is specific to its growing cash economy and its financing and manipulation of credit and debt. The discomfort of some sectors of medieval society with the growth of an economy based on money is well known, especially as it accompanies the practice of interest.[19] Earning money by lending money or speculating on its value was considered by the Church to be profiting from unnatural category violations, from confusing natural or spiritual productivity with the growth of empty abstractions or dead matter. For example, a number of Chaucerians have argued that the Pardoner and his trade in holy commodities exemplify the threat of spiritual infertility. In this line of thinking, his nihilism is the logical extreme and divorce of spirit from the world: the whole of material creation, and of the body in especial, is just dead matter and, because already dead, unable to die.[20] Medieval discourse treating monetary interest

---

18 See Lacan, *Seminar VII,* 135–41 on art, anamorphosis, and seeing from the standpoint of *Das Ding.*
19 Thomas Hahn, "Money, Sexuality, Wordplay, and Context in the *Shipman's Tale,*" reviews sources for the prohibition of usury in biblical injunction and natural law, showing how the tale's associations of sex and money play on a concept of usury as "a make-believe sexual entanglement" that is "a sin against society" and, for Dante, a "sin against self, neighbor, and God" (243).
20 H. Marshall Leicester, Jr., *The Disenchanted Self: Representing the Subject in the Canterbury Tales* (Berkeley: University of California Press, 1990) reads the Pardoner through Lacanian theory to give an invaluable reading of the Pardoner and to redirect thinking about Chaucer's pilgrims as a whole; for the Pardoner, see esp. 35–64, 161–94. He accounts for the Pardoner's subjectivity as "the structure of the space within which his self-presentation occurs and of which it is a subset" and describes it "as a form of disenchantment" (63). See also Carolyn Dinshaw's portrait of the Pardoner as a fetishist, drawing on the mechanism of disavowal as Freud and Octave Mannoni describe it, "I *know* but even *so...*" (176), in *Chaucer's Sexual Poetics* (Madison: University of Wisconsin Press, 1989), 156–84. Further consideration of the Pardoner's objects goes beyond the limits of this chapter. In a complex treatment of how discourses produce literary character, Elizabeth Fowler, *Literary Character: The Human Figure in Early English Writing* (Ithaca: Cornell University Press, 2003), examines

argued that lenders profited from time, which was not theirs to give, and the paradoxical substance of money that would grow was the ultimate source of suspicion and anxiety. Metaphoric language underlines the ambiguous status of the reproduction of inorganic matter as profit. The Shipman points out "Of chapmen, that hir moneie is hir plough" (l. 288), aligning cash with an instrument like a plough that works to promote natural reproduction. Laboring over his accounts, "To rekene with hymself ... how that it with hym stood ... And if that he encressed were or noon (ll. 78–79, 81), the husband's activities seek to generate and account for increase. In both illustrations of the unnatural category violation, the merchant husband works on his own, with no need of the Other for the act of generation. And yet, as *The Shipman's Tale* reminds us, an economy is in fact necessary to produce something from no/thing.

A cash economy demands a willingness to take risk; it rewards flexibility and the exploitation of circumstance. Anomalously for its *fabliau* form, *The Shipman's Tale* voices an anxious fear of the transience of fortune and of change, and specifically of the effects of transience on money-making.[21] Its characterization of the mer-

> "three principles" underlying "theoretical discussions of money in the middle ages: its *sterility,* its *consumptibility,* and its *atemporality"*(78), arguing that each of these is evoked by the Pardoner. His performance deploys consumptibility as a kind of gluttony and fraud: it "is a quality of money that classifies it with wine. Wine cannot be sold again after it is consumed; thus neither can money. In this view, of course, illicit financial transactions are associated with gluttony, waste, and sexual activity devoid of the intention to procreate" (80). See 76–87 for the condensed review of canonical thinking on money. I am indebted to Fowler's concept of character, even while "consumptibility" does not clearly figure in *The Shipman's Tale,* except perhaps in its analogous anxiety about using up Fortune and change as a consumption of time.

21 For Patterson, in *Chaucer and the Subject of History,* the tale's concern and the source of its anxiety, is "exchange per se" (350), which he defines as "the primary condition of economic man" (351), rather than money and interest. Patterson provides a valuable review of a medieval Aristotelian tradition of economic thinking that provides a background for Chaucer's tales about marriage and commerce (351–58). His emphasis on "a fallen and alienating history" (356) may lead to

chant husband's obsessive study of his accounts – his worry about the need to take advantage of opportunity, to carry on trade, to buy and to take on debt, to profit from loans and exchange rates – demonstrates the necessity that the merchant "gooth ... faste and bisily / Aboute his need, and byeth, and creaunceth [obtains credit]" (ll. 302–3) is the representation of a new mentality that was entering into and upsetting more traditional forms of economic behavior. Although markets and urban production had flourished in medieval England alongside rural agriculture, in the later half of the fourteenth century trade expanded, new forms of organizing production developed, and financial innovations appeared.[22] Just as the figure of the merchant would be a source of anxiety in a developing economy, the merchant's activities keep him in a consistently anxious state, keeping him "in drede," in fear of the very change he also depends on: "therefore have I greet necessitee / Upon this queynte [complicated, curious] world t'avyse me; / For everemoore we moote stonde in drede / Of hap and fortune in oure chapmanhede" (ll. 235–38), with connotations of the signifiers *queynte* and *stonde* witnessing again how sexual and financial anxieties are intertwined in this tale. The merchant seems to be mastered by his concerns, and if he presses on circumstance, having to "dryve forth the world as it may be" (l. 231), he is equally driven by a powerful inner compulsion, since merchants may not rest until death, until "we

>   an overstated reading of the Shipman's merchant husband as a model for "fallen man" who "preserves vestiges of the primal innocence he has lost" (357), but the description of the husband's prudence and his ethical behavior does show how he is an exception in a setting in which "the domestic becomes an extension of the commercial" where "everything has its price" (351).
> 22 Rodney Hilton, *Class Conflict and the Crisis of Feudalism* (London: Verso, 1990), gives a full and focused study of the changing economy of late medieval England, with an emphasis on class conflict and class anxiety from a Marxist point of view: "The problem, especially between about 1380 and 1450, was seen by ... contemporaries as a general upward move of the whole of the lower class, as much as social climbing by individual parvenus" (174). The Shipman's Merchant represents an emergent social figure from a status group "that had to be included" in a traditional "tripartite image" of society.

be deed" (l. 233). The need to profit when it is possible, *while one has good reputation*, "whil we have a name" (l. 289), recognizes temporal limits to warding off the threatening extreme of poverty: "goldlees for to be, it is no game" (l. 290). Imminent ruin hangs over the merchant. Compulsive activity – obsessively calculating accounts and constantly coming and going to manage financial ventures – are means to ward off anxiety, to protect against the fear of the loss of wealth that is a disaster or catastrophic end waiting to happen. Yet again, chance is also the merchant's element, risk his means of gain as well as loss, and the manager of his *oikos*, his home economy, is of course also risky and unreliable, at once sexually and financially. In this tale, so to speak, Lady Luck is as fallible and uncertain as her supposed victims. Hence her husband, rather than punishing her, turns a kind of complicit eye toward her transgressions.

Anxieties about making money and Fortune's temporality are introduced at the very start of the narrative. The narrator's opening complaint against transience is connected to money generally, to the profit and loss of expense, "dispence" (l. 5), but in particular to the honor and status men may gain from spending on their wives' display. "Swiche salutaciouns and contenaunces / Passen as dooth a shadwe upon the wal" (ll. 8–9): reputation is insubstantial, as well as fleeting. Yet the image of insubstantial worldly pleasure, because it carries the weight of centuries of Platonic, neo-Platonic, and Augustinian thought, resonates not simply in its context's focus on money, women, and clothing, but extends to embrace materiality as such. A shadow appears on a wall as the trace of an absent cause, just as in the traditional image of vanity the material forms of the world are reflected in a mirror; the implication in both cases is to question the reality of matter, to make the concrete source of shadow or reflection even less substantial than its trace. Money and sexual pleasure, dependent as that pleasure is on women, along with the honor dependent on women's desire and conveyed in part through their clothing, are all insecure, and the conjoining of money and desire under the appearance of clothing will be a special concern of the narrative.

New anxieties about money are therefore connected in *The Shipman's Tale* to traditional and pervasive anxieties about women's desires and worldly mutability in general. The trouble with money lies not only in its dead materiality, or its lack of a rational foundation for profit, or the insecurity of its possession; not only was money considered infertile, but loaning and borrowing were especially suspicious because abstract. Complex financial operations seemed to be especially opaque. Without value in itself but signifying value and with the power to determine value, money is transformed in financing as an object of calculation. The relation to money of the Shipman's merchant is not the sensuous enjoyment of Marlowe's Barabus, who revels in the aura of gold pieces, but the substance of a continual mental activity that carries enjoyment, the peculiarly painful pleasure of the drive. The merchant may set out his records and his bags of wealth on his table – "His bookes and his bagges many oon / He leith biforn hym on his countyng-bord" (ll. 82–83) – but his purpose is to calculate, to "rekene with hymself" (l. 78), not to fondle or gaze on coins but to draw up accounts, "how that it with hym stood, / And how that he despended hadde his good, / And if that he encressed were or noon" (ll. 80–81). He may promise his wife a cash present, "silver in thy purs" (l. 248), but he is never shown to be physically handling pieces of money, and his promise is delivered in the context of a directive about good husbandry (ll. 244–46).

Functioning as an abstraction and a cause of calculation, money brings enjoyment to the merchant as the object of an obsession; it is a signifier in reckoning, an abstraction to manage, and as a signifier, a representation of an absence. Thinking about money is his symptomatic enjoyment. And as with any obsessive, the insistence on the one kind of enjoyment prohibits any other; he cannot enjoy sex while he enjoys calculating, his wife complains, and in the end, it is his knowledge of his financial profit that enables sex, as the *for* of causation indicates: "And hoom he gooth, murie as a papejay / For wel he knew he stood in swich array" (ll. 369–70). But no sooner is the sexual activity finished than the husband returns immediately to reckoning accounts. *The Shipman's Tale* adds to the traditional concept of greed a more contemporary insight into passional calculation and the historical patterning of *jouissance* more generally.

The merchant husband's intellectual management of the rarified, esoteric instruments of finance emerging in the late medieval economy may perhaps be related to the teller of the tale. For the Shipman, brawny drinker, dangerously armed "good felawe" (*General Prologue,* l. 395), canny profiteer, and by innuendo a killer – "By water he sente hem hoom to every lond" (*General Prologue,* l. 400) – is skilled in the complex arts of navigation: "But of his craft to rekene wel his tydes, / His stremes, and his daungers hym bisides, / His herberwe, and his moone, his lodemenage, / Ther nas noon swich from Hulle to Cartage" (*General Prologue,* ll. 401–4). The accumulation of specialized terms is hyperbolic, but it indicates a mastery of technique – in some accounts, the beginnings of a science.[23] Mastering the skills to measure routes and determine locations involves abstract operations similar to those enabling advanced trade and financing. Both the narrator and his character are dependent upon such new instruments of calculation. If *The Shipman's Tale* was originally intended for the Wife of Bath, Chaucer arguably found an even more powerful place for it in the mouth of the Shipman. Chaucerians have long noted the gender instability evident in the voice of the narrator whose opening comments introduce the narrative and suggest its moral: the distribution of pronouns in the introductory passage show that it is spoken by a woman. The resulting uncertainty about the speaker's identity and position is commonly ascribed to Chaucer's original intention to give the tale to the Wife of Bath.[24] The tale's concerns are indeed consistent with those of the Wife of Bath, who is a weaver, covered in voluminous material in her portrait, concerned with feminine display in her prologue, and like the Shipman's wife, a self-trading commodity who exchanges her body for the wealth of aging husbands. However, *The Shipman's Tale* uniquely emphasizes links between the exchange of money and women and anxieties

---

23 For a brilliant contemporary study of ship navigation and the psychology of extended (and enactive) cognition, see Edwin Hutchin's *Cognition in the Wild* (Cambridge: MIT Press, 1996).

24 William Witherle Lawrence discusses the attribution of the tale in "Chaucer's *Shipman's Tale,*" *Speculum* 33, no. 1, summarizing manuscript evidence, 58–60.

about Fortune and transience to a new *jouis-sens* of abstract calculation absent in the Wife's performance and in other *fabliaux*.

The apparent discrepancy in the person of the narrator is a radical example of the anonymous subjectivity the narrative sponsors. As well, it may be explained by what John M. Ganim discusses as "Chaucer's theatricality"[25]: in a performance situation – and Chaucer's tales may well have been intended for oral delivery – an accomplished narrator might imitate the voices of characters. Throughout the tale, the fictional narrator imitates the diction and tone of the wife in direct quotation of dialogue, establishing a flexible voice, by turns assertive, querulous, demanding, self-justifying and self-pitying, and sly, a complexity that produces an evasive and un/canny subjectivity-effect; so too the narrator may in the introduction be ventriloquizing her speech in indirect quotation. The seemingly incongruous pronouns in the introduction – "He moot us clothe, and he moot us arraye / ... In which array we daunce jolily. / ... Thanne moot another payen for oure cost, / Or lene us gold, and that is perilous (ll. 12, 14, 18–19) – would then indicate mimicry, the narrator's impersonation of the woman's voice and his engagement of her desire.[26] Pronouns by definition are shifters, and they appear as

---

25 See John M. Ganim, *Chaucerian Theatricality* (Princeton: Princeton University Press, 1990).
26 One could argue, and many have argued, of course, that Chaucer's report of female speech is always an impersonation and hence an appropriation by a dominant discourse. E. Jane Burns suggests a potential method for "feminist readers of medieval texts" that would affirm "the multiple, heteronomous nature of female subjectivity and begin to read 'for the female' in the margins and interstice of hegemonic discourses ... actively listening for ways in which female characters might be heard as resisting, speaking against, and dissenting from the very discourses that construct female nature." See her chapter "This Prick Which Is Not One: How Women Talk Back in Old French *Fabliaux*," in *Feminist Approaches to the Body in Medieval Literature*, eds. Linda Lomperis and Sarah Stanbury (Philadelphia: University of Pennsylvania Press, 1993), 195. Burns deploys such a critical method in analysis of Old French courtly romances and *fabliaux* in *Bodytalk: When Women Speak in Old French Literature* (Philadelphia: University of Pennsylvania Press, 1993). Arguably, of course, we are

dangerously malleable, not only in a woman's voice by also in the monk's conversations with the husband. This malleability comports with the tale's assertion overall of an abstract equivalence between subjects, and between subjects and their objects, that defuses traditional antifeminist demonization of woman's unreliability in favor of identificatory links between all signifiers that circulate in hope and fear in Fortune's new economies of desire.

The articulation of the feminine voice at the start follows directly upon the complaint about the transience of worldly enjoyment, and then leads to a warning about the expense of and for women: anxiety about money, transience, women's desire. The introduction's impersonated feminine speech is linked to what appears to be a general truth: women want clothing and display. The tale invites us to see it as an exemplum of this warning, illustrating the dangerous and transgressive desire of woman. In their desire for clothes, women ensure that their desire will remain secret and perpetually enigmatic. "The symbolism of clothes is a valid symbolism," Lacan states, because textile "at any given moment ... concerns disclosure or concealment."[27] Clothing is a metonym for the body, since it is a covering lying next to the body, and also a metaphor, substituting for the body; perhaps, then, in desiring *arraye,* the wife exemplifies a feminine desire of and for the body. However, as a screen for the body, the wife's desire for clothing is perhaps also, or even instead, a desire for signification rather than for the body as such – a desire for masquerade, enjoyment, and exchange. It is the wife's desire for clothing, not for the monk's body, that winds the clock of this tale, though her sexual frustration is duly noted. The objects of feminine desire multiply when the wife, in an enumeration condensing the Wife of Bath's investigations of feminine desire, instructs the monk about what women want with an extended list of desirable objects: "wommen naturelly / Desiren thynges sixe as well as I: / They wolde that hir housbondes sholde be /

> all impersonations, but, e.g. when "men" impersonate "themselves," different drives and intersubjective effects might be involved.

27 Jacques Lacan, *The Seminar of Jacques Lacan, Book VII: The Ethics of Psychoanalysis, 1959–1960,* ed. Jacques-Alain Miller, trans. Dennis Porter (New York: W.W. Norton, 1992), 226.

Hardy, and wise, and riche, and therto free, / And buxom unto his wyf, and freshe abedde" (ll. 173–77). The convictions of a popular current of medieval misogyny are validated, from the embedded voice of the woman: the lesson is that woman's desire is an endless metonymy, all-inclusive and insatiable, and comes at men's expense. But this very endless desire is also seen to generate signification, in the form of warnings, laments, examples, stories.

Further, if clothing displays male honor on the body of the woman, the display also screens the desires of men – their lack – and the risks they take in pursuing their enjoyment, perhaps even their enjoyment of risk itself, without which neither honor nor monetary profit are possible. Again, the husband's tactful silence about what he might or might not believe about his wife's activities suggests that he is also unwilling to give up on the uncertain profits of honor and reputation and prefers to continue his association with his errant wife. The tale signals a preoccupation with woman's endless desire and hence the anxiety produced by sexual difference, but also shows us a larger anxiogenic context of exchangeability and abstractability that makes the projection of uncertainty exclusively onto women seem almost nostalgic.

Lacan's claim that clothing "shows and hides at the same time" associates clothing with the phallus, the object that is hidden and revealed in being hidden, by a veil. The phallus for psychoanalysis is both an object and a signifier of desire. Not a biological organ, it is the image of an organ capable of enjoyment and reproduction; a heterosexual woman's desire is for the phallus as the object of sexual enjoyment. This woman also wants to be the phallus, to give to her partner what he does not have – since no man possesses the phallus – and so to cover his lack as well as hers; veiling herself in clothing, the woman may entice a quest to find what is not present and to create herself as a woman, the object of masculine desire. The feminine is hence a masquerade, a substitute and disguise, alluding to what is absent for both the heterosexual man and the heterosexual woman. At the same time, clothing, like the phallus incarnated in a woman, is a signifier of desire, and functions like a language.

Clothing in fact composes the material of a cultural language. Lining up like signifiers in language, articles of clothing are combined according to a grammar that determines what is worn where, and by whom. Margaret F. Rosenthal points out that clothing acts "as material and symbolic currency ... Fashion, clothing, dress, and costume ... must be understood as elements of sign systems produced by historically specific material conditions."[28] It is just because clothing is a species of discourse that the *General Prologue* can indicate the pilgrims' stations (and transgressions thereof), personalities, and singularities by focusing on the details of what they wear. Especially in societies dependent on visual spectacle, like late medieval England, clothes declare class, so that the matter of clothes was repeatedly regu-

28 Margaret F. Rosenthal, "Introduction: Cultures of Clothing in Later Medieval Europe," *The Journal of Medieval and Early Modern Studies 39*, no. 3 (Fall 2009), 459–82, writes that clothing and its parts "acted as material and symbolic currency": "Fashion, clothing, dress, and costume, then, must be understood as elements of sign systems produced by historically specific material conditions. Each part of the system acted in different ways in negotiations between dominant groups and cultures and the lower echelon of society" (462). In the same issue, Maria Giuseppina Muzzarelli focuses on sumptuary laws in "Reconciling the Privilege of a Few with the Common Good: Sumptuary Laws in Medieval and Early Modern Europe," *The Journal of Medieval and Early Modern Studies* 39, no. 3 (Fall 2009): 597–617, showing how "they privilege the symbolic and social significance of clothing: its role in maintaining and reinforcing individual and collective identities as well as distinctions between social groups" (599). Emphasizing their regulation of social identity, she claims that "sumptuary legislation could be formed with a design to integrate society while still maintaining distinctions and subordination" (601). In addition, Muzzarelli emphasizes the effect of such regulations on women "who acted as indicators of the social position of their husbands and fathers" and who as a result were enabled to "satisfy aesthetic sensibilities but also to create social visibility" (600).

For a discussion of clothing and the body's accessories as composing a semiotic system in the medieval period, see E. Jane Burns, *Courtly Love Undressed: Reading Through Clothes in Medieval French Culture* (Philadelphia: University of Pennsylvania Press, 2002), where she develops the concept of the "sartorial body." For a more extensive discussion of cloth, see also E. Jane Burns, *Sea of Silk: A Textual Geography of Women's Work in Medieval French Literature* (Philadelphia: University of Pennsylvania Press, 2009).

lated in sumptuary laws that attempted to make display accord with income, beginning with Edward III.[29] As is well known, clothing also signified group membership and association, since patronage alliance was indicated in retinues' colors, while marginal groups, such as European Jews, were confined to wearing stipulated material, recognizable hats and (beginning with a regulation by the Fourth Lateran Council in 1215) armbands. Prostitutes were required to wear armbands and other identifying signs. Such spectacular organization of material signs seeks to approximate an ideal of semiotic transparency visible in a social display. And if clothing composes a material discourse, in *The Shipman's Tale* discourse conveys the material effectiveness of the signifier, not only in the wife's desire for clothes but in the tale's characteristic use of the indicative article, *this*. Repeatedly, *this marchant, this monk,* and *this wyf* point to characters who are assigned presence by the referential indicator; similar use of the indicative pronoun appears in *The Miller's Tale*. Likewise the Shipman's indicative in *thise hundred frankes* (l. 293) gives substance to the matter of the money circulating in the empty form of a loan.

Signifying Desire

To be clothed is the human condition. Lacan explains that "Textile is first of all a text," and that man "begins to be individualized, ... begins to organize himself as clothed, that is to say, as having needs that have been satisfied."[30] The etymology of "text" in Latin *textile* associates the materiality of clothing with the materiality of the signifier. Anglo-Saxon poetry describes making verse to be a weaving of words. R. Howard Bloch shows that the "coat as representation and representation as a coat have a

---

29 That the uses of wealth were a late medieval subject of popular thought is indicated by *Wynnere* and *Wastoure,* an alliterative poem from the early 1350s, that centers on a debate between allegorical figures representing expenditure and saving, or commodity consumption and capital accumulation, held with much pageantry before a ruling figure who in all probability represents Edward III.
30 Lacan, *Seminar VII*, 227, 228.

long history in the Middle Ages," going back to Macrobius, for whom "the relation of Truth – Nature – to its representation or image ... is that of the body to clothes," and Bloch argues that particularly in French *fabliaux* – tales about theft, deception, and scandalous sex – "tale and coat are linked in the assimilation of deceit ... to poetic invention."[31] The nexus of the deceptive sexual body, clothing, and money that runs through the Shipman's *fabliau* is made explicit in the pun on *taillynge,* whose differing senses expand in the wife's speech that ends the tale and in the narrator's final, concluding prayer.[32]

The tale concludes as it begins, with the introductory words of a woman and with the woman of the narrative in debt. The circulation of desire is completed, returning to its start in the lack of the object that causes desire. Her lack may well be a figure of castration, but castration understood not as the woman's missing something, not as an absence of what should be present, but as her position in sexual division, a relation to the phallus that neither sex can claim for itself. Moustafa Safouan points out that for a woman "the fact that she understands immediately that she hasn't the phallus means that castration has already taken place. That means she is not caught up in castration. It doesn't mark her body as closely."[33] There is no exception to castration for woman, but woman is not all in castration, so she can more easily live with limitation and therefore go beyond it. Perhaps, too, because a woman more readily accepts lack, she is more readily (and defensively) figured in heteronormativity as the source of desire.

---

31 R. Howard Bloch, *The Scandal of the Fabliaux* (Chicago: University of Chicago Press 1986), 24, 25, 26.
32 C. David Benson, *Chaucer's Drama of Style* (Chapel Hill: University of North Carolina Press, 1986), 104–16, and Laura Kendrick, *Chaucerian Play: Comedy and Control in the Canterbury Tales* (Berkeley: University of California Press, 1988), 90–93, explore the punning in detail. Lee Patterson's account of the substitutions and displacements in the tale in *Chaucer and the Subject of History* is elaborate and revealing.
33 Moustafa Safouan, *The Seminar of Moustafa Safouan,* eds. Anna Shane and Janet Thormann (New York: Other Press, 2002), 85.

In the end, the wife carves out a lack in her husband and insists on what he does not have, reminding him of his castration, and thereby ensuring the continual circulation of desire among objects. She covers over his lack with the promise of a surplus of enjoyment in place of money for the missing loan, "giving" the body that is supposed to incarnate the lost object of desire, which she does not have, and which he cannot possess. By choosing to compromise, they each make do with what they do not have in marriage.

The wife, to hide her deception, comes up with a pun that condenses the husband's desire for money and her desire for sex, punctuating the tale with a concluding series of surprises. Her specious speech is the unexpected, happy solution to the deceptions and dissatisfactions of desire. Drawing on the idiom of "the marriage debt"[34] – the responsibility of partners to satisfy the other's desire for sex – she will *score,* or "mark," the debt, as if writing an account, on her *taille,* metonym of her body, the rear end. As well, *tailler* in Old French signified "castration" to imply that, as subjects of desire, both husband and wife will have to settle for less than full enjoyment.[35] As it evolves in modern French, *tailler* is to cut or cut out and to shape, in fashioning clothes, for example, illustrated in the idiom *tailler un habit,* to cut out a coat. Thus feminine deception is subsumed in textual instability, in the variant meanings of signifiers.[36] But the pun on *taille,* like any pun, points to the separation of the signifier from the signified in speech as well as writing, for its wit is a function

---

34 Thanks to Jane Alison Minogue, whose unpublished paper, "Merchants in Love and Debt: Chaucer's View in Three Tales," delivered at the Medieval Association of the Pacific Annual Conference, University of New Mexico, March 5, 2009, suggests the uses of the marriage debt in the tale.

35 See Henri Rey-Flaud, *La nevrose courtoise* (Paris: Navarin, 1983), 73: "in Old French '*tailler*' signifies very precisely 'castration'" (my translation).

36 Dinshaw's *Chaucer's Sexual Poetics* does not treat *The Shipman's Tale* in detail, but Dinshaw's nuanced development of the relation of traditional treatments and metaphors of textuality to gender and the sexual body, and to the sexed body of woman especially, illuminates the wife's linking of sex and story-telling.

of the proliferation of meaning under a single sound. That the signifier is also linked to the signified by the vulnerable processes of memory, attachment, and convention, only complicates such proliferations.

The wife's desire for sex, clothing, and money is projected into a future of marital happiness and surplus enjoyment of speech. Her play with the possibilities of language to tell the truth by lying is generative and opens out a widened perspective in an end that keeps desire in motion, not only for the couple but for the audience: the audience gains the pleasure of grasping the unanticipated pun, and its attention is recalled to the tale's language. So here the concluding scene introduces an expanded inner space, as the wife's prompt, unexpected verbal agility deftly maps out a compromise to respond to the lack of sexual relation. The scene takes place in a much reduced physical space, the confined dimensions of a private setting in which at "night in myrthe they disette" (l. 375). The sound of the wife's opportune speech, especially in contrast to the husband's thoughtful silence, is amplified by the couple's solitude.

The tale's having shifted from the present of the narrative to the future of the marriage partners, in an ultimate shift the Shipman narrator's last words address the presence of the pilgrim audience and extend to future audiences beyond. The desire of the audience is directed to the anticipation of a surplus enjoyment that telling tales produces: addressed to the audience, "and God us sende / Taillynge ynough unto oure lyves ende" (ll. 433–34), the narrator's prayer links yet another layer, now of homophonic blessings, to *taillynge,* to signify "telling," the narration or "telling" of stories. Even while the echo of *taillynge* as debt remains as a reminder of the judgment of a final accounting at death, it sponsors continuing enjoyment in the meanwhile, as indeed does the "end" of the *Canterbury Tales,* under the sign of Libra. The tale then becomes the object of the desire for audience present and to come. Secular pleasures may be insubstantial and fleeting, but they provide the matter to tell in narrations about pleasure. "Getting" the pun is also an opening in the unconscious, as the audience unpacks the metonymic chains the pun condenses, and leads to a momentary expansion of consciousness that accompanies its recognition. The Shipman's narration is resolved in an expansive, momentary timelessness opening on an anticipated, infinite future of pleasure in the pursuit of fleeting objects of desire – of what Freud called "scarcity value in time."[37]

---

37 Sigmund Freud, "On Transience" (1916), in *The Standard Edition of the Complete Psychological Works of Sigmund Freud,* vol. 14: *On the History of the Psycho Analytic Movement (1914–1916),* ed. and trans. James Strachey with Anna Freud (London: The Hogarth Press, 1957), 303–7, at 305.

CHAPTER 4

Some Rules of the Game: *The Miller's Tale*

The *Canterbury Tales* that focus on sexual division and the absence of sexual rapport all begin with the unexpected speech: a single signifier, or a long sequence of words, or a collocation of articulate sounds that calls up a response from the Other. The conclusions are economical. They use the condensations and displacements of metonymy and metaphor to undo the psychic expenditures and accumulated energies built up in developing story telling. Pleasure is delivered with the release of these energies and by the intellectual satisfaction of "getting" the economy of the language in a spark of recognition. The scenes have the structure of jokes. Given that these tales are *fabliaux,* none of these observations is meant to be especially startling. But why is Chaucer so drawn to these forms, what does he use them for, and how do his texts see the connection between the joke and the absence of sexual rapport? Is the former always "about" the latter?

In *The Miller's Tale* the surprising eruption of the overdetermined signifier water condenses the strands of the plot and brings about its climax. Both *The Friar's Tale* and *The Summoner's Tale* end with the internal audiences' attention on a clinching argument that leads to a surprising conclusion. *The Miller's Tale* is a *fabliau*: its formulaic but complicated narrative of sexual betrayal in marriage depends on lies and aggression; duplicitous scheming is the means to having sex and satisfying aggression. The narratives of both *The Friar's Tale* and *The Summoner's*

Tale are not overtly concerned with sexual division and nonrelation, but, like *The Miller's Tale,* with the language of lying, scheming, and aggressive debasement. Aggression and anality function in these tales to punish those guilty of violating social norms, the resolutions of which in unexpected language follow the rules of jokes to contain aggression and pleasure within the rules of social exchange. "Holes" in these tales frequently open up the question of the lack that powers desire. The performance of aggression leads to an enactment of drive so that hostility is allowed expression – again, frequently anal – but unconscious energies are recontained in the end, made "privee," within the regulation of a social regime.

In *Jokes and Their Relation to the Unconscious,* Freud accounts for the economy of language in jokes and for their mechanisms.[1] The rules determining jokes follow the rules of unconscious structure; they release the drives while avoiding censorship and lifting repression. Freud shows how jokes may tell the truth by lying: many jokes illustrate Lacan's conviction that human language is correlative to the capacity to lie and, conversely, that unconscious truth is manifested in the lie. The exemplum of *The Friar's Tale* demonstrates that because the human subject of speech is split between a position of enunciation and a statement, lying ironically tells the truth. In this tale, speech is true if it aligns with the subjective intention, and it is guaranteed by symbolic law that does not deceive; in the absence of any guarantee offered by the social or spiritual system it dramatizes, truth in *The Summoner's Tale* is reduced to a trace produced by the body. All three tales work, like jokes, to suture community by offering the chance to be "in the know"; they are concerned with an ethics of social belonging. The resolution of *The Miller's Tale* asserts the norms of social regulation of desire; however, Alisoun is unpunished, and community remains troubled in *The Friar's Tale* and problematic in *The Summoner's Tale.*

---

1   Sigmund Freud, *The Standard Edition of the Complete Psychological Works of Sigmund Freud,* vol. 8: *Jokes and Their Relation to the Unconscious (1905),* ed. and trans. J. Strachey with Anna Freud (London: The Hogarth Press, 1960), 120.

The Work of Jokes

The previous chapter's analysis of the final scene of *The Shipman's Tale* points to an unstable movement between telling the truth and lying. The conversation between the Shipman and his wife demonstrates the couple's implicit, mutual understanding of what is at stake in their mutual deception – for his silence can only be willful, an interval during which he puts things together, and an obstinate refusal of her agency or her power, and it issues in his warning that she not repeat her behavior. It too is a kind of lie. Theirs is a mutual deception that fails to deceive. The agreement to accept their lies is a kind of alliance, a means of dealing with the lack of rapport that is cynical and pretends to be realistic. This is one way to make up for the absence of sexual relation.

The Host's response to the conclusion indicates that the tale works, that the narrator has aroused an appropriate response to his performance, at least in the Host. The Host's is a normative judgment that enjoys the tale's aggressive purposes: the husband has been cuckolded; the wife too has been exposed for her adultery and covetousness; and the monk's treachery and greed stand as a moral warning against trusting men of the religious orders with one's privacy, or even one's hostelry – "Draweth no monkes moore unto youre in" (l. 441). But what the Host initially emphasizes and praises in his first words is the language of the teller: "Wel seyd" (l. 435), he exclaims in response to the Franklin's performance. It is surely the manipulation of "*taillynge*" that catches the Host's attention and makes his appreciation a tribute, while preparing for his own witty play on "hood" – "The monk putte in the mannes hood an ape, / And in his wyves eek, by Seint Austyn!" ("the monk has made a fool of the man, a monkey," ll. 440–41), signifying the husband's victimization, the wife's genitals, and the monk's order, in a condensation that imitates the Shipman's language play. The host's appreciation of the Shipman's performance focuses on the imbrication of deception and aggression in its language.

The concluding scene of *The Shipman's Tales* offers a perfect example of what Freud calls the short-circuit that results from the condensation of several "circles of ideas that are brought together by the same word."[2] In *Jokes and Their Relations to the Unconscious,* Freud emphasizes that it is the technique, in his words the joke-work, that brings pleasure; simply stating, for example, that having sex, keeping financial accounts, and telling stories are linked activities would not get a laugh. The joke-work acts like a bribe. It calls attention to itself, to a verbal surface, and recognition of the joke's content follows upon "getting" the language. Joke-work depends on the structure of unconscious grammar: condensation conveys the pleasure of economy, producing in an instant an awareness of similarities that are ordinarily repressed; in contrast, displacement evades the censorship of content that would otherwise be painful or objectionable, providing instead, in many cases at least, a pleasurable haunting, teasing, sense of mystery. The Shipman's wife comes up with a displacement when she answers with "a diversion of the train of thought from one meaning to another";[3] to respond to the husband's questioning whether the monk has returned money to her, if "he yow hadde an hundred frankes payed" (l. 389), she claims that she didn't keep the money, "I kepe nat of his tokenes never a deel" (l. 403). She changes the subject; in Freud's terms, her answer "make[s] a diversion from the suggested train of thought."[4] At the same time, she admits indirectly that she has received the money, even if she hasn't kept it. The wife provides an illustration of what Freud thinks of as sophistry, or faulty reasoning; however, within the tension of the dramatic context, the question of whether the husband will understand what she has done may override the surface wit, although any tension finally prepares for a greater punch in the narrator's condensation of *taillynge.* The wife's ploy illustrates Freud's argument for the "necessity of not confusing the psychical processes involved in the construction of the joke (the 'joke-work') with the psychical process involved in taking in the joke (the work of understanding)."[5] In the context of the husband's testing of his wife, attention is on the characters' "work of understanding."

2   Ibid.
3   Ibid., 53.
4   Ibid.
5   Ibid., 54.

The wife's argument in fact resembles closely Freud's primary illustration of "tendentious" aggressive jokes. If Freud's example is an expression of anti-Semitic aggression, appealing to his contemporaries' biases, it is also a metajoke, a joke about jokes:

> Two Jews met in a railway carriage at a station in Galicia. "Where are you going?" asked one. "To Cracow," was the answer. "What a liar you are!" broke out the other. "If you say you're going to Cracow, you want me to believe you're going to Lemberg. But I know that in fact you're going to Cracow. So why are you lying to me?"[6]

The first speaker knows that the other may not tell the truth; he anticipates a lie but gets the truth, so he does not know what to think. The Shipman's wife illustrates what Freud's first speaker asserts, for she is "lying when [s]he tells that truth and is telling the truth by means of a lie."[7] Lorenzo Chiesa follows Lacan by claiming that "man as a being of language is definitely the only animal who has the ability to pretend to lie" so that a subject must assume a "supposition of deceit"[8] in another speaker: "The hub of the function of speech is the subjectivity of the Other, that is to say, the fact the Other is essentially he who is capable, like the subject, of convincing and lying."[9] Hence, Chiesa argues, "The dimension of 'true lies' or 'lying truths' – to which all (symbolic) truths as fictions ultimately belong – together with the related dimension of doubt can thus provide us with a minimal definition of a symbolic order that functions properly; this is well captured by Freud's famous Jewish joke."[10] Speakers may lie, but conversely, language depends upon a law, a "non-deceptive

---

6   Ibid., 115.
7   Ibid.
8   Lorenzo Chiesa, *Subjectivity and Otherness: A Philosophical Reading of Lacan,* (Cambridge: MIT Press, 2007), 112.
9   Jacques Lacan, *The Seminar of Jacques Lacan, Book III: The Psychoses, 1955–1956,* ed. Jacques-Alain Miller, trans. Russell Griff (New York: W.W. Norton, 1993), 65.
10 Chiesa, *Subjectivity and Otherness,* 112.

element,"[11] for Lacan the phallus, acting as the signifier of signification: "The dialectic correlate of the basic structure which makes of ... speech that may deceive is that there is also something that does not deceive."[12]

At stake in Freud's joke is the potential of any speech situation: because a statement might always be a lie, might always present what is not the case, neither about the speaker's motives nor about the state of things, it is always susceptible to the judgment of its audience. The metajoke is illuminating and especially funny because it raises the stakes to show that one might deceive by telling the truth. It introduces the larger question concerning the basis of truth, "the more serious substance" of "what determines the truth .... Is it the truth if we describe things as they are without troubling to consider how our hearer will understand what we say? Or ... does genuine truth consist in taking the hearer into account and giving him a faithful picture of our own knowledge?"[13] The wife is indirectly telling the truth, reporting what happened, as the external audience understands it; the question remains whether the husband grasps the full impact of her speech.

Freud's joke illustrates that speaking the truth may deceive and serve to convey a lie. Conversely, a lie or a mistake or slip in speech may indicate the truth; the effectiveness of free association in psychoanalysis is predicated on such a possibility. The subject of psychoanalysis is the subject who speaks and is therefore alienated in language from wholeness or transparency, and split by an unknown, unconscious knowledge. The split of the subject shows itself in Lacan's elaboration of the distinction between statement, what is spoken, and enunciation, the act of speaking. The speaking subject of the unconscious is divided between both and yet is in neither position, neither in (the "I" of) what is said nor in the conscious act of saying. The summoner in *The Friar's Tale* and the friar in *The Summoner's Tale* refuse this split, performing as masters of language and rejecting subordination to the law, so that they become dupes of the truth they disavow.

11 Ibid.
12 Lacan, *Seminar III*, 64.
13 Freud, *Jokes and Their Relation to the Unconscious*, 115.

The Shipman's wife takes advantage of that split, using a lie to tell the truth: it is the case that the monk gave her the money, not, however, to return the loan, as the husband may presume, nor to reciprocate for hospitality and to honor her, as she claims, but to pay for sex; as well, she did spend a hundred francs to buy clothing. Her deceptive speech delivers pleasure to the audience, in part because it deftly both transgresses and reinforces the symbolic pact of language, that is, the expectation that speakers tell the truth. The silence of the husband suggests his implied collaboration with her deception. He gets the joke, which is at his expense, as well as hers. His conclusion is an insight: "This marchant saugh ther was no remedie, / .... Sith that the thing may nat amended be" (*Shipman's Tale,* ll. 427, 429), which indicates his sane capacity to acknowledge that speech may lie and doubt is sometimes useful. The wiggliness of speech is also acknowledged by the tautological form given to the husband's insight: he saw there was no remedy, because [he concluded] there was no remedy. The closure offered by this piece of *fabliau* "widom" is almost purely formal; there is only the slippage between something stated as a fact ("the thing may nat amended be") and the "seeing" of it (he "saugh ther was no remedie").

The whole of the wife's elaborate excuse is a joke. The joke is tendentious for its reliance on the conviction that women deceive men, but if the audience objects to that conviction or sympathizes with the husband, the pleasure of the language, the "joke's work," may disappear. In either case, what remains is an exemplification of the reality that the truth of a statement may take the form of a lie, because the intention of a speaker is never apparent, not even to the speaker. The husband puts a good face on things, which is perhaps one cynical means of coming to terms with sexual division – adopted, as well, by the Miller. The Miller declares explicitly that he does not need to know the truth; he doesn't not to concern himself with his wife's doings, with her privacy or secrets, and not God's either. The Shipman's husband, behaving like the creditor he is, tries to make the best of a bad deal. He chooses to accept the argument, since, as she points out, it is in his own self-interest and nothing can be done anyway. He also tries to control her future behavior.

The husband's compromise is a concession to the wife's seeming compromise, to exchange one kind of *taillynge* with another, which is not really a compromise since she gets what she wants – that is, the money and sex – while it is also an admission revealing the truth, that she, like so many of her male counterparts, trades money for sex. At the same time the elaborate play on *taillyinge* is a new, powerful technique of the joke work that indirectly reveals the truth and appears to sponsor a trust in language that the wife's casuistry has complicated. A near-tautology is not much to go on. It works because it provides a modicum of rhetorical pleasure.

Jokes' rhetorical techniques are "the sources from which jokes provide pleasure,"[14] according to Freud. The joke *is* the jokework; the pleasure derives from the verbal processes, "the mere activity, untrammeled by needs, of our mental apparatus."[15] The condensation and displacement of signifiers and the gap between the enunciated and the enunciation at the source of irony, or what Lacan treats as the unconscious process of "negation," are the tropes that are the work of unconscious primary processes, dreams, and jokes. Condensation undoes repression in an apprehension of a surplus of meanings joined by sound or likeness; displacement liberates from censorship by insinuating through juxtaposition what should not or may not be said. In the jokework both techniques bring pleasure by avoiding an expenditure of energy. Hence the joke's frequent reliance on economy or brevity. The function of jokes "consists from the first in lifting internal inhibitions and in making sources of pleasure fertile which have been rendered inaccessible by these inhibitions."[16] The single signifier *taillyinge* is economical, in that it both condenses the separate exchanges of sex, money, and language and lifts internal inhibitions in its promise of future pleasures.

Hence Freud concludes that jokes are paradigmatic of psychic activity as a whole: "Dreams serve predominantly for the avoidance of unpleasure, jokes for the attainment of pleasure; but all

---

14 Ibid., 130.
15 Ibid., 179.
16 Ibid., 130.

our mental activities converge in these two aims."[17] Lacan adds that unpleasure too can be a source of *jouissance*. The analyses of *Jokes and Their Relation to the Unconscious* that frequently appeal to a psychic energetics are typical of Freud's use of analogies from mechanics to explain the "economy" of mental processes that bring pleasure by avoiding an expenditure of energy. His ultimate conclusion is that jokes, and the comic generally, conserve psychic effort by "regaining from mental activity a pleasure which has in fact been lost through the development of that activity."[18] Getting a joke, grasping its logic of condensation and/or displacement, involves both complex mental activity and the surplus pleasure such activity delivers. Jokes are, in other words, in the realm of play, in the sense of *not-work*. By lifting repression and evading censorship, jokes produce a reconfiguration of psychic space. Language has effects on the unconscious Real of drive and enjoyment and on the organization of symptoms and defenses. Many of Chaucer's endings are economical: they halt and restart the action; they recall the totality of the narrative, the full arc that has been submerged in the ongoing present of the telling; and they alter the perspectives of the narrations by introducing a wider space or an extension into the future, even if that extension takes the form of a frustrated commitment to keep on going. Shifting the angles of perception breaks down subjective obstacles and inhibitions that limit access to reality and, therefore, to opportunities for pleasure. The unanticipated emergence of the key signifiers gives a sudden access to repressed material that jolts consciousness and enlarges its scope.

Lacan points out that it is always the frame of our desire that gives access to reality, so that "we make reality out of pleasure."[19] Since the subject's sense of reality is determined by desire, Lacan can claim that Freud's "reality principle" follows the pleasure principle: "The reality principle consists in making the game

---

17 Ibid., 180.
18 Ibid., 236.
19 Jacques Lacan, *The Seminar of Jacques Lacan, Book VII: The Ethics of Psychoanalysis, 1959–1960,* ed. Jacques-Alain Miller, trans. Dennis Porter (New York: W.W. Norton, 1992), 225.

last, that is to say, in ensuring that pleasure is renewed."[20] It follows that subjectivity is implicated by the subject's orientation in social reality, the unconscious frame of desire, and already figures in any reality that the frame constructs. Manipulation of the signifier can alter the subjective frame and change perspective, stripping away accustomed pleasures but accessing desire and enlarging psychic potential. In no case does psychoanalysis attain a final, transcendent reality; it uses language to change subjective perspective only to offer the truth of the unconscious. In contrast, a social system that is founded on and supported by a transcendent reality governing the universal laws of nature can secure the truth of language in "a nondeceptive apriori which is itself symbolic."[21] A transcendent providence governing the laws that carry out God's purposes and are reflected in nature, functions in the Christian middle ages "as an unmediated Real that ultimately assures its own symbolically mediated forms in everyday reality as well as the inherently deceptive dimension of the symbolic Other."[22] This is to say that God's existence and his creation operate as the "external non-deceptive" foundation of the truth of language: as the O, not the barred O that is variable and is made up of blindness as well as insight.

Any symbolic structure depends on law, and speech depends on the trust that speakers will tell the truth. A particular symbolic structure also depends upon a social consensus composing the "game" or the particular practice giving the parameters of language use and its understanding. The fact of such a consensus is not ideology, which confines and fixes meaning, but rather the possibility of any language at all, situated in a historical moment, although the key significations of the consensus do compose an ideology. What counts as truth therefore depends upon the situation of social reality that allows for and limits the creation of meaning. The truth of the statement depends upon the rules of a

---

20 Jacques Lacan, *The Seminar of Jacques Lacan, Book II: The Ego in Freud's Theory and in the Technique of Psychoanalysis,* ed. Jacques-Alain Miller, trans. Sylvana Tomaselli (New York: W.W. Norton, 1989), 84.
21 Chiesa, *Subjectivity and Otherness,* 113.
22 Ibid., 112–13.

particular language, the truth of the enunciation of unconscious desire.

Desire is bound up with social law and hence the laws of language governing the unconscious and structuring desire. Lacan argues that it is with the commandment "Thou shalt not lie" when "the intimate link between desire, in its structuring function, with the law is felt most tangibly .... In "Thou shalt not lie as law is included the possibility of the lie as the most fundamental desire'."[23] Prohibition invites transgression, motivating both desire and the lie, so that lying is caught up in desire, as is witnessed in the structure of the pervert. It may be possible, as Moustafa Safouan points out, that the commandment to forbid lying is "a crazed commandment in any other mouth save that of a God," but the injunction operates inherently as the law of language: "It is a law such that speech, no matter how much it were to exploit the guarantee that truth is to be found there ... would still not evade it" because the lie must present itself as a semblance of truth in order to be believed.[24] The fact that language is tied to what may not deceive, so that speech may approximate truth, and the consequent, necessary relation between the lie and the law it transgresses is the foundation for an ethics.

Uses of Aggression

Freud categorizes the metajoke that scrambles the difference between telling the truth and lying under the heading of tendentious jokes. Taking the form of a conversation between two Jews, it ridicules the cagy, shrewd, and suspicious thinking characteristic of the anti-Semitic stereotype of his time. Tendentious jokes give voice to aggression; while Freud distinguishes two kinds of aggressive jokes, "the hostile joke (serving the purpose of aggressiveness, satire, or defense) or an obscene joke (serving the purpose of exposure)," they "can be subsumed under a single heading."[25] He demonstrates that in fact obscenity is a form of aggression, meant to embarrass and weaken the woman to

---

23 Lacan, *Seminar VII*, 81–82.
24 Moustafa Safouan, *Speech or Death?* (Houndmills: Palgrave, 2003), 17.
25 Freud, *Jokes and Their Relation to the Unconscious*, 97.

whom it is directed, and that it serves a demeaning purpose, even when, in the absence of a woman, it takes place between men. Notwithstanding Freud's sexist analysis of the "smut" of obscenity that is intended to further sexual seduction, his emphasis on sexual aggression demonstrates that tendentious jokes, like innocent jokes, also derive their pleasure from the joke-work and that they have the same purpose of escaping repression and censorship: "They make possible the satisfaction of an instinct (whether lustful or hostile) in the face of an obstacle that stands in its way. They circumvent this obstacle and in that way draw pleasure from a source which the obstacle had made inaccessible."[26] The tales of sexual division and marital trouble spell out the course of desire overcoming obstacles to attaining pleasure, and they develop the techniques of jokes to deliver a surplus pleasure in language. As they enact desire, they uncover an unconscious truth, and also the truth that the pleasure the joke delivers is *jouissance* endlessly deferred.

These tales of course are other and more than jokes. They are extended and complicated narratives, while jokes are short and simple and depend on the instantaneous effect of a punch-line. The tales do in fact behave like jokes as they culminate on a single signifier, argument, or message that condenses or displaces the narrative's metonymic chains and delivers the pay-off economically, to release the energy of repression in a sudden insight. *The Miller's Tale* uses joke-work to carry out aggression: the Miller's hostility toward the Reeve is expressed in his characters' intentions to mock, shame, debase, and challenge others. If the dramatization of aggression works, we are bribed by the techniques, simply by pleasure in the language of the narration. If we put emphasis on the narrative content, we may protest the ridicule, in spite of the advice in the *Miller's Prologue* that "men shal nat maken ernest of game" (l. 3186). But Chaucer's tales are situated in specific fictional communities whose responses ideally would mirror or at the least guide an audience response, and the fictional pilgrim community of the tales as a whole is situated in the cultural context of late fourteenth-century England by realis-

26 Ibid., 101.

tic description, common idiomatic language, and contemporary references.

Freud's discussion of jokes pays little attention to their social function, although they operate in a social context, one reason jokes can easily become dated. The formalization of aggression in especial exemplifies the social use of jokes to regulate consensus, strengthen social norms, and discipline excessive or threatening modes of behavior. Jokes generally have the conservative function of containing within a given context just what they ridicule, and they typically reinforce the norms and expectations of their audience; the apprehension of the joke-work delivered by repeated formulaic endings returns the audience to a social community to recontain the energies they liberate. Conforming to a society's rules and demands may limit individual gratification, but the endings sponsor the ethical conviction that a good society enables the pleasures of desire, if not the transport of *jouissance*. Individual desire may be aligned with the good of the general welfare, while the impossibility of satisfaction (for all) is also registered.

The Miller's Tale plots aggression in outrageous and extreme action in support of regulating pleasure in agreement with social norms. In the first place, as the lower class Miller's travesty of the Knight's performance of courtly love conventions, it might be understood to express class resentment. *The Miller's Tale* might also be seen as an attempt – many think a successful one – to beat the *Knight's Tale* on the score of *jouis-sens*, the remainders or echoes of *jouissance* pointed to by the signifier. The tale is also felt by the higher status Reeve as an attack out of personal animosity, rather than simply part of the pilgrims' competitive game of quitting. The Miller is acutely sensitive to status difference, as exemplified in the summary comment that caps the description of Alison within a class context: "She was a prymerole, a piggesnye, / For any lord to leggen in his bedde, / Or yet for any good yeman to wedde" ("she was a primrose, a pig's eye flower for any lord to lay in his bed or yet for any good yeoman to wed," ll. 3268–70). This is a cagy, if harsh, appraisal of the power of privilege. Finally, acts of aggression motivate the narrative structure, a tight design of interdependent performances of masculine competition intended to humiliate rivals.

Each move in the plot, moreover, is generated by a lie, and the end result of each lie is to expose the drive that fuels the desire of each of the men. The husband is duped by Nicholas, his rival for his wife, to believe that Noah's flood is coming again, and is persuaded to hang from the roof three tubs that will serve as lifeboats.[27] Much of the narrative develops the scheme to engage the husband in this plot. The younger, higher-status and more learned student humiliates the older workman, harming his arm, the engine of his work and his autonomy. The exposure of the husband's credulity demonstrates the impotence of his excessive will to control and possess an inappropriate mate, and critiques a marriage in violation of the rule that like should marry like, that "man sholde wedde his simylitude" (l. 3228), upon which the Merchant's tale is also predicated. The rival lover, the clerk Absolon, is tricked by Alison's promise of a kiss into confronting, in place of her face, the woman's rear end, extended out the window; he receives a fart instead of a kiss. Seeking revenge against Alison, Absolon fetches a hot iron and, with the intention of striking Alison, instead scalds Nicholas "in the towte [buttocks]" (Nicholas having foolishly substituted his bottom for Alison's). Both plots – the gulling of John and the suitors' reciprocal subjection to displaced kisses – carry out the intergenerational hostility of the young. Each strand of the plot carries out an intensifying series of acts of debasement that simultaneously satisfies anal enjoyment, and each act is set in motion by a lie, in the form of a deception, that leads to the truth. The ultimate punishment of each man is the ridicule of the social community that witnesses the domestic circulation of displaced desire, diverted by the demand of drive.

The marriage of John, the "riche gnof [churl]" (l. 3188), to the teenage Alison is a spectacular instance of the sexual nonrelation, the discrepancy between their ages marked for trouble. In the social register, this nonrelation takes the form of a marriage market, the marketing of brides, controlled by wealthy old men. Young men without property were compelled to delay

---

27 For the carpenter husband's mistaking of the biblical story and the warning that accompanies it, see Lawrence Besserman, *Chaucer's Biblical Poetics* (Norman: University of Oklahoma Press, 1998), 114–16.

marriage until they could gain stature and condemned to official abstinence in the meantime, while ambitious young women grabbed up the wealthier, ancient prospects. Oh to be a merry widow! For, certainly, it was not so much fun to be a maiden. The inevitable result was hostility between the male generations, resentment tingeing the sexual relation between young wife and husband and between young men and women, and competition between men within an age group in an economy of scarcity and rivalry that could lead to social disorder.[28] Predictably also the

28 Ruth Mazo Karras, *From Boys to Men: Formations of Masculinity in Late Medieval Europe* (Philadelphia: University of Pennsylvania Press, 2003), 109–50, discusses rebellious and violent behavior, including charivari, by young workers who "resented it bitterly when an older man took one of the women whom they considered their potential future partners. This inability to marry – the relegation to prostitutes, the dependence on a master rather than heading one's own household – had significant effects on these young men's concept of their own manhood. Their opportunities for expressing their masculinity were limited to the informal and even illicit, including violence" (148). Much of Karras's evidence of youth gangs that "used rape as a tool of social control" and of fraternities of young men, intended "to channel the rebellious energy of men between about eighteen and thirty-six years old" (149), is taken from urban environments in France and Italy in the fifteenth century. Similar sources are studied in Jacques Rossiaud, *Medieval Prostitution* (Oxford: Blackwell, 1988). Roussiaud discovers that "nearly one-third of the marriageable girls and 'remarriageable' women under thirty years of age were claimed by men who were 'established,' if not elderly" and concludes "such age gaps seem to me to have caused both a certain amount of social tension between penniless and wifeless young men and more fortunate men who had both; and, even more, a rivalry between marriageable young men and married men or widowers of over thirty years of age" (18). Evidence of youthful violence is less available for England and is more concerned with urban commerce and guild regulation of apprentices; see the reading of Chaucer's *Cook's Tale* by David Wallace, "Chaucer and the Absent City," in *Chaucer's England: Literature in Historical Context,* ed. Barbara Hanawalt (Minneapolis: University of Minnesota Press, 1992), 59–90, for an emphasis on "a restless personal energy" (72) of young men and on their "act of association" figured "as constructive or destructive of social and moral order" (73) and of the established hierarchy.

old husband should and would be suspicious of his wife and behave like John: "Jalous he was, and heeld hire narwe [closely] in cage" (l. 3224). Just as predictably, the woman would try to escape constraint. The plot of *The Miller's Tale* is proof that jealous surveillance is an ineffective response to the sexual non-relation. The confining cage of the Miller's image also appears in the Franklin's narration – "Love wol nat been constreyned by maistrye. / Whan maistrie comth, the God of Love anon / Beteth his wynges, and farewell, he is gon!" (ll. 764–66) – and in *The Manciple's Tale,* where Phoebus holds his wife and crow in similar constraints. The Franklin's imagery literalizes release from repression, as the God of Love flaps his wings and takes flight, in a metaphor for desire breaking free. Lacking the idealization of *The Franklin's Tale,* the debasing technique of the Miller's *fabliau* results in the reduction of desire to its grounds in anarchic drive, and it confirms the principle that prohibition stimulates desire and simultaneously introduces an excess enjoyment delivered by the violation of the law.

Because the marriage of old and young was commonly viewed as a transgression of natural order and an ignoring of the imperative to direct sex to reproduction, and since the resulting tensions of such unequal marriages could end in violent behavior, communities publicized disapproval and reasserted norms by means of informal yet organized practices. Charivari has been widely studied as a means to keep unruly women in line and to shame husbands who surrendered dominance, but it could also be aimed at unequal, inappropriate unions. Charivari, or what in England was called "rough music," was a rite organized and carried out by a local group and directed at an individual or a couple who had acted inappropriately, and was accompanied by noise and, in some cases, disguise.[29] It enacted idiomatic justice

---

29 See E.P. Thompson, *Customs in Common: Studies in Traditional Popular Culture* (New York: The New Press, 1991), 467–538.
Thompson's material generally begins with the eighteenth century, but popular customs were remarkably stable; compare an illustration Michael Camille presents in *Image on the Edge: The Margins of Medieval Art* (Cambridge: Harvard University Press, 1992), 144, from "a manuscript of the *Roman de Fauvel* made in Paris in 1316" showing

in a collective, extra-judicial punishment of behavior out of line with community expectations. It also problematized the status of expectations in the first place, by revealing how wealth and sometimes rank could appear to subvert the law of nature. And Nature, according to Lee Patterson, was central to "peasant" ideology at this time of social unrest.[30] The Miller's narrative of course does not literally enact a charivari, but the tale's concluding scene performs a ritual of communal disapproval and leads directly to communal participation and judgment.[31]

When the carpenter husband cuts the cord and falls to the ground in his tub in response to the sound of "water," and Alison and Nicholas raise the cry of alarm, a local crowd gathers: "the neighebores, both smale and grete / In ronnen" (ll. 3826–27). Their reaction is to stare, "to gauren" (l. 3827) and to ridicule, "laughen" (l. 3840). Reacting to the lovers' description of what they explain as the husband's mad fantasy, which the lovers have themselves sponsored, group opinion blames the duped victim: "They seyde, 'The man is wood [crazy], my leeve brother'; / And every wight [person] gan laughen at this stryf" (ll. 3848–49). Moreover, they refuse John's excuses, add-

---

a procession of men wearing masks, some hitting drums or cymbels, accompanied by children in wheelbarrows and carrying men displaying their "arses," while they are "observed by urban spectators from the sides" (145).

30 Lee Patterson, *Chaucer and the Subject of History* (Madison: University of Wisconsin Press, 1991).

31 Peggy Knapp points to such rituals in stating that the "gross disparity in age between the bride and groom" is a reason for them, but adds that on this occasion "the young men are not engaging in a traditional form of social ridicule ... but a private, self-interested reaction to the inappropriate marriage," in *Chaucer and the Social Contest* (London: Routledge, 1990), 36. The qualification is fitting but does not account for the community's response; the argument here is that the action performs as an accidental, comically appropriate ritual like a charivari. Knapp also draws on Robert Darnton, *The Great Cat Massacre* (Princeton: Princeton University Press, 1983), for later, "eighteenth century eruption of this kind – younger, poorer men acting out a ritualized violation of their landlord's household" (36) that similarly use disruption to act out communal disapproval and insult.

ing to his humiliation. Gossip and ordinary surveillance in rural villages and towns limited privacy, as is illustrated by Absolon's knowledge that the blacksmith must be at work early at his forge and by his reliance on local knowledge of neighbors' habits when he seeks information about the carpenter's whereabouts before going to court Alison. The carpenter's unequal marriage was, of course, public knowledge. As well, although the narrator frequently describes the male suitors as acting *pryvely,* in secret, Absolon's initial, unwelcomed courtship is loud enough to wake the husband at the least and so possibly the neighbors too. In the end, the concluding scene exposes and shames the husband who marries inappropriately and is complicit in his own duping, thereby reconfirming sexual conventions believed to accord with nature. The conclusion also both humiliates and encourages the young men engaged in a disruptive rivalry with John and with each other. That rivalry, a competition for the woman, is both a critique of the marriage and an expression of frustrated exclusion. The outcome satisfies the gathered audience that reads it in solidarity with the triumphant young, as "every clerk anonright heeld with oother" (l. 3847), but at the same time it punishes the young men who threaten social instability.

The concluding scene, then, has the force and function of a fortuitous charivari, fortuitous because it is inflicted by those who are themselves reciprocally shamed by the unintended consequences of their desire. Put differently, the social community that conventionally upholds and enforces norms and passes judgment on their violation – through gossip, exclusion, ridicule – acts as a witness approving the debasing enjoyment the men who pursue Alison inflict upon each other as well as their humiliation of the husband. The group response reenacts a containment of what might have remained a private scene and private desire within a larger, public setting, recalibrating desire in accord with social norms. Narrative action builds towards the extended, climactic window scene to release inhibition and repression and at the same time to punish the violation of conflicting norms in a series of debasing acts. One of the effects of this plot dynamic is to reassert the arbitrary power of the law: on this level, it matters not whether the various forms of law at stake in the tale cohere. Or, they cohere only on the level of their power to structure expectations and exact payment for violations. Whatever you do, draw the line at prying into "pryvetee," or you are likely to become one of those publicly shamed. But who can resist the temptation? And if we can't, we are at the mercy of the tight bond between the law and "sin."

The window, one among the many openings in the domestic architecture that Charles Muscatine savored as functional detail of Chaucer's naturalism,[32] is the setting for the narrative's climax and a metaphor for the effect of the joke-work. An escape from confinement or repression, similar to the door on a cage, the window also functions as the figure for a permeable screen or frame fixing the boundaries of unconscious phantasy, like the doors the Miller can butt through with his head. It opens to give way to the drive. Breaking through the frame will not lead to any final, full reality; as in Magritte's painting, *The Human Condition,* in which a picture on an easel, standing before a window, covers over but represents the landscape it conceals and corresponds to, with the view of the landscape itself cut by the window, any perspective, any view of reality is framed. But the carpenter's window can be opened to expose what is kept off limits. The various openings within John's and Alison's home are then potentially escapes from repression and, simultaneously, opportunities for surveillance. Marking the division of private and public space, the permeability of windows and doors in the tale's familiar space invites intrusion into privacy,[33] as when the husband observes Nicholas in his room through the cat door and the servant breaks down the door to get in; the servant, described as "a strong carl for the nones" (l. 3469), is a trace of the narrator, "a stout carl [churl] for the nones" (*General Prologue,* l. 545), who butts

---

32 Charles Muscatine, *Chaucer and the French Tradition* (Berkeley: University of California Press, 1957), 225.
33 Gila Aloni, "Extimacy in the *Miller's Tale,*" *Chaucer Review* 41, no. 2 (2006): 163–84, problematizes distinctions between private and public by means of Lacan's notion of extimacy, indicating "both proximity to and distance from an object" (163). The object is both within, in a relation to the subject that is the structure of desire, and without, a part of the body the subject has been separated from and seeks in an other. As such, it complicates divisions of space.

doors with his head, indicating the same impulse to defy limitation that also drives the narrative.³⁴ The cumulative details of the openings imply both release and the always present possibility of social oversight of personal relations.

The outrageous power of the scene depends on the mutual implication of law and the enjoyment of its violation that is *jouissance*. Law makes violation possible, and violation conversely supports the law: "we accept the formula that without transgression there is no access to *jouissance*, and, to return to Saint Paul, that that is precisely the function of the Law. Transgression in the direction of *jouissance* only takes place if it is supported by the oppositional principle, by the forms of the Law .... Sin needed the Law, Saint Paul said, so that he could become a great sinner – nothing of course, affirms that he did, but so that he could conceive of the possibility."³⁵ The acts of aggressive debasement violating practices of courtship and reproductive sex – the misplaced kiss, the unanticipated fart in Absolon's face, and the scalding of Nicholas "amydde the ers" ("amid the buttocks" or "ass," l. 3810) – are a means to drive satisfaction. The accumulation of deceptions and mistakes follows a seemingly perverse logical relay that in actual fact follows inexorably from the insistence of drive to focus on the anus as the site of painful intrusions on the body and of unbearable enjoyment, ignoring distinctions between aggressive and sexual intentions and between law and its violation.

---

34 In "Private Practices in Chaucer's *Miller's Tale*," *Studies in the Age of Chaucer* 28 (2006): 141–74, a wide ranging study of the tale's various meanings of "privetee" and its derivates, referring to property, space, the body, and the soul, Maria Bullón-Fernández relates the "Hitchcock-like appearance of Robyn the Miller in his own story" to the tale's pattern of "the construction of and transgression against private and public boundaries" (141) and shows "that there is an inherent paradox in the notion of privacy: the act of creating private boundaries contains the seeds of privacy's own violation" (154). Since she covers the demands on limited urban space and on boundaries, especially among merchants and artisans, her discussion applies also to *The Shipman's Tale*, given its location in an urban world of merchants, although Bullón-Fernández considers ramifications only in the First Fragment.
35 Lacan, *Seminar VII*, 177.

Aggression is a source of drive enjoyment, but since sexual and aggressive aims are indistinguishable at the level of drive, drive is ambivalent, diverting its aim. Drive emerges at the openings of the body to circle around an object that is given to or taken from the Other. So both the sources and the objects of drive are partial: oral, anal, genital, scopic, invocatory. Ultimately, however, for Lacan, all drive is death drive: "the drive, the partial drive, is profoundly a death drive and represents in itself the portion of death in the sexed living being."[36] "Death drive," then, is not directed at the literal extinction of the subject but at an overwhelming pleasure-pain kept at bay by the Law as it is reduced in desire. Hence, for Freud and Lacan, the necessity of castration setting a limit on enjoyment, one somewhat debased version of this being the "civility" that "is supposed to set us on the most reasonable path to temperate or normal desires."[37] What is perceived to be consistency of character is the manifestation of a fixed orientation to a particular object; character is habit. But drive is labile and plastic, since it may change direction and object to achieve satisfaction, finding opportunities in any number of body openings. Drive may be transformed into its opposite, as, for example, the anal object may be withheld or expelled, the oral object ingested or spit out, and the object is "extimate," located both in and outside the body, but not in either place. The malleability of drive, its lack of discrimination, is suggested by the frequently noted rhymes of the tale – the pun on "queynte" ("curious," "cunt," ll. 3275–76) and its echo in "yqueynt" and "ybleynt," "jalousye" and "nether ye" (3852), "kisse" and "pisse" (ll. 3797–98). Aggressive debasement is indifferent to social standards and sublimation: the difference between a lofty kiss and piss is merely the distinction between a "k" and a "p." These rhymes also show that the system of signifiers is indifferent to meanings, that all sounds are equal and mark only a systemic difference.

36 Jacques Lacan, *The Seminar of Jacques Lacan, Book XI: The Four Fundamental Concepts of Psychoanalysis,* ed, Jacques-Alain Miller, trans. Alan Sheridan (New York: W.W. Norton, 1978), 205.
37 Lacan, *Seminar VII,* 177.

The developing scene at the window, when Absolon is waiting for his kiss and Alison thrusts her bottom out, builds up anarchy by means of substitutions of objects, diversions of drives, refusals of genital normativity, and accelerating pace. The masculine rivalry and homoerotic implications of the action have been widely noted. Elaine Tuttle Hansen has drawn attention to the ambiguity of the reference to Alison's "hole": "the term 'hole' shifts attention from something that is anatomically female, the 'queynte,' to something ... that is anatomically undifferentiated in males and females, the anus ... expos[ing] the humiliating and frightening lack of difference between male and female bodies."[38] Viewed differently, however, the window scene revels in the versatility of polymorphous bodies whose every opening can be a source of excessive pleasure/pain. Debasement is pleasurable here, a rivalrous satisfaction, and it issues in the *jouissance* of a return to the potentials of infantile corporeality, undeterred by any normative organization or direction of drive or by an unconscious identification with a position in sexual difference enforced by castration. As well, drive easily vacillates between sublimity and debasement: Lacan points to the case of Domna Ena presented by the troubadour Arnaud Daniel, the case of a Lady "who orders her knight to put his mouth to her trumpet" and thereby presents a problem "to be resolved in terms of the moral casuistry of courtly love."[39] Alison intends to ridicule Absolon's offer of an uninvited and presumptuous courtship; functioning in a parody of courtly passion, she does not intend to "test the worthiness of his love, his loyalty and his commitment,"[40] as did Arnaud's Domna Ena. The narrative leads to a scene in which enjoyment disregards gender differences and distinctions between sexual and aggressive purposes and between passive and active positions. The window frames a fantasy of undeterred libidinal satisfaction.

---

38 Elaine Tuttle Hansen, *Chaucer and the Fictions of Gender* (Berkeley: University of California Press, 1992), 228.
39 Lacan, *Seminar VII*, 162. See Erin Felicia Labbie, *Lacan's Medievalism* (Minneapolis: University of Minnesota Press, 2006), 91–101, for a discussion of Arnaut's poem.
40 Ibid.

The humiliations of the husband and of the feminized young clerks, Nicholas and Absolon, exceed the pleasurable aggressions coiled within the notion of just punishment presumably desired by their community. Many feminist critics object to the tale's demeaning of womankind; especially they object to the kiss that calls on a "conventional association or conflation of (female) genital and anal functions, of women's sex (or sex with a woman) and dirt, decay, and dissolution."[41] For Karma Lochrie, the tale follows a "*fabliau* logic ... with the determined force of an algebraic function: [cuckolded] old man and young" wife.[42] This conventional plot depends, for Lochrie, on the "functioning of patriarchal relations of power" and the "masking of homosocial relations created and enjoyed through such exchanges."[43] The addition of a second, competing lover is a complication in this formulaic triangle and in the rivalry leading to the travesty of homosocial relation that puts just such patriarchal power into question – though, of course, it could equally well be argued that rather than complicating and parodying anything, the addition of a second lover just doubles the fun. Alison disappears after the kiss, as Lochrie points out, the butt of a joke who has been reduced to an object. This is an apt reading, consistent with Freud's analysis of the joke, but I suggest it neglects the implications of Alison's reaction to the kiss: "'Tehee!' quod she, and clapte the window to" ("tee-hee, said she, and snapped the window closed," l. 3740). With abbreviated finality, she signals her satisfaction in the ruse she has herself initiated, nor does she cease speaking later in the narrative. Further, as many critics have noted, she herself goes unpunished, whereas the analogues to the story are not so merciful.

The intervention of the narrator with a rhetorical question at this point directs audience response by affirming that Alison's trick is intended to be at Absolon's expense: "Who rubbeth now, who froteth [wipes] now his lippes / With dust, with sond, with straw, with clooth, with chippes / But Absolon" (ll. 3747–49)?

---

41 Hansen, *Chaucer and the Fictions of Gender*, 227.
42 Karma Lochrie, "Women's 'Pryvetees' and *Fabliau* Politics in *the Miller's Tale*," *Exemplaria* 6, no. 2 (1994): 288.
43 Ibid., 289.

Absolon, not the woman, is the object of the humiliation. Yet his homophobically painted effeminacy is also evident in the portrait that links his hair care to that of the Squire and the Pardoner. His repulsion and surprise at encountering the woman's anal body are symptoms of a squeamish, fastidious vanity as well as cluelessness: "wel he wiste a womman hath no berd / He felte a thyng al rough and long yherd" (ll. 3737–38) is framed as a report of his state of mind; it presents his perception, and it indicates his inexperience with heterosexual sex.[44] Absolon is confused in his misreading of sexual division, encountered in mistaking "a face, only not any longer a woman's, for he knows that a woman does not have a beard," but "not exactly a man's either,"[45] for he takes gender markings to be determinants of sexual difference. The confusion signals an encounter with a real threat of subjective annihilation. Mark Miller defines the trauma exactly: "if the shifting character of the object's identity is humiliating, the course of its transformation is even worse .... Absolon not only does not know what he has done, he does not know what he has become."[46] Disabling as the encounter is for Absolon, it is a putatively justified punishment for his narcissistic fixation on a pretentious ego supported by an ascetic disdain for the sensuous, unperfumed body. The encounter is also an undoing of a disowning of knowledge: trauma is a return of the repressed, in this case, of an unconscious knowledge Absolon does not want to know about.

Hansen's emphasis on a humiliation redirected at Alison pays too little attention to the ridicule of Absolon. Though she usefully underscores the potential threat to Alison of the hot coul-

---

44 If the "shot wyndowe" is in reality intended to function for defection, as Peter Brown indicates in "'Shot wyndowe' (*Miller's Tale*, l. 3358 and l. 3695): An Open and Shut Case?," *Medium Aevum* 69 (2000): 96–103, Absolon's choice of a site for courting is also a symptom of his obsession with repugnant tastes and smells.
45 Mark Miller, *Philosophic Chaucer* (Cambridge: Cambridge University Press, 2004), 75.
46 Ibid., 76. See also Glenn Burger, *Chaucer's Queer Nation* (Minnesota: University of Minnesota Press, 2003), 23–36, for the ways the scene destabilizes normative masculinity.

ter: though "nothing happens to Alison, readers never seem to notice what Absolon intended to do with the hot coulter,"[47] and Alison is rescued by her lover's one-upmanship. Absolon's intention to harm her signals his petty viciousness. Alison acts upon her own desire in collusion with Nicholas – as Peggy Knapp claims, Alison "makes up her own mind ... Her sexual nature is not ignored ... nor is it denied"[48] – and she has her own reasons for hostility towards Absolon.[49] In addition, the anus is not an exclusively male source of enjoyment nor is taking it as an object a symptom of sexual lack of distinction: heterosexual anal intercourse is widely practiced today as a form of birth control, and it was not unknown as a source of pleasure in the past.

Anal aggression is acted out in the narrative, but narrowing its ramifications to Freud's treatment of feminine castration and the critique of normative patriarchal domination threatens to perpetuate, rather than treat, an imaginary configuration of castration centered on woman's lack and of the phallus as an arbitrator of imaginary gender difference. Freud's account is a starting point in a further psychoanalytic elaboration. For Lacan, symbolic castration imposes the phallus as the signifier of language, "the privileged signifier of that mark in which the role of the logos is joined with the advent of desire."[50] The phallus installs a limit by prohibiting a full enjoyment – one that in any case cannot be achieved by any subject other than the mythical father. Under the phallus, as the Name-of-the-Father, drive is

47 Hansen, *Chaucer and the Fictions of Gender,* 232.
48 Knapp, *Chaucer and the Social Contract,* 35.
49 Bullón-Fernández emphasizes Alison's agency and autonomy and attributes to her a realism that accords with woman's subjectivization in castration: "Alison recognizes the limits of her agency and, as it were, works with the limitations of any attempt to mark private spaces, that is, with the fact that private spaces are bound to be violated" (166). Every human subject is both subject and object, an unstable position more marked by women, perhaps because women have in fact been legal property.
50 Jacques Lacan, "The Signification of the Phallus," in *Écrits: A Selection,* trans. Alan Sheridan (London: Routledge, 1989), 220. See also Samuel Weber, *Return to Freud* (Cambridge: Cambridge University Press, 1991), 139–51, for the phallus as signifier.

superseded by desire in language. It is the mark of a real sexual division, not the sign of "the actual and feared lack of distinction between men and women,"[51] but a signifier structuring a position for any speaking being.[52]

In *The Odd One In: On Comedy*, Alenka Zupančič[53] offers a Lacanian reading of character in comic theatre that has suggestive implications for the action at the Miller's window. Adding to Freud's analysis of jokes and its emphasis on psychic expenditure in the sudden release of energy, Zupančič develops the relation of the comic character to its others: mirroring others of identification and rivalry, objects of drive, and the Other of language. Comedy in theater, she shows, undoes the imaginary unity of the identity of the ego, as others escape its control, as objects perform independently, and as signifying constellations interpolate the characters.[54] The various eruptions of the libidinal body at the carpenter's window in the aggressive acts of Nicholas and Absolon and in their responses to debasement challenge each character at the point where a fixed trait tries (and fails) to give cohesion to identity. Drive seems to act on its own, almost in spite of conscious control or motivation, and enjoyment accelerates as a consequence of obstacles, crossed purposes, deceptions, and mistakes that defy expectations, with the effect of increasing instability. In Zupančič's terms, the unity of the self decomposes as drive separates from ego.

Zupančič argues further that in comic theatre, character is not a complex, affective individual but one that appears in the form of a single trait which is the mark of a "singular coincidence or short circuit between the signifier and the body," a trait manifest-

51 Hansen, *Chaucer and the Fictions of Gender,* 230.
52 This equation of the phallus with the master signifier has of course been extensively critiqued by the "French feminists" and more recently by Bracha Ettinger. See, for example, Bracha Ettinger, *The Matrixial Borderspace* (Minneapolis: University of Minnesota Press, 2006).
53 Alenka Zupančič, *The Odd One In: On Comedy* (Cambridge: MIT Press, 2008).
54 Zupančič here extends Henri Bergson's theory of comedy, *Laughter: An Essay on the Meanings of the Comic,* trans. Cloudesley Brereton and Fred Rothwell (Copenhagen: Green Integer Books, 1999), that focuses on human action appearing in mechanical, automatic forms.

ing "the person's passionate attachment to a singular object or activity."[55] Character is attacked at just the point of the ideal trait in order to detach and to put the object of desire in motion; the object seems to take on its own, independent trajectory, drawing desire after it. The ego, the support for the "single trait" that defines character, breaks down under the pressure of the drive. In its aspiration to live up to an ideal, to see itself and to be seen as an object worthy of love, the ego is a defense against desire. The ego is not exactly a lie but rather a false conviction of coherent, substantial being, propped up by the outline of the body and composed of identifications with all those figures of the subject's erotic history. As an illusion, the ego conceals the truth of the subject by clinging to protection against an unconscious attachment to the object.

Absolon, then, would incarnate the "beautiful soul" preening and guarding an idealized ego from bodily degradation, from repelling odors and tastes in particular. He is attacked at just this attachment when drives breaks through the ego's defenses. His jealous protection of an isolate, inviolate ego ideal defends against a fascination with just what would endanger it: obsession with defilement of the contained self is the very manifestation of anal drive. His character is an incarnation of the mechanism of reaction formation: his ambivalent attractions follow the pattern of neurotics who "are often captured in a vexing paradox – they are drawn into an increasingly intimate relationship with the very thing that they claim to despise or fear …. obsessive cleaning rituals bring the neurotically conscientious person into an ever-closer relationship with the supposedly polluting and corrupting dirt (or invisible bacteria) that the repetitive wiping and scrubbing activities are designed to eradicate."[56] In the dual, imaginary relation that forms the ego, idealization and debasement are mutually determining affects.

Nicholas gets at Absolon where it matters to him, but, like Absolon, he erects a defensive ego that is broken down by his rival's reciprocating attack. Nicholas has an obsessive concern

---

55 Zupančič, *The Odd One In*, 66.
56 Henry Bond, *Lacan at the Scene* (Cambridge: MIT Press, 2009), 219–20.

with the details of his domestic décor: "His Almageste, and bookes grete and smale, / His astrelabie, longynge for his art / His augrym stones layen faire apart, / On shelves couched at his beddes heed" ("his astrology book and others great and small, his astrolabe belonging to his art, his calculating cubes lay nicely arranged on shelves at the head of his bed," ll. 3208–11). And he is likewise preoccupied with sweet smells, his room "fetisly ydight with herbes swoote" (l. 3205). The word "fetisly" and the reference to "lycorys" link him to the obsessive Absolon. Nicholas and Absolon are reflecting images of one another, each figuring in the other his own mirroring ego form and each standing as an ally for identification, both educated and vain and both defying the older male generation, but easily moving from allies to rivals, from identification to hostility. It is the very identification of the ego with the other that turns into rivalry with that other who stands in the ego's place.

Nicholas's defensive ego attachment, however much it protects against an enjoyment of the anal object, is not the narcissistic attachment of Absolon but, rather, is directed outward to intellectual work. Taking advantage of the jealous husband's desire and of his investment in his labor as an artisan, Nicholas manipulates the carpenter into accepting the lovers' scheme, but his elaborate deception, a prolonged mental exercise, brings its own pleasure. The energy of seduction is diverted into Nicholas's obsessive plotting to carry out a deception; the result is that the plot that is set up as access to the woman becomes itself an object of desire. What is a means towards pleasure turns into an end; the elaboration of work is a source of pleasure for Nicholas, satisfying the obsessive's compulsion to prolong unsatisfied desire by erecting obstacles to it. In other words, the scheme intended to give access to the woman as object of desire and to ridicule the husband becomes the object of desire precisely because it puts off the satisfaction of access and ridicule.

Husband and lover are united by an obsessive work that diverts attention from Alison as object of desire onto just that work that would secure the object, that is, Nicholas's plot to engage and convince John of the coming of the Flood and John's decision to follow the advice to make and hang the tubs. Like Nicholas's elaborate plotting, the husband's work is eroticized, as it diverts desire for the woman onto their mutual labor. What may be a homosocial relation of rivalry enacted over the body of the woman but superseding it[57] leads the carpenter to an expansion into the work of building culture, of making something, what Freud treated as the widening out of Eros at the source of civilization, as the carpenter labors away on his own for the salvation of the three. Nicholas takes advantage of the homosocial alliance, since the carpenter's work is set up as an elaborate hoax, but his devotion to his labor, a consequence of his excessive devotion to his wife, makes the husband's gulling poignant.

Poignant but not necessarily sympathetic: commiseration for the husband's broken arm at the end contradicts the unanimous agreement of the spectators to dismiss his pain. John chose to marry Alison, after all, and thereby invited a highly probable disappointment, the consequence of his disavowal.[58] He knows that the marriage between old and young calls for jealousy, but accepts Nicholas's advice without suspicion or guard. His disavowal of responsibility for the tub scheme is consistent with his disavowal of the likely consequences of his lechery. Suspicion need not be the result of intimacy in itself. It is not an inevitable response to intimacy; it is, rather, an attempt to master alterity, to keep the unknowability of other minds "narwe in cage." Jealousy is one outcome of the absence of sexual relation, a consequence of a failure to control sexual division.

Jealousy is only encouraged by the conditions governing male sexuality in marriage: patriarchal dominance, ego control, wom-

---

[57] Eve Kosofsky Sedgwick, *Between Men: English Literature and Male Homosocial Desire* (New York: Columbia University Press, 1985), is the classic source for the analysis of homosocial relations in a circuit through the woman.

[58] See the Miller's fine and careful analysis of the dynamics of the Miller's inconsistent relation to desire (ll. 50–57). The comments that follow respond to his provoking analysis in terms that refer also to other tales' dramatization of the ways sexual division inflects what Miller approaches through a problem with "intimacy." In contrast, the account here of the Miller's compromise with jealousy attributes it to a decision, or in Miller's terms, the production of self-reflective agency, so that the refusal to question his wife's "pryvetee" might be an ethical act.

an's otherness, the fragility of gender determination. The conditions of marriage in the tales, then, exaggerate the mis-fit, the real lack of symmetry and correspondence, between the subject who loves and the desire of the other. The lover can never be sure of the desire of the Other, nor ever have direct access to an other subjectivity, nor, for that matter, can the subject of the unconscious have direct access to its own desire. Januarie in *The Merchant's Tale* chooses to counter jealousy with surveillance, to no effect; surveillance may forestall anxiety, but an insecure man can never have enough security. The Miller, by contrast, knows jealousy is inefficient protection and decides not to inquire too far into his wife's privacy, not to believe himself a cuckold: "Yet nolde I .... / Take upon me moore than ynough ... / I wol bileve wel that I am noon" (*The Miller's Prologue,* ll. 3159, 3160, 3162). A disavowal of sorts also, but his refusal to pry and think ill of others signals at least a conscious determination to avoid jealousy, even if his description of Alison implicates him in his male characters' desires; the *Tale* itself, after all, is also a seduction: the Miller is the one man on the scene who knows what women want. He does not take responsibility for his own lechery, but, consistent with his belief that he can beat down heavy doors with his head, at least he will not take account of the desire of the Other. The Host, propped up by cynicism and misogyny, chooses likewise to ignore possible deception with "lat alle whiche thynges go" ("Epilogue," *The Merchant's Tale,* l. 2430). The alternative is to entertain a jealousy that must feed on itself and destroy the subject; skepticism, a refusal to imagine the other as a subjectivity like one's own, is another.[59] John is brought to suffer as a result of his self-indulgent choice of a mate in defiance of social ideals (if not realities), and he also suffers from the possessive jealousy that tries, hopelessly, to alleviate the threat of loss. Unlike the Miller –

---

59 Much of the work of Stanley Cavell concerns the ethical limitations of skepticism, the problem of the relation to other minds to which the subject has no direct access. See especially Stanley Cavell, *Disowning Knowledge in Seven Plays of Shakespeare* (Cambridge: Cambridge University Press, 2003), 125–42, for the way the problematic of suspicion and patriarchal intolerance of woman as the Other sex is worked out in *Othello.*

as his own performance constructs him – John is not a stand-up man, and the Miller wins the contest, as he so loves to do.

The unfolding of Nicholas's scheme and its consequences absorbs each of the men at the point of their object attachments, and it absorbs the audience as well and diverts its attention as it is bribed by the surface of the plot to be unprepared for the climactic explosion of libido. In fact, Nicholas's intended seduction and scheme are both completed after the lovers creep out of their tubs and off to bed. The narrative could conclude with the lovers in bed. The light delicacy describing their proceedings – "Ther was the revel and the melody; / And thus lith Alison and Nicholas, / In bisynesse of myrthe and of solas" (ll. 3652–54) – continues until sacred sound explodes: "the belle of laudes gan to rynge / And frères in the chauncel gonne synge" (l. 3655). The intrusive sound, echoing the "melody" of making love, is a euphemistic substitute for sexual climax and is a kind of fade-out on the coupling. Yet the narrative does not stop with the euphemistic interlude, but regathers energy and starts again, as it were, picking up to focus on Absolon and working through the unintended consequences of the logic of the narrative and of the characters' drives. The misdirected actions that follow appear to be mistakes, but they satisfy libidinal investments. What seems to happen by accident or mistake in comedy achieves what is desired, in Zupančič's terms, "much to everyone's surprise – the demand manages to find an unexpected satisfaction .... somewhere else than where we expect it or wait for it."[60] The satisfaction of anal drive disrupts the composed egos of the young men; the composure and mastery of the husband's ego is attacked. And the Miller wins the ram again.

The action "directs and engages our attention elsewhere than where the point of the joke will pass"[61] in the narrative, when the turf-cutter iron, the kiss, and the fart, lead unexpectedly to the climax with the sudden appearance of the signifier "water." The overdetermination of this signifier may obscure the joke-work for a time, but the joke comes to a head and closes on the action when the narrative momentum suddenly halts with the

---

60 Zupančič, *The Odd One In*, 132.
61 Ibid., 133.

eruption of "water," of which, of course, there is none. The sudden word recalls attention to the joke's work, and thereby rearranges knowledge that has been repressed. The cut of the signifier's appearance halts the steady insistence of the drive, ending its repetitive enactment. Nicholas's cry for "water" is a demand cast into the unknown, an address to the Other to respond to a bodily need and alleviate his pain, Levinas's cry. It delivers an immediate truth that overcomes the lies or half-truths that have motivated this climax, that is, the deception directing the lovers' scheme and their efforts to dupe Absolon. The cry for "water" reinstalls truth, the truth of the human condition, our vulnerability, our inability to foresee, our need for balm. Despite its simplicity, however, the enunciation is a condensation, collapsing the several metonymic chains that are the lines of the narrative in a single metaphor and collecting the senses to which the separate chains lead. The surprise delivered by the joke-work in the condensation "water" is, again, overdetermined: for Nicholas, it signifies relief from his wound; for John, the return of the Flood; a means of purification for Absolon; and perhaps the release of sexual climax in seminal fluid.[62]

62 In Boccaccio's *Decameron* (Book III.vi), a wife berates her husband, who thinks he has been making love to another woman, exclaiming, "But thanks be to God, it was your own land you were tilling and not some other man's, as you fondly imagined .... But with God's help, I saw to it that the stream took its natural course." Giovanni Boccaccio, *The Decameron,* trans. G.H. McWilliam (London: Penguin, 2003), 234. "Stream" here translates the Italian "l'acqua." A more literal translation is "the water ended up in the right direction," as translated by Mark Musa and Peter E. Bondanella in their edition (New York: New American Library, 1982), which preserves the sense of semen as water. I thank Misha Grudin for confirming this reference. Patricia Simons, "Manliness and the Visual Semiotics of Bodily Fluids in Early Modern Culture," *The Journal of Medieval and Early Modern Studies* 39, no. 2 (Spring, 2009): 331–73, explores "a semen-otic system of fluids," showing the equivalence of Latin "verbs for urinating, piddling, or pissing, like *meiere* and *mingenere*"with ejaculation, and argues, "Almost as significant as the release of semen was the emission of any kind of fluid from the male organ, as long as it was represented as assertive, confident, and forceful" (340). Evidence from painting and of sculpted fountains of putti urinating water or wine may also suggest

The cut produces a stop and a turn that opens up psychic space. It redirects perspective from the enclosed, focused scene to the wider social background that comes into the foreground. The narrative has all along been preparing for the surprise, but engrossed in the process of narration, drawn into the intricacy of the exchanges, the focus of the narrative is caught up in the present moment of each thread in the action until the appearance of the signifier that economically condenses the plot: when John falls in his tub, the audience then remembers and puts together in an instant the knowledge it has suspended. Charles Muscatine explains the climax as an effect of retrospection in which "focal images – the flood, the carpenter in his tub, the axe and cord – are suddenly brought to our conscious attention, not from nowhere (with an effect of mere surprise and chance) but from the semiconscious storage of previous acceptance, unanticipated, perhaps, but inevitable."[63] The appearance of the signifier produces a short circuit: the energy of the several plots that dispersed attention is now funneled into the single outlet in the cry for water; the accumulated charge is more than the outlet can handle. This is the "economy" of the joke that produces the release of laughter in a charge of pleasure.

The climax not only condenses the past in the signifier; the narrative comes to a stop, changes gear, and prepares for a wider social scene and for the judgment of the Other that will devolve. The cry has aroused the neighbors' attention, and a public audience converges at the house. The signifier reverberates to alter perspective and to enlarge the scale of the action, as the domestic scene is enclosed within the social scene, itself to be enfolded within the ongoing setting of the "rowte," the pilgrim audience. The internal audience composed of the gathered neighbors witnesses the end of an intrigue it can easily reconstruct, and it can be satisfied by the humiliation of the jealous, old husband and of young male pride.[64] The effect is democratizing, levelling; no one

---

   an association of flowing liquids with semen, although Simons's examples are drawn from fifteenth century Italian art.
63 Muscatine, *Chaucer and the French Tradition*, 225–26.
64 H. Marshall Leicester, Jr., *The Disenchanted Self: Representing the Subject in the Canterbury Tales* (Berkeley: University of California

escapes the law of human limitation, however rich a "gnof" or clever a student one may be. The external audience receives the surplus pleasure of the unexpected intrusion of the word that brings about the climax, and its attention returns to the surface of language. But there is the effect of the Miller's triumph.

If the Miller's narration succeeds, the joke-work will overcome inhibition and allow the audience to enjoy the outrageous satisfactions generated by the plot; at the very least, the audience may recognize the economy of the joke-work and the elegance of the narrative's architecture. It will not work if the signifier's pay-off is not sufficient to distract moral condemnation or, more seriously, ethical conviction. However, *The Miller's Tale* anticipates and molds its reception through the internal audience's laughter, which signals approval of its outcome; the silence of the characters at the end reinforces their necessary acquiescence to the collective judgment. The conclusion affirms the conventions of its society while it both allows for and contains aggression and transgression against social norms. If the tale's performance is liberating, it is also conservative – ironically, in asserting the power of the law that levels all – not only in the economy of its construction or the reduction of psychic expenditure achieved by the joke-work but also in its affirmation of unconscious truth supporting lies.

The tale is in this sense also conservative in its conclusion. To whatever degree a marriage is a private arrangement responding to the absence of sexual relation, it is a social institution of exchange as well, and this marriage is submitted very publically to the judgment of society. John, the husband – old, well established, wealthier then most, inappropriately married to a younger wife of whom he is jealous – is of course the object of ridicule, without effective speech, a cuckold as well as a fool. Social ridicule is directed at the husband, and implicit communal knowledge of the lovers' transgressions remains silent. The community is witness to a charivari carried out by the objects of ridicule. Ridicule

---

Press, 1990), adds that the audience's ridicule is supported by "the class solidarity of Nicholas's brethren: 'For every clerk anonright heeld with oother' (I. 3847)" (11), which need not imply that the audience is composed exclusively of clerks, sympathetic to the young men.

and silence serve as forms of communal judgment, as means of controlling transgression and enforcing norms. Marriage, as one means of making do with the absence of sexual relation, is kept in line, checked while not directly regulated, by social consensus. Unless you count the *Tale*'s triumphant assertion of the Miller's prowess in the telling jokes.

To Beat the Devil

The division in speech between statement and enunciation exemplified in Freud's metajoke is the symptom of the alienation that necessarily affects every speaker. Alienation is apparent in the referential function of the pronoun, in the fact that the pronoun is a shifter that is indifferent to the identity of the speaker, so that, for example, "I" may indicate any language user. The speaking subject is displaced in what is enunciated, that is, in the statement, and disappears in the act of enunciation, in the process of speaking, by the interference of the unconscious in meaning.[65] The subject is neither in what is said nor in the act of saying but in the gap between the two; language causes a division of the subject in the unconscious, implicating subjectivity in the effects of speech that appear in dreams, lapses, and apparent nonsense to show that what is said and what is unsaid both exceed conscious intention. The non-coincidence of the subject with itself, more than any conscious intention to deceive, is the source in psychoanalysis for explaining how lies reveal the truth.

Because the signifier is detached from the signified, not hooked to a single reference, meaning slides under what is spoken. Meaning is produced retroactively, by the punctuation of a halt in an ongoing string of signifiers, and by context. In addition, and consequently, a signifier may gather unconscious strings in condensed form. The Shipman's wife's pun on *taiyllinge*, for example, condenses chains referring to money, sex, and narrating; the Milller's *water* brings to a head several lines of action; while the Franklin's *trouthe* represents an ideal trait governing disparate models of behavior. As well, because signifiers evoke

---

65 Lacan discusses the alienation of the subject of language in the seminar of May 27, 1964, Chapter 16 of *Seminar XI*, 203–15.

associations with other signifiers both "abstract" and "concrete," they may produce both literal and figurative meanings.

As in *The Miller's Tale,* narrative voice is apparently uncomplicated in *The Friar's Tale* and *The Summoner's Tale,* consistent with the social station and dramatic purposes of the pilgrim character. The Friar and the Summoner are locked in imaginary rivalry, and their narratives are intended to serve their aggression. Each believes himself a master, in control of the law, but neither can evade the unconscious effects of speech that subject him to law. Each attempts to manage speech by rejecting any limit to his language, and each attempt only produces a further loss of mastery. The tales are concerned with resolving a true meaning of language in a reconciliation of literal statement with signifiers' figurative, indeterminate potentials.

The problem of determining the truth of meaning in *The Friar's Tale* devolves upon the question of intention: the Friar works to show that speech is true when it accords with a speaker's intention. Subjective *entente* is demonstrated to be a guarantee of truth that secures the speaker's meaning, despite unconscious distortion, the slippage of the signified under the signifier, and perpetual failure of language to be tied to the literal.[66] The apparent paradox is that it should be a devil who understands and can teach the difference between what is stated and what is intended, for the devil's "lord" (l. 1427) is the Father of Lies. Yet this is an apparent paradox only, since the tale gives the assurance that the truth of language, its attachment to meaning, can be determined because the devil serves God, his ultimate Lord, and, hence, because intention can be known, if not by supernatural means, then by adherence to the moral law or *trouthe,* that is, subjectivity in accord with moral law.

---

66 Lacan's early seminars from 1953–55 develop the notion of "full speech," whose meaning Dylan Evans summarizes: "Full speech articulates the symbolic dimension of language" and is "closer to the truth of the subject's desire," whereas empty speech articulates the imaginary dimension" and is reduced to signification. Full speech "becomes established in the recognition of one person by another." Dyman Evans, *An Introductory Dictionary of Lacanian Psychoanalysis* (London: Routledge, 1996), 191.

The Friar's summoner is a literalist who takes people at their word.[67] He glosses badly, reading speech like a jurist who does not account for figurative meaning, and he takes personal advantage of the letter of the law. He thinks he is an exception to the law, and he counts on power to determine truth. He is a liar, and he intends to lie; he wants to close the gap between statement and enunciation, choosing to evade the law because he thinks he has knowledge and the power to determine what truth is. Denying a subjective split, he derives an excess enjoyment of *plus-de-jouir,* an enjoyment in the letter of language emerging from his supposed control of the signifier and its effects; he depends upon others' subjection to the law that he thinks he evades. He makes himself an instrument of the lack of the Other in order to extract enjoyment while remaining resistant to his own implication in the Other of language and hence to any lack.

The subjective gap nevertheless becomes evident when the operation of the law manifests unconscious truth despite conscious intention. Pledging fidelity to the devil, "My trouthe wol I holde, as in this cas .... / My trouthe wol I holde to my brother / ... For to be trewe brother in this cas" (ll. 1525, 1527, 1529), the summoner inadvertently, in other words, ironically, reveals a knowledge that he doesn't know he has in statements that mean more than he intends. He says what he means just when he doesn't mean to say what he is saying. He thereby demonstrates his subordination to God's law as well as the laws of the Other that he would deny: he *is* eternally tied to the devil he

---

[67] Linda Georgianna describes the summoner's literal-mindedness as a profound misreading of the world, both physical and metaphysical, that ultimately damns the summoner and implicates us in "Anticlericalism in Boccaccio and Chaucer," in *The* Decameron *and the* Canterbury Tales: *New Essays on an Old Question,* eds. Leonard Michael Koff and Brenda Deen Shildgen (Teaneck: Fairleigh Dickinson University Press, 2000), 164. Although she differentiates the setting of *The Friar's Tale* from the "feudal village, where the interests of parish clergy, villagers, and feudal lord are tightly bound," of *The Summoner's Tale* she describes a crisis of faith both tales present, the problem faced by "the rural, English, Catholic community of believers defined not as an enlightened or liberated laity but as a group in need of pardon and the clerical practices meant to provide access to it" (160).

claims as his brother, bound in sin and condemned to hell. The irony is articulated in his repeated assertions of "my trouthe," a commitment to law and consistent fidelity belied by his corruption. Tying the signifier to the purposes of his will to power, he remains oblivious to signifying effects beyond conscious control and so tells the truth when he means to lie. So despite the devil's instructions and ironic insinuations, the Summoner refuses to admit to his companion's identity, one he should be able to recognize.

The tale demonstrates a lesson in *entente* (intent) as the devil uses experience to instruct the summoner in language use. Coming across the carter cursing his horse, "'The feend,' quod he, 'yow fecche, body and bones, / ... The devel have al, bothe hors and cart and hey'" (ll. 1544, 1547), the summoner mistakes what he hears for the truth. The carter is not lying; he just does not mean his curse, as the devil shows: "'Nay,' quod the devel, ... / 'It is nat his entente, trust me weel. Axe hym thyself, if thou nat trowest me'" (ll. 1555–57). The carter has merely given voice to a momentary frustration, not desire, as he immediately demonstrates when the horse draws the cart and he expresses the piety accordant with his will: "'Heyt! Now,' quod he, 'there Jhesu Christ yow blesse, / And al his handwerk, bothe moore and lesse! / ... I pray God save thee, and Seinte Loy'" (ll. 1561–62, 1564). The devil extracts the general principle from the illustration, that is "'The carl spak oo thing, but he thoghte another,'" (l. 1568), and accepts the result that he cannot take possession of the horse. The principle delivers the instruction: speech does not always accord with conscious intention. The carter did not speak literally, did not want his horse to go to the devil. The illustration showing that the meaning of a speaker's word must be aligned with the truth of the heart provides the criterion for judging truth. Entente is the hidden or unconscious meaning to be read in the enunciation; *entente* cannot be deceptive, although it may be concealed by a lie.

The summoner thinks he knows how things are done, believing he is in charge of the law, rather than being its subject, so he answers with a performance intended to instruct and outdo his instructor. He needs an audience as an onlooker before whom he may play out his challenge to the law. The irony of the pervert's position is his need for the very law from which he exempts himself; he demands that the law show itself. The devil is made an accomplice, because he is positioned by the pervert's need for "an Other that seems to coincide with 'the authorities,' or 'the powers that be.'"[68] His performance reiterates the lesson of the carter. Picking on a generic victim, a poor old widow, emphasizes his cruelty, and his spurious accusations are a hyperbolic accumulation of lies leveled to instill fear of the power that allows him to collect fees for the acquittal of unjust charges. The devil is modest, and he sticks to simple, direct language: "Is this youre wyl in ernest that ye seye?" (l. 1627) he questions the widow. She reacts to the summoner's charges as a slander directed at the truth, and she reaffirms her curse, "Unto the devel blak and rough of hewe / Yeve I thy body and my panne [penny] also!" (ll. 1622–23), and, to confirm her intent, does so again when she repeats her curse to the devil who has taken her words literally: "'The devel,' quod she, 'so fecche hym er he deye, / And panne and al, but he wol hym repente!'" (ll. 1628–29). Piety, a faith in "my savacioun" (l. 1618), and her virtuous chastity, "my body trewe" (l. 1621), back up the curse. To be "trewe" here is not only a matter of character, but of fidelity to the truth of speech accordant with law. The summoner's effort to beat the devil at his own game enforces the lesson that what is said is true when it is spoken from the heart.

Truth aligns statement with enunciation, and material or literal meaning with metaphoric meaning. The devil's literal claim, in accord with the widow's literal, stated intention, is delivered as the punch line. "Thy body and this panne been myne by right" (l. 1635) is a joke on the summoner that ridicules his assumed knowledge and punishes his refusal of the law of speech. The summoner reveals the truth of his subjective intent by refusing to show mercy – "the foule feend me fecche / If I th'excuse" (ll. 1610–11) – and his statement turns back on his self as an appropriate curse, revealing the subjective split he denies. His statement asserts the literal consequences of the faulty logic of the conditional. Spiritual loss replaces material profit, retroactively redefining the senses of "wynne" (ll. 1421, 1453), "wynnyng" (l. 1478), "purchas" and "preyes" (ll. 1530, 1472), when the

68 Bond, *Lacan at the Scene,* 42.

summoner loses both his anticipated money and the soul he has already lost. Thus the devil's claim on the summoner reinstates the power of the Law and the truth of language, confirming the "non-deceptive element" of divine law operating in the world. The widow's curse becomes a performative speech act since the literal presence of the devil is the context for its force; the context accounts for the economy of the joke, that is, its comedy, rightness, and weight. *The Friar's Tale* supports such a belief, especially because the presence of the devil provides the immediate, felicitous condition for her trust, ensuring the efficacy of her speech, although she is unaware of his presence. But even in the absence of a judge, in any context, a belief in a non-deceptive Providence ensures that a pious statement is efficacious by nature, since the Law is always present as an active condition of truth.

The Friar-narrator draws the moral conclusion for his audience: "Disposeth ay youre hertes to withstonde / The feend, that yow wolde make thral and bonde"("the fiend who would make you a slave and (put you) in bondage," ll. 1659–60). *The Friar's Tale* is an elaborate curse that gives the fictional summoner what he deserves and satisfies the narrator's aggression against his rival, the pilgrim Summoner. For all the devil's pragmatic method and moderate language, his instruction is a form of aggression that attacks the summoner's fixed ego attachment to invulnerability and to his claim to exemption from symbolic law. The summoner is outwitted by a higher power; he loses by his own terms, in playing by the rules he makes up. The devil teaches the summoner his limits and gives proof that he is subject to the law he both denies and makes appear: the summoner is a perverse subject "in a socially coded context of subversion and sabotage,"continually protesting "against externally applied limits and boundaries" but determined to risk no status or standing in doing so.[69] That the devil should be the narrative's means of carrying out justice, properly a summoner's calling as a carrier of ecclesiastical court summonses, ironically reinforces the omnipotence of divine Law.[70] The devil knows his limits, acknowledging that

69 Ibid., 34.
70 Nicholas Havely, "Chaucer, Boccaccio and the Friars," in *Chaucer*

he is in service to his ultimate Lord. In the position of the tale's spokesperson, he is beyond history and so can serve to transmit a timeless doctrine, giving the assurance of an orthodox belief in a providential design, delivered in a lecture the summoner characteristically fails to take in (ll. 1483–502). In a transient world, ultimately under the design of Providence governing the natural creation and social arrangements according to law, evil is only apparent: "sometyme we been Goddes instrumentz, / And meens to doon his comandementz, / Whan that hym list, upon his creatures" (ll. 1483–85). The pains of the body and sufferings of the soul, if they be the devil's work, are defined as disguised trials of faith, leading to salvation, despite devils' "entente," which are powerless against God's will. The devil himself, then, teaches the Boethian conviction that all creation, all contingency even, is for the good. As an instrument of Providence, the devil is able to distinguish between body and soul, as the summoner cannot – in fact, the tale is proof that devil's work is correlative to such a skill. Dante's sinners and Marlowe's Mephistophilis likewise acknowledge their subordination to the Law when they admit that suffering the deprivation of sharing in the good of God's presence is the greatest pain of the damned. It should, of course, be understood that in Lacanian terms such a God is the (unbarred) Other, Being that embodies rather than submitting to the Law.

The division of the human subject, alienated in language and split between statement and enunciation, can be thus consoled only at a remove to the Divine. Through misspeaking, misstatement, or denial, essentially through lies, truth will emerge: "Even through his body," Lacan claims, "the subject emits a speech, which is ... a signifying speech which he does not even know he emits. It is because he always says more than he means to,

---

and the Italian Tradition, ed. Piero Boitani (Cambridge: Cambridge University Press, 1983), 249–68, points out analogies in "collections of material for preachers" (264) for the tale. As well, he relates the friar's several references to furthering the building of his abbey (ll. 1718, 1977, 2102) to "a preoccupation of antifraternal criticism," and of "Lollard propagandists," in particular with "building programmes" (258).

always more than he thinks he says."⁷¹ Animals can camouflage themselves, but the butterfly will not announce that it is a butterfly in disguise. For the subject of language, "reality is defined by contradiction."⁷² Conditionals and subjunctives, not exactly lies but not yet the truth, state what is not the case by "saying otherwise"; they give speakers the power to imagine and change themselves and the world as it is. For psychoanalysis, all language is figurative, a substitute for an absent object, made absent precisely by the substitution, and for the unspeakable and unavailable real object of the subject's desire, posited at the limit of the symbolic. For *The Friar's Tale* truth is determined in the coincidence of speech and the truth of the soul, that is, in the subjective entente aligned with the true, transcendent good.

What the Fart Said

In contrast to *The Friar's Tale*, any assurance of truth is absent in *The Summoner's Tale*. The master signifier here is a fart, a literal enunciation whose very materiality suggests that its meaning should be clear, yet it becomes open to interpretation just because its materiality can not be put into words. The Summoner's friar John abuses his office to extort money rather than bring consolation to the sick Thomas; he masters a speech that cajoles and manipulates, extends oily sympathy and sermonizes in his own interest, in defiance of the symbolic contract of speech that inserts the subject in an exchange anchored in truth. His message comes back to him in an inverted form when he is given a fart in return for his groping for reward. Thomas's fart, and the accompanying instruction to distribute it to his brethren, need not be interpreted, since both are a sufficient degradation of friar John and of his order. John's consequent recourse to his lord to plead for justice and to interpret Thomas's directions only opens him to further ridicule.

---

71 Jacques Lacan, *The Seminar of Jacques Lacan, Book I: Freud's Papers on Technique, 1953–1954*, ed. Jacques-Alain Miller, trans. John Forrester (New York: W.W. Norton, 1988), 266.
72 Ibid., 267.

The fart is Thomas's effort to attain certain meaning. Neither a self-sufficient material trace of a presence nor a sign that represents something to someone, it is expelled as a speech act, a bodily performance directly and unambiguously signifying hostile aggression, and it needs no glossing to convey insult. It attempts to reduce subjectivity to a transparent corporeality and, by merging statement with enunciation, to come close to being a literal truth. The production of the fart appears in the context of the tale's several comparisons of humans to animals: the wife claims that her husband snorts like a boar: "He groneth lyk oure boor, lith in oure sty" (l. 1829); moreover, his fart is louder than that of a work horse (ll. 2150–51); the enraged friar "looked as it were a wilde boor; / He grynte with his teeth" (ll. 2160–61). Yet the fart, and not merely the injunction to the friar to divide it among his brethren, does invite interpretation. At the least, the fart means that money, the object of the friar's demand, is nothing but shit and that the friar's bombast is full of wind and foul odors.[73] The message returns to the sender in an inverted, literal

---

73 Much recent critical interpretation of the fart reads it in the context of Lollard controversy. See especially Peter Travis, "Thirteen Ways of Listening to a Fart: Noise in Chaucer's *Summoner's Tale*," *Exemplaria* 16, no. 2 (2004): 323–48. Travis is concerned primarily with the relations between the tale's "heterglot" (346) sounds and the *vox confusa* of popular discontent (326), and he considers not only the philosophic problem the fart presents but criticism of "ecclesiastical materialism" (338), and Wycliff's concern for the redistribution of church riches.

Paul Strohm, "Chaucer's Lollard Joke: History and the Textual Unconscious," *Studies in the Age of Chaucer* 17 (1995): 23–42, points to Lollard controversy about the Eucharist during the 1380s and '90s to unpack the Pardoner's reference to cooks "turnen substaunce into accident" (*The Pardoner's Tale*, l. 539) as a joke referring to the sacramental transformation of Christ's body. Strohm's succinct summary of the contemporary Lollard threat to orthodoxy and to the terms of the debate is equally relevant to the problem the fart presents, especially to the relation between matter and spirit it poses.

Gregory Heyworth, "Ineloquent Ends: *Simplicitas,* Proctolalia, and the Profane Vernacular in the *Miller's Tale*," *Speculum* 84, no. 4 (2009): 956–83, points out that a fart could be intended as an exorcism or mode of apotropaic magic to ward off the devil, and although his concern is with *The Miller's Tale,* his study applies as well to the

form. The instruction to divide the fart, on the other hand, means as a metaphor; it says that the whole order is as worthy of insult as the friar.

The lord, however, along with the friar who petitions for the lord's justice, insists on reading speech literally, and his servant, Jankyn, caters to the demand for literalism with a clinching solution that condenses satiric distaste with the corruption of the spiritual orders in a single, elaborate image. The solution would work like the punch-line of a joke were it not such a sophisticated intellectual feat of engineering: from the center of a cartwheel, the friar is to emit a fart that will be distributed to twelve of his brethren, crouched with their noses to the spokes of the wheel. As Freud explains, "the joke loses its effect" when it requires "an expenditure of intellectual energy" whose "awakening of conscious intellectual interest"[74] forestalls the economy of the jokework. Engrossed in the construction of the answer to the enigma of the fart's distribution, the noble audience appreciates the "subtiltee / And heigh wit" (ll. 2290–91) of the servant. As well, perhaps the onlookers also appreciate that the joke is at the lord's expense, that the servant betters his superior and displays a more profound wit.[75] Glossing the fart may produce the satisfaction of solving a puzzle, but it does not end in a discharge of the drive.

The friar is ridiculed for his insistence on literalism and his corruption, but no law, norm, nor principle functions in his

---

Summoner's: "Common medieval superstition, therefore, held that farting was an expulsion of the devil or that a fart could repel him" (975).

75 Freud, *Jokes and Their Relation to the Unconscious*, 179.

75 Fiona Somerset, "'As just as is a squyre': The Politics of 'Lewed Translation' in Chaucer's *Summoner's Tale*," *Studies in the Age of Chaucer* 21 (1999): 187–207, relates the squire's solution to an "uneasiness about potential lay judgment and argumentation" (191) among anti-Wycliffites concerning lay reading of vernacular translation of the Bible, teachings and sermons that might contradict doctrine and clerical practices, and lay use of argumentative techniques. The "lay judgment" of "Thomas's answer has turned it into a problem posed in terms of the lord's knowledge of natural science" and is a "scientifically informed solution" that "validates the scholastic interest the lord has found in it" (206).

world as an authority that would effectively punish violation and draw a limit to transgression. The joke on the friar and his order, and indirectly on the secular court, does not threaten the stability of a compromised social arrangement. The Summoner's narrative lacks the security of a credible, enunciable position that might provide a gauge for the truth, and hence it cannot offer a non-deceptive element for speech. Lacking a source for consoling doctrine or belief, and without dramatizing a guarantee of social justice, the Summoner reduces true speech to an immediate, unelaborated certainty ascribed to the body's exertions. Nor does his tale dramatize a basis for consensus in a social community that would support secure standards; the historical background of dissent and repression, as well as of popular opinion that goes unrecorded, to be detected only in the margins of written records,[76] is the context that leaks into the tale. The Summoner's friar is the representative of what was widely felt to be an endemic transgression of spirituality and of institutional corruption in Chaucer's society, and the victim's sick body and its emissions infect the tale with a tone of desolate sterility and paralysis. Introduced by a vision of friars streaming from under Satan's tail like a flow of excrement and culminating with the image of friars kneeling at the spokes of a wheel that distributes the odors of a fart to their noses, the tale leads to no future.

---

76 See Steve Justice, *Writing and Rebellion: England in 1381* (Berkeley: University of California Press, 1994). While Justice treats the representation of popular opinion of the rising of 1381, similar problems of reading against the grain of written sources confront the history of later religious dissent, although more material is available in this case, given the Wycliffite emphasis on lay access to the printed word.

CHAPTER 5

The Sweet Life: *The Nun's Priest's Tale*

The Nun's Priest's Tale is a beast fable, a genre that traditionally treats animal behavior as analogous to human behavior. Deftly handled, the juxtaposition is humorous, even while the ultimate intention of the fable is serious: to accentuate the "fruit," the instruction, of the narrative, and the laws, symbolic and otherwise, that underlie its narrative logic. The form puts nature in tension with culture in order to deliver a moral lesson, one that the Nun's Priest explicitly spells out in his conclusion with an address to his audience. The moral of the narrative is ostensibly to guard against flattery: "Lo, swich it is to be reccheles [careless] /And necligent, and truste on flaterye" (ll. 3436–37). The cock who, in his pride, has been taken in by the flattery of the fox, is the recipient of the lesson, though the story, remarkably, also allows the fox to deliver his own moral. The story, then, functions to convey the importance of self-knowledge, for the cock who gains from his experience, the fox also, and for the audience that might profit from reading or hearing the tale.

The cock, Chauntecleer, is known for his outstanding voice: "In al the land, of crowyng nas his peer" (l. 2850). His singing, the defining trait that introduces and characterizes him, is described as unique, peerless. It is the source of an ego ideal that would make his self admirable, loveable, and desirable; at the same time pride in his talent makes him vulnerable and defenseless. Although his voice proudly and regularly greets the sun each morning, when *The Nun's Priest's Tale* opens, Chauntecleer awakens moaning in terror. He has had a dream that he relates to Pertelote, his wife: a frightening, unknown beast, brightly colored and "lyk a hound" (l. 2900), has made him afraid, almost to death, so that "for feere almost I deye" (l. 2906). The beast's eyes, "glowynge eyen tweye" (l. 2905), are especially terrifying: the predatory gaze. The cock's elaboration of the vivid detail and of his intense absorption in the dream reveals that he has been captivated by the gaze that has appeared to him. He prays God "my swevene [dream] recche [interpret] aright, / And kepe my body out of foul prisoun!" (ll. 2896–97). Terror draws Chauntecleer into the dream in which he loses himself. He is both troubled and aroused by the fascination in which he is lost.

Captivated by the gaze of the dream, Chauntecleer is susceptible when he comes upon the fox who resembles the phantasmatic beast. Rather than serving as a warning, the dream sparks an excitement drawing him into danger. The issuance of warning, the promulgation of the law, is so likely to invite transgression instead. So the seduction of the fox is a repetition of the dream, of the beast that appeared to him, fulfilled in experience. Seduced by the fox to sing for him, Chauntecleer begins by shutting his eyes, as if shut in the voice filling up the real: "This Chauntecleer stood hye upon his toos [toes], / Strecchynge his nekke, and heeld his eyen cloos, /And gan to crowe loude for the nones" (ll. 3331–33). He is disarmed, immersed in narcissism. The posture is a representation of the pride enclosing him in pleasure in the self and in the *jouissance* of the voice.

Chauntecleer's susceptibility to flattery is an expression of what the Middle Ages called pride, and his pride gives access to *jouissance*. Both the gaze materialized in the dream and the voice that captivates Chauntecleer are immaterial objects of *jouissance*. They have effects without having materiality, presence in their absence. They give substance to the excessive enjoyment beyond pleasure that overcomes and overwhelms the subject, that makes of him only an object. Chauntecleer is "ravysshed" (l. 3324), taken out of himself, by *jouissance*, ravished by the voice and fascinated by the dream. *Jouissance* accompanies a disappearance of his being that causes him to fade away as a subject, and become prey.

Mladen Dolar theorizes the voice as an immaterial object with which the subject is identified: "The source of the voice can never be seen, it stems from an undisclosed and structurally concealed interior."[1] Operating as an "effect without a proper cause," because it is known only through its effects, the voice "appears from the void from which it is supposed to stem but which it does not fit."[2] Although it is a material object, the voice functions within language without being grasped, corresponding to "any material modality of its presence." It is a support of speech that cannot be grasped. It can be conceived as "coinciding with the very process of enunciation: emerging from the breath, it epitomizes something that cannot be found anywhere in the statement, in the spoken speech and its string of signifiers ... the voice as the agent of enunciation sustains the signifiers and constitutes the string, as it were, that holds them together, although it is invisible because of the beads concealing it. If signifiers form a chain, then the voice may well be what fastens them into a signifying chain."[3] When it appears as an object of *jouissance* rather than a support of language, the voice threatens the coherence of subjective experience, as Chauntecleer is threatened by *jouissance* of the voice of his song and by the gaze of his dream, the desire of the Other.

The Known World

Chauntecleer's dream follows the form of a *somnium,* an enigmatic dream that "conceals with strange shapes and veils with ambiguity the true meaning of the information being offered, and requires an interpretation for its understanding," in the words of A.J. Spearing.[4] Despite Pertelote's insistence that dreams are meaningless, Chauntecleer knows his dream has significance, but he does not know what it signifies. The dream is a cipher for him: it's only clear meaning is that it means, that it should be interpreted. And indeed, the dream does presage his encounter

[1] Mladen Dolar, *A Voice and Nothing More* (Cambridge: MIT Press, 2006), 70.
[2] Ibid.
[3] Ibid., 22–23.
[4] A.J. Spearing, *Medieval Dream-Poetry* (Cambridge: Cambridge University Press 1976), 10.

with the fox. The dream, then, might not simply be an enigma, a *somnium,* but can also be a *visio,* "or prophetic vision" that "shows something which 'actually comes true'."[5]

Much of the Nun's Priest's narrative is given over to a debate between Chauntecleer and Pertelote on the nature of dreams, Pertelote arguing that they are insignificant, Chauntecleer that they can foretell the future. Much of that debate consists of Chauntecleer's exemplification of his argument in stories that demonstrate dreams' foreknowledge. The argument between the cock and hen, a transposition onto animals of the absence of sexual relation for human beings, is the frame for the ensuing narrative. Clearly the narrative does demonstrate that dreams convey knowledge. However, despite his conviction that dreams convey foreknowledge, Chauntecleer does not attend to his dream's warning, so that although its knowledge is disavowed, foreclosed from consciousness, the dream insists. The *jouissance* of the dream is repeated until its danger is consciously rejected. The dream's action, then, could be said to be therapeutic, an *ascesis* of the ego's pretensions to the sempiternity of the abstract image; acceptance of danger means acceptance of creaturely vulnerability, and the chance to embrace living on newly realistic and invigorated terms.

Chauntecleer is a creature of *jouissance,* in accord with his natural state. Although he and Pertelote are humanized, capable of language and of learning, the law does not function for them. They are not ruled by the incest prohibition. He has seven wives, hens "Whiche were his sustres and his paramours" (l. 2867), with "paramours" suggesting objects of illicit enjoyment. Like the father of a primal horde who is outside of the law, he has access to all the females whose purpose is to carry out his will, "for to doon al his plesaunce" (l. 2866). Spending their days in unrestrained leisure, neither the cock nor his wives need to work. They are unaware that their fertility has been captured by an Other economy, and unaware that they are, at the very least, under the Law of Nature. In the course of the tale, Chauntecleer will learn to substitute the good of pleasure for an enjoyment that cares not about death, and to recognize the law of the father.

5   Ibid.

Pertelote's response to Chauntecleer's feverish recitation of the dream is to engage him in an argument intended to mitigate his fear. Their argument plays out the absence of rapport as a natural condition: Chauntecleer and Pertelote seem to know sexual division instinctively and without question, as human beings do not. Each exaggerates a position both to contradict and to impress the other. Chauntecleer stresses his learning, performing masculinity as a parade. Pertelote emphasizes her argument by drawing on a gendered femininity to fashion the absence of rapport into a form of persuasion; she is one of Chaucer's "eloquent" wives, as David Wallace once characterized them.[6] Her refusal to support his vanity is deliberate.

Characterized as a courtly lady and described by the language of courtly romance, Pertelote presents gender as a learned role, as it is for humans, not nature but an acquired practice: the masquerade, in fact.[7] She is "faire damoysele Pertelote" (l. 2870), courteously titled, and conventionally elegant: "Courteys she was, discreet, and debonaire, / And compaignable" (ll. 2871–72). Her manners are sophisticated and aristocratic. The humor foregrounds the incongruity of the description, of nature crafted into performance – she "bar hyrself so faire, / Syn thilke day that she was seven nyght oold" (ll. 2872–73) – while it insists on the fabricated character of any display of gender. Her self-presentation inspires the devotion of her mate, so "That trewely she hath the herte in hoold / Of Chauntecleer, loken in every lith [locked in every limb]; / He loved hire so that wel was hym therwith" (ll. 2874–76). She acts conventionally as a physician of love, ministering a sense of pleasurable well being. The diction conveys ambivalence as well: she inspires love, but "loken" insinuates ensnarement or bondage. The tale presents elaborate displays and selective mating as part of "nature," but asks the human whether its arts of presentation are so very different.

---

6 See David Wallace, *Chaucerian Polity: Absolutist Lineages and Associational Forms in England and Italy* (Stanford: Stanford University Press, 1997).

7 See Joan Riviere, "Womanliness as Masquerade," *The International Journal of Psychoanalysis* 10 (1929): 303–13.

In her argument, Pertelote plays out a courtly fiction of the lady whose desire is to admire and reward her idealized lover. Claiming to be appalled by the cowardice displayed in his fear of the dream, she doubts Chauntecleer's masculinity. Her words might be construed as part of an act, a pretense intending to call upon and to renew his courage, that is, his bravery and his spirit. In this sense, that is, acting out a performance, she takes on a role, assuming anger, disappointment, and petulance, nagging at him and implying that he should fear the loss of her respect rather than fearing the dream. Her diction and overwrought tone are parts in a masquerade, the exaggerated rhetoric and overstatement calculated for effect:

> "Avoy!" quod she, "fy on yow, hertelees!
> Allas!" quod she, "for, by that God above,
> Now han ye lost myn herte and al my love!
> I kan nat love a coward, by my feith! (ll. 2908–11)

> Fie, quoth she, fie on you, coward!
> Allas! quoth she, for, by that God above,
> Now have you lost my heart and all my love!
> I cannot love a coward, by my faith!

She is Lacan's "inhuman partner," spewing out demands like an automaton.[8] If her most powerful argument is to question his masculinity – "Have ye no mannes herte, and han a berd? / Allas! And konne ye been agast of swevenys? ("And can you be aghast of dreams?", ll. 2920–21) – the purpose is not only to shame but also to encourage him. She appeals to an ego ideal of male conduct and demeanor that he should fulfill. Her concluding statement reinforces this ideal as it calls upon his male lineage and draws on the father as a model for imitation: "Be myrie, housbonde, for youre fader kyn! / Dredeth no dreem; I kan sey you namoore" (ll. 2968–69). The fox's strategy will likewise be to remind Chautecleer of his father, as an object of competition as well as imitation. Again,

---

8 See Jacques Lacan, *The Seminar of Jacques Lacan, Book VII: The Ethics of Psychoanalysis, 1959–1960*, ed. Jacques Alain-Miller, trans. Dennis Porter (New York: W.W. Norton, 1997).

the humor enjoys the absurdity of family pride among animals, but also makes fun of family pride among humans.

Pertelote takes a leaf from Chauntecleer's book, too, by enlisting contemporary learning in an extended dismissal of dreams' importance in order to dispel Chauntecleer's fear. She claims that his dream is nothing more than a *somnium naturale,* the physiologic effect of bodily disquiet, the product of "replecciouns, / And ofte of fume and complecciouns" (ll. 2924–25). The dream expresses his humor, that is, the temperament defining his character in medical terms, which is choleric: "Ye been ful coleryk of compeleccioun / ... repleet of humours hoote" (ll. 2955, 2957). According to her medical advice, he should "taak som laxatyf" (l. 2943) and eat a worm. Convinced or not, his response to her argument is an exaggerated display that will reassert the ideal of potent manhood: "He fethered Pertelote twenty tyme, / And trad hire eke as ofte, er it was pryme. / He looketh as it were a grym leoun" (ll. 3177–79). He uses sex with Pertelote to reassert his prowess but also to negotiate the absence of sexual relation even after ending the argument before feeling rejuvenated enough to have sex.

For the narrator, Chauntecleer's dismissal of his dream is a reenactment of the Fall: convinced by The Woman, man loses his innocence by following her advice, just as the cock is misled by the hen. The Nun's Priest offers this moral as one interpretation of his fable:

My tale is of a cok, as ye may heere,
That tok his conseil of his wyf, with sorwe, ...
Wommennes conseils been ful ofte colde;
Wommennes counseil broughte us first to wo,
And made Adam fro Paradys to go,
Ther as he was ful myrie and wel at ese. (ll, 3252–53, 3255–59)

My tale is of a cock, as you may hear,
That took counsel of his wife, sorrowfully
Women's counsels full often are fatal;
Women's counsel brought us first to woe,
And made Adam from Paradise go
From there where he was fully merry and well at ease.

Such misogyny is one response, both popular and authoritative, to the absence of sexual relation, and, of course, it appears in other tales. It might suit a Priest, particularly one serving the Pilgrim Prioress who has pretensions to worldly sophistication, whose excesses are rebuked by comparison to the poor widow caring for the farm at the tale's start. The complicated assertion and disavowal of blame fails to avoid misogynistic intent:

> If I conseil of wommen wolde blame,
> Passe over, for I seyde it in my game.
> Rede auctours, where they trete of swich mateere,
> And what they seyn of wommen ye may heere.
> Thise been the cokkes wordes, and nat myne;
> I kan noon harm of no womman divyne. (ll. 3261–66)

> If I the counsel of women would blame,
> Just pass over that, for I said it in play.
> Read authors who treat of such matter,
> And what they say of women you may hear.
> These are the cock's words, and not mine;
> I can conceive no harm of no woman.

The double negative at the end of the passage is ambivalent in Middle English, both a negative and a positive assertion, and the rhetoric of the excuse is ambivalent as well. The injunction to "pass over" what was said in game, like its echo in Chaucer's excuse for the Miller's salacious tale, does not, and cannot, deny the speaker's language, the fact that he said what he said. Nor can responsibility for the misogyny be shifted to the cock who, after all, is Chaucer's fiction, like the Nun's Priest, the supposed speaker.

The purpose of Pertelote's argument is to recall Chauntecleer's courage; she is not the cause of what the narration emphasizes as his deliberate failure to take the measure of the fox. His response to the encounter with daun Russell foregrounds the egotistical disregard and childish self-satisfaction that characterize him, exposing him to danger. The fox issues a challenge that will arouse that ego in a competition with the father. Respect for Chauntecleer's presumed peerless status, and acknowledgement of his unique voice – "ye have as myrie a stevene [voice] / As any aungel hath that is in hevene" (ll. 3291–92) – is put in question by the sound of the father: "Save yow, I herde never man so synge / As dide youre fader in the morwenynge" (ll. 3301–2). The fox's repeated reference to the father's discretion and wisdom calls attention to Chauntecleer's refusal to acknowledge the father, and the echo of Chauntecleer's posturing in the fox's description of the father's posture, as he "stonden on his tiptoon [tiptoes] therwithal, / And strecche forth his nekke long and smal" (ll. 3307–8), undoes any unique status of the son. The clinching move of the fox's tactic, his ultimate challenge, casts doubt on Chauntecleer's very being: "Lat se; konne ye youre fader countrefete [imitate]?" (l. 3321). The challenge issued in the invitation insinuates that Chauntecleer is a phony replica, lacking identity and substance. His only option is to assert his being by singing and thereby prove he is more than equal to the father.

Following Chauntecleer's capture, the narrative of the cock and the hen suddenly is elevated to epic proportions, and contemporary political significance, the elaborate classical references culminating in Pertelote's shriek and the cries of her sisters. It is Pertelote's sensitivity and alert response to danger that enables Chauntecleer's rescue. The hens' unanticipated noises interrupt the course of the narrative; mixing studied rhetoric with barnyard action, the tonal shift prepares for the tale's conclusion. That providential ending is a most richly elaborated exemplification of the concluding type-scene that has played out in the four other tales covered in this study. Following the narrator's lamentations for Chauntecleer's impending doom, the setting expands to open up the narrative space to the dimensions of the human space enclosing the chickens', and the visual perspective widens. The sounds of the hens' fear sets off the attention of the humans who tend the farm, the widow and her two daughters, along with the farm animals giving chase. Sound is emphasized. The lengthy interlude of the formulaic type-scene – the accelerating cacophony and the expanded external space of the narrative and widening arena that places the animals' world in perspective – leads to the conclusion: "Lo, how Fortune turneth sodeynly" (l. 3403).

In parallel to the expansion of external space, a sudden eruption of insight emerges from within consciousness. Chauntecleer's suggestion that the fox defy the approaching rescuers is a surprising wakening from a characteristic passivity: Chauntecleer takes charge, manipulating the fox into defiant speaking and letting go; he thereby escapes into a tree, rejecting any further engagement. Chauntecleer's refusal to be fooled again, "to synge and wynke with myn eye" (l. 3430), to be taken in by flattery, implicitly admits that he is responsible for his own deception. Such an acknowledgment displays the "wisedom and discrecioun" (l. 3318) the fox's challenge had attributed to the father. Simultaneously, Chauntecleer's sudden prudence is a refusal of *jouissance*: it is the acceptance of limits on enjoyment. As well, it is also, implicitly, a rejection of the posture of self-sufficiency: his gift of song is transmitted by the law of the father, subjected by limits and dangers. Rather than an object of rivalry the fox deployed, the father is understood to be the source of an inheritance, the kinship invoked by Pertelote's incitement of courage, "Be myrie, housbonde, for youre fader kyn!" (l. 2968). The autonomous self is subordinate to a place in a lineage.

To characterize Chauntecleer's transformation as an approximation of the oedipal crisis is perhaps to lose perspective on what is, after all, a tale of a cock and hen. But the tale's premise is that these chickens are very like a human couple, within limits. The bravura interlude of condensed references to epic tradition and contemporary history leading to the sudden transition to good fortune, as well as the narrator's explicit interpretation of the tale's import, for "ye that holden this tale a folye [folly], / As of a fox, or of a cok and hen" (l. 3439), invite the reading and interpretation of Chauntecleer and Pertelote in complex, human terms.

The Nun's Priest's concluding address to the audience acknowledges the tale's complexity. That complexity is structural, as well as thematic. It is composed of a collage of material, laid out in blocks juxtaposing diverse themes: sexual division and the absence of sexual relation; the truth of dreams and their relation to the unconscious; the relation between nature and culture; the influence of predestination and free will in worldly action; the history of England. Likewise, the tale's complexity is produced by the juxtaposition of several blocks of generic material, among them beast fable, courtly love, enigmatic dream poem, debate, epic battle, advice to princes. Peter Travis, in *Disseminal Chaucer,* finds in *The Nun's Priest's Tale* "literary features of Menippean satire,"[9] a form he describes as "a mixture, mish-mash, or 'hodge-podge' of styles and forms, a 'paradoxical jumble of disparate things'."[10] Narrative instability is also a product of juxtaposed elements.

The narratorial instability is one instance of the many forms of instability – textual, rhetorical, thematic, narrative, generic – in the tale. The source of the narrative shifts between Chauntecleer and the Nun's Priest, producing an unstable position of enunciation for the narrator, and interjections are inserted, increasingly towards the end of the tale, without clear ascription. As well, the constant changes of tone, along with the changing location and time of the narrative, result in the tale's shifting, enunciative position. The effect of the various, unsteady, and unstable sources of a speaker produces what Slavoj Žižek calls "subjectivity without [a] subject-agent."[11] Such displacement of the subject of language is not exactly a postmodern disappearance of the author. Rather, in the absence of a single, stable foundation for speech, an anonymous subjectivity is the source of a voice that secures continuity and consistency to the narration of the tale. Ultimately, the voice of an absent, anonymous subjectivity replaces the reassuring presence of a speaker in the tale.

Worlds upon Worlds

The instability of the tale's narrative source and narratorial position responds to the tale's concern with the sources of human knowledge and the limits of knowing. In his study of *The Consolation of Philosophy,* John Marenbon discusses the "Modes of Cognition Principle," Boethius's concept that knowledge is suited to the capacity of the knower: "'everything that is known is cognized not from its own nature but from that of those who

9   Peter Travis, *Disseminal Chaucer: Reading The Nun's Priest's Tale* (Notre Dame: University of Notre Dame Press, 2010), 78.
10 Ibid., 76.
11 Slavoj Žižek, "Leave the Screen Empty!," *lacanian ink* 35 (2010): 156.

grasp it'."[12] Each of "the four different cognitive faculties – sense, imagination, reason, and intelligence," has a "different object," that is, "the particular, material thing, ... a sensible image, ... an abstracted universal form, ... and the Form – that is to say, God himself. Yet [they] are all ways of cognizing the same thing, which is known in different ways – more perfectly by higher faculties, less perfectly by lower ones."[13] Chauntecleer obviously knows the world within his limits: he does possess the faculties of sense and imagination, and he has a capacity to illustrate general principles, but clearly he lacks abstract intelligence, the human power Boethius names "the heyeste strengthe" (Chaucer, *Boece*, Book V, Prosa 4, l. 170) of the mind. Arguing for dreams' prescience, Chauntecleer can draw conclusions from narrative examples and buttress his positions by appealing to authorities, and he learns from experience. But he has no interest in philosophy, with the problem of divine foreknowledge and necessity, whether "what that God forwoot moot nedes bee" (l. 3234), or with free choice, "Wheither that Goddes worthy forwityng [foreknowledge] / Streyneth [constrains] me nedely [necessarily] for to doon a thing" (ll. 3243–44) – or the niceties of logical principle, with "necessitee conditioneel" (3250), all issues that trouble the narrator.[14]

Chauntecleer and his mate complicate the modes of cognition principle as they extend the conventions of the genre that ally human with animal features and characteristics as the basis for imagining them as animals. On the other hand, Chauntecleer pursues a limitless desire in the blissful idyll of an exclusively

12 John Marenbon, *Boethius* (Oxford: Oxford University Press, 2003), 131–32. Chaucer's translation of the passage in *Boece*, Book V, Prosa 4, ll. 138–43, reads: "for al that evere is iknowe, it is rather comprehendid and knowen, nat aftir his strengthe and his nature, but aftir the faculte (that is to seyn, the power and the nature) of hem that knowen" (l. 379).
13 Marenbon, *Boethius*, 133.
14 Marenbon's argument that Boethius's discussion of the faculties and of knowledge as being "relativized to their knowers" (338) contributes to an argument about free will, necessity, and God's foreknowledge, applies precisely to the issues the narrator brings up, ll. 3230–50, and dismisses, just as the fox is about to be introduced.

feminine, contained world; their paradise *is* desire without the father. Pertelote, along with her sister hens, passes the day in the sun, splashing in water, "[f]aire in the soond" (l. 3267); Chauntecleer sings like a mermaid[15] and idly watches a butterfly. They follow their pleasure, happy in a sweet, natural enjoyment, innocent of the law and of sin, and so "Moore for delit than world to multiplye" (l. 3345), oblivious to hazard or obstacle before the intrusion of the fox. No demands are placed on them. However, the horizon of their pleasurable reality is the world of human effort surrounding them, and the chickens exist as if unaware of the caretakers responsible for their idyllic existence, feeding, sheltering, and protecting.

For humans as well, rather than opposing pleasure, the reality principle operates in the service of the continuation of the pleasure principle: as Lacan claims, "In truth, we make reality out of pleasure."[16] For Lacan, unconscious desire is the frame through which the subject understands and negotiates what is taken for reality; each subject is limited by the structure of desire that lays out a reality according to the paths of pleasure. Lacan's discussions of desire insist on the imbrication of the pleasure principle, the reality principle, and the good[17] that he traces throughout Western thought, and he especially acknowledges Saint Augustine's claim that "everything that is, is good, because it is the work of God."[18] It follows for Lacan that "the question of

---

15 Trevor Whittock points out in *A Reading of the* Canterbury Tales (Cambridge: Cambridge University Press, 1968) that this "comparison of Chauntecleer's song to that of the mermaids refers to the Sirens whose song, in the medieval Latin bestiary, symbolizes deceitful worldly pleasures, and is generally renowned for the sweet temptation that lured men to their doom" (244). The reference should properly be associated with Pertelote, the female splashing in water, although Chauntecleer's identification is with the voice, the object that gives consistency to Chauntecleer's being, and as such is the object of the fox's seduction.

16 Jacques Lacan, *The Seminar of Jacques Lacan, Book VII: The Ethics of Psychoanalsysis 1959–1960,* ed. Jacques-Alain Miller, trans. Dennis Porter (New York: W.W. Norton, 1992), 225.

17 See esp. ibid., chapter 17, "The Function of the Good," 218–30.

18 Ibid., 220.

the good is situated athwart the pleasure principle and the reality principle," and that the enterprise of the psychoanalytic should be characterized as "no more than an invitation to [the subject's] desire."[19]

The Nun's Priest's narrative issues in a secure assurance of the continual operation of a beneficent order that has designed the creation and protects continuing pleasure for the good. The tale is resolved by the surprising emergence of the manifestation of that order. Motivating Chauntecleer's deliverance from capture is the higher order of the human reality, the domestic staff that caters to the chickens' comforts, as if in the natural functioning of things: the widow and her two daughters with their domestic animals, that is, "Colle oure dogge, and Talbot and Gerland, ... / cow and calf, and eek the verray hogges" and "dogges" (ll. 3383, 3385–86), helped by "Malkyn, with a dystaf in hir hand" (l. 3384), the personal names indicative of the familiar, homely relation between humans and their animals. The human order, over which the widow presides, is the representative of law. It draws the parameters of the chickens' reality and establishes its reach; the chickens are affected by that larger environment, but their perspective does not account for it. Nor can their perspective account for Providence: an animal only, even while he is endowed with speech, Chauntecleer lacks the capacity for insight into a higher, transcendent good.

Until the unanticipated conclusion, the perspective of the audience is limited to the parameters of the chickens' dimensions. The widow and her farm retreat after their initial appearance, not appearing and never mentioned again until the end. All the work of the narrative has repressed audience awareness of the human background: limiting point of view; enclosing any representation of human reality within the chicken's perspective; framing any presence of human beings within Chauntecleer's report of his dream; and consistently characterizing the chickens in human terms. The dimensions of the chickens' space has excluded the containing, framing space of human reality until the human frame reenters to bring salvation at the end. That larger perspective, encasing the narrative of Chauntecleer, is reintro-

19 Ibid., 224, 221.

duced suddenly, with an eruption of noise, of "berkyng ... / And shoutyng of the men and wommen eeke" (ll. 3386–87), sounds signaling the presence of the Other that enables Chauntecleer's escape from capture by the fox. The noises signal the opening of an extended perspective, jolting the internal, rural audience into action, calling up Chauntecleer's consciousness and wit, and setting off the memory of the tale's external audience to take in the narrative arc as a whole. For the audience, the eruption of memory, the return of what has been excluded in the course of the narrative, is like an opening onto the unconscious, a reemergence of what we don't know we know.

By analogy, what the surrounding human world is to chickens in the tale, providential design is to human life. The narrative technique of enclosing scene within scene (the chickens' coop, the setting for Chauntecleer's narration of a dream that encloses foreign, human settings, for example) produces a regression of enclosed framing scenes that unfolds and flips outward in the conclusion with an intimation of an extended fictional space, itself enclosed within even wider possible spaces. Supervening from outside the limits of transient being is the transcendent Providential reality of law operating for the good in the created world and for salvation in the next. Animals, according to their modes of cognition, are unaware of Providence; the rescue of the chickens erupts as a kind of miracle, an intrusion into their sphere but, after all, in accord with the world surrounding and ensuring their pleasure. So too the limited sphere of the earth is governed by the laws of a higher power, an order higher intelligence may contemplate. Caught up in "worldly joy," we forget the sovereign, transcendent design and its promise of the greater good, also directed to our future pleasure. The Nun's Priest reminds us that woe inevitably follows joy, but the tale calls to mind that joy may follow woes, in this world and the next.[20]

20 Arthur Chapin, "Morality Ovidized: Sententiousness and the Aphoristic Moment in the *Nun's Priest's Tale,*" *The Yale Journal of Criticism* 8, no. 1 (1995): 7–33, describes the ending as "a comic apotheosis, an un-solemn, sensuously alive elevation, in which earthly life is lifted, for a moment, back into innocence, enjoying a state of enlightenment" (20). Although Chauntecleer's trajectory moves him

Sexual difference and the absence of rapport between sexed human beings may lead to conflict but also provide continuing opportunities for pleasure. The repeated, formulaic type-scene concluding the five tales that have been studied here bring about the comedy of the endings, opening onto possibilities for reconciliation of discord and for future pleasures. The formulaic conclusions end with "joye and great solas" affirming the good of Providential design and of pleasure in the created world.

beyond innocence, the conclusion is certainly an apotheosis, an insight into a transcendent power ruling earthly life.

Bibliography

Althusser, Louis. "Ideology and the Ideological State Apparatuses." In *Lenin and Philosophy and Other Essays,* translated by Ben Brewster, 170–77. London: New Left Books, 1971.

Aloni, Gila. "Extimacy in the *Miller's Tale.*" *Chaucer Review* 41, no. 2 (2006): 163–84. https://www.jstor.org/stable/25094350.

Apollon, Willy. "A Lasting Heresy, the Failure of Political Desire." In *Psychoanalysis, Politics, Aesthetics,* edited by Willy Apollon and Richard Feldstein, 31–44. New York: State University of New York Press, 1996.

Bakan, David, Dan Merkur, and David S. Weiss. *Maimonides' Cure of Souls: Medieval Precursor of Psychoanalysis.* Albany: SUNY Press, 2009.

Barthes, Roland. *Mythologies.* Translated by Annette Lavers. New York: Hill and Wang, 1972.

———. *Writing Degree Zero.* Translated by Annette Lavers and Colin Smith. New York: Hill and Wang, 1968.

Benson, C. David. *Chaucer's Drama of Style.* Chapel Hill: University of North Carolina Press, 1986.

Benson, Larry D. *The Riverside Chaucer.* 3rd edition. Boston: Houghton Mifflin, 1987.

Berson, Henri. *Laughter: An Essay on the Meanings of the Comic.* Translated by Cloudesley Brereton and Fred Rothwell. Copenhagen: Green Integer Books, 1999.

Besserman, Lawrence. *Chaucer's Biblical Poetics.* Norman: University of Oklahoma Press, 1995.

Bleeth, Kenneth. "The Image of Paradise in the *Merchant's Tale*." In *The Learned and the Lewed,* edited by Larry D. Benson, 45–60. Cambridge: Harvard University Press, 1974.

Bloch, R. Howard. *Medieval Misogyny*. Chicago: University of Chicago Press, 1991.

———. *The Scandal of the Fabliaux*. Chicago: University of Chicago Press 1986.

Boccaccio, Giovanni. *The Decameron*. Translated by G.H. McWilliam. London: Penguin, 2003.

Bond, Henry. *Lacan at the Scene*. Cambridge: MIT Press, 2009.

Brown, Norman O. *Life against Death: The Psychoanalytic Meaning of History*. Middleton: Wesleyan University Press, 1986.

Bullón-Fernández, Maria. "Private Practices in Chaucer's *Miller's Tale*." *Studies in the Age of Chaucer* 28 (2006): 141–74. DOI: 10.1353/sac.2006.0008.

Burger, Glenn. *Chaucer's Queer Nation*. Minneapolis: University of Minnesota Press, 2003.

Burnley, J.D. *Chaucer's Language and the Philosophers' Tradition*. Cambridge: D.S. Brewer, 1979.

Burns, E. Jane. *Bodytalk: When Women Speak in Old French Literature*. Philadelphia: University of Pennsylvania Press, 1993.

———. *Courtly Love Undressed: Reading through Clothes in Medieval French Culture*. Philadelphia: University of Pennsylvania Press, 2002.

———. *Sea of Silk: A Textual Geography of Women's Work in Medieval French Literature*. Philadelphia: University of Pennsylvania Press, 2009.

———. "This Prick Which Is Not One: How Women Talk Back in Old French *Fabliaux*." In *Feminist Approaches to the Body in Medieval Literature,* edited by Linda Lomperis and Sarah Stanbury, 188–212. Philadelphia: University of Pennsylvania Press, 1993.

Butler, Judith. *Gender Trouble: Feminism and the Subversion of Identity*. New York: Routledge, 1990.

Bychowski, M.W. "Trans Textuality: Dysphoria in the Depths of Medieval Skin." *postmedieval* 9, no. 3 (2018): 318–33. DOI: 10.1057/s41280-018-0090-6.

Camille, Michael. *Image on the Edge: The Margins of Medieval Art.* Cambridge: Harvard University Press, 1992.

Cavell, Stanley. *Disowning Knowledge in Seven Plays of Shakespeare.* Cambridge: Cambridge University Press, 2003.

Chapin, Arthur. "Morality Ovidized: Sententiousness and the Aphoristic Moment in the *Nun's Priest's Tale.*" *The Yale Journal of Criticism* 8, no. 1 (1995): 7–33.

Cheyette, Frederic L. *Ermengard of Narbonne and the World of the Troubadours.* Ithaca: Cornell University Press, 2001.

Chiesa, Lorenzo. *Subjectivity and Otherness: A Philosophical Reading of Lacan.* Cambridge: MIT Press, 2007.

Coontz, Stephanie. *Marriage, a History: From Obedience to Intimacy or How Love Conquered Marriage.* New York: Penguin Books, 2005.

Copjec, Joan. *Read My Desire.* Cambridge: MIT Press, 1994.

Crane, Susan. "The Franklin as Dorigen." *The Chaucer Review* 24, no. 3 (1990): 236–52. https://www.jstor.org/stable/25094124.

Curtius, Ernst Robert. *European Literature and the Latin Middle Ages.* New York: Harper & Row, 1963.

Darnton, Robert. *The Great Cat Massacre.* Princeton: Princeton University Press, 1983.

Davoine, Françoise, and Jean-Max Gaudillière. *History Beyond Trauma.* Translated by Susan Fairfield. New York: Other Press, 2004.

Delany, Sheila. *Medieval Literary Politics: Shapes of Ideology.* Manchester: Manchester University Press, 1990.

Dinshaw, Carolyn. *Chaucer's Sexual Politics.* Madison: University of Wisconsin Press, 1989.

Dolar, Mladen. *A Voice and Nothing More.* Cambridge: MIT Press, 2006.

Duby, Georges. *Medieval Marriage: Two Models from Twelfth Century France.* Baltimore: Johns Hopkins University Press, 1978.

———. *The Knight, the Lady, and the Priest.* New York: Pantheon, 1983.

Ealy, Nicholas. *Narcissism and Selfhood in Medieval French Literature: Wounds of Desire.* New York: Palgrave, 2019.

Edmondson, George. *The Neighboring Text: Chaucer, Boccaccio, Henryson.* Notre Dame: University of Notre Dame Press, 2011.

Edwards, Robert R. "Narration and Doctrine in the *Merchant's Tale.*" *Speculum* 66, no. 2 (1991): 342–67. DOI: 10.2307/2864148.

———. "Rewriting Mendon's Story: *Decameron* 10.5 and the *Franklin's Tale.*" In *The* Decameron *and the* Canterbury Tales*: New Essays on an Old Question,* edited by Leonard Michael Koff and Brenda Deen Shildgen, 226–46. Madison: Fairleigh Dickinson University Press, 2000.

Ettinger, Bracha. *The Matrixial Borderspace.* Minneapolis: University of Minnesota Press, 2006.

Evans, Dylan. *An Introductory Dictionary of Lacanian Psychoanalysis.* London: Routledge, 1996.

Evans, Ruth. "Historicism, Sexuality Studies, Psychoanalysis." *postmedieval FORUM,* October 2011. https://postmedievalforum.wordpress.com/forums/forum-i-responses-to-paul-strohm/evans/

Flyer, John M. "Love and Degree in the Franklin's Tale." *The Chaucer Review* 21, no. 3 (1987): 321–37. https://www.jstor.org/stable/25094007.

Fowler, Elizabeth. *Literary Character: The Human Figure in Early English Writing.* Ithaca: Cornell University Press, 2003.

Fradenburg, Louise Olga [Aranye]. *City, Marriage, Tournament: Arts of Rule in Late Medieval Scotland.* Madison: University of Wisconsin Press, 1991.

———. *Sacrifice Your Love: Psychoanalysis, Historicism,* Chaucer. Minneapolis: University of Minnesota Press, 2002.

———. "'Voice Memorial': Loss and Reparation in Chaucer's Poetry." *Exemplaria* 2, no. 1 (1990): 169–202. DOI: 10.1179/exm.1990.2.1.169.

Freud, Sigmund. *Jokes and Their Relation to the Unconscious* (1905). Edited and translated by James Strachey. New York: W.W. Norton, 1960.

———. "On Transience" (1916). *In The Standard Edition of the Complete Psychological Works of Sigmund Freud,* Vol. 14: *On the History of the Psycho Analytic Movement*

(1914–1916), edited and translated by James Strachey with Anna Freud, 303–7. London: The Hogarth Press, 1957.

———. *The Standard Edition of the Complete Psychological Works of Sigmund Freud,* Vol. 8: *Jokes and Their Relation to the Unconscious* (1905). Edited and translated by J. Strachey with Anna Freud. London: The Hogarth Press, 1960.

Fumerton, Patricia. *Cultural Aesthetics: Renaissance Literature and the Practice of Social Ornament.* Chicago: University of Chicago Press, 1991.

Ganim, John M. *Chaucerian Theatricality.* Princeton: Princeton University Press, 1990.

———. "Double Entry in Chaucer's *Shipman's Tale:* Chaucer and Bookkeeping Before Pacioli." *The Chaucer Review* 30, no. 3 (1996): 294–305. https://www.jstor.org/stable/25095934 .

Gaylord, Alan T. "From Dorigen to the Vavasour: Reading Backwards." In *The Olde Daunce: Love, Friendship, Sex and Marriage in the Medieval World,* edited by Robert R. Edwards and Stephen Spector, 177–200. Albany: State University of New York Press, 1991.

Geertz, Clifford. "Deep Play: Notes on the Balinese Cockfight." In *The Interpretation of Cultures,* 412–53. New York: Basic Books, 1973.

Georgianna, Linda. "Anticlericalism in Boccaccio and Chaucer." In *The* Decameron *and the* Canterbury Tales: *New Essays on an Old Question,* edited by Leonard Michael Koff and Brenda Deen Shildgen, 148–73. Madison: Fairleigh Dickinson University Press, 2000.

Gherovici, Patricia. *Please Select Your Gender.* New York: Routledge, 2010.

Gilbert, Jane. *Living Death in Medieval French and English Literature.* Cambridge: Cambridge University Press, 2011.

Griffin, Miranda. *Transforming Tales: Rewriting Metamorphosis in Medieval French Literature.* Oxford: Oxford University Press, 2015.

Grossberg, Lawrence. "On Postmodernism and Articulation: An Interview with Stuart Hall," *Journal of Communication Inquiry* 10, no. 2 (2016): 45–60. DOI: 10.1177/019685998601000204.

Guéguen, Pierre-Gilles. "The Extraordinary Case of Jean Genet." *lacanian ink* 34 (2009): 94–105.
Hahn, Thomas. "Money, Sexuality, Wordplay, and Context in the *Shipman's Tale*." In *Chaucer in the Eighties,* edited by Julian N. Wasserman and Robert J. Blanch, 235–49. Syracuse: Syracuse University Press, 1986.
Hall, Stuart. "The Problem of Ideology: Marxism without Guarantees." In *Critical Dialogues in Cultural Studies,* edited by David Morley and Kuan-Hsing Chen, 25–46. London: Routledge, 1996.
Hansen, Elaine Tuttle. *Chaucer and the Fictions of Gender.* Berkeley: University of California Press, 1992.
Havely, Nicholas. "Chaucer, Boccaccio and the Friars." In *Chaucer and the Italian Tradition,* edited by Piero Boitani, 249–68. Cambridge: Cambridge University Press, 1983.
Hersh, Cara. "'Knowledge of the Files': Subverting Bureaucratic Legibility in the *Franklin's Tale.*" *The Chaucer Review* 43, no. 4 (2009): 428–51. https://www.jstor.org/stable/25642124.
Heyworth, Gregory. "Ineloquent Ends: *Simplicitas,* Proctolalia, and the Profane Vernacular in the *Miller's Tale.*" *Speculum* 84, no. 4 (2009): 956–83. DOI: 10.1017/S0038713400208154.
Hilton, Rodney. *Class Conflict and the Crisis of Feudalism.* London: Verso, 1990.
Hollywood, Amy. *Acute Melancholia and Other Essays: Mysticism, History, and the Study of Religion.* New York: Columbia University Press, 2016.
Hume, Kathy. "Domestic Opportunities: the Social Comedy of the Shipman's Tale." *The Chaucer Review* 41, no. 2 (2006): 138–62. https://www.jstor.org/stable/25094349.
Hutchin, Edwin. *Cognition in the Wild.* Cambridge: MIT Press, 1996.
Justice, Steve. *Writing and Rebellion: England in 1381.* Berkeley: University of California Press, 1994.
Karras, Ruth Mazo. *From Boys to Men: Formations of Masculinity in Late Medieval Europe.* Philadelphia: University of Pennsylvania Press, 2003.
Kendrick, Laura. *Chaucerian Play: Comedy and Control in the Canterbury Tales.* Berkeley: University of California Press, 1988.

Kittredge, George Lyman. "Chaucer's Discussion of Marriage." *Modern Philology* 9, no. 4 (1912): 435–67. https://www.jstor.org/stable/432643.

Knapp, Peggy. *Chaucer and the Social Contest.* New York: Routledge, 1990.

Kolve, V.A. *Telling Images: Chaucer and the Imagery of Narrative II.* Stanford: Stanford University Press, 2009.

Koff, Leonard Michael. *Chaucer and the Art of Storytelling.* Berkeley: University of California Press, 1998.

Kristeva, Julia. *Desire in Language: A Semiotic Approach to Literature and Art.* Edited by Léon Roudiez. Translated by Thomas Gora and Alice Jardine. New York: Columbia University Press, 1980.

Kruger, Steven F. "Claiming the Pardoner: Toward a Gay Reading of Chaucer's *Pardoner's Tale."* *Exemplaria* 6, no. 1 (1994): 115–39. DOI: 10.1179/exm.1994.6.1.115.

Labbie, Erin Felicia. *Lacan's Medievalism.* Minneapolis: University of Minnesota Press, 2006.

Lacan, Jacques. *Écrits.* Paris: Éditions de Seuil, 1966.

———. *Le séminaire, livre IV: La relation d'objet.* Edited by Jacques-Alain Miller. Paris: Seuil, 1994.

———. *Le séminaire, livre VIII: Le transfert.* Edited by Jacques-Alain Miller. Paris: Seuil, 1991.

———. "Seminar on 'The Purloined Letter'." Translated by Jeffrey Mehlman. In *The Purloined Poe: Lacan, Derrida and Psychoanalytic Reading,* edited by John P. Muller and William J. Richardson, 28–54. Baltimore: Johns Hopkins University Press, 1987.

———. *The Seminar of Jacques Lacan, Book I: Freud's Papers on Technique, 1953–1954.* Edited by Jacques-Alain Miller. Translated by John Forrester. New York: W.W. Norton, 1988.

———. *The Seminar of Jacques Lacan, Book II: The Ego in Freud's Theory and in the Technique of Psychoanalysis.* Edited by Jacques-Alain Miller. Translated Sylvana Tomaselli. New York: W.W. Norton, 1989.

———. *The Seminar of Jacques Lacan, Book III: The Psychoses, 1955–1956.* Edited by Jacques-Alain Miller. Translated by Russell Grigg. New York: W.W. Norton, 1993.

———. *The Seminar of Jacques Lacan, Book VII: The Ethics of Psychoanalysis, 1959–1960.* Edited by Jacques-Alain Miller. Translated by Dennis Porter. New York: W.W. Norton, 1992.

———. *The Seminar of Jacques Lacan, Book XI: The Four Fundamental Concepts of Psychoanalysis.* Edited by Jacques-Alain Miller. Translated by Alan Sheridan. New York: W.W. Norton, 1978.

———. *The Seminar of Jacques Lacan, Book XX: On Feminine Sexuality, the Limits of Love and Knowledge, Encore 1972–1973.* Edited by Jacques-Alain Miller. Translated by Bruce Fink. New York: W.W. Norton, 1998.

———. "The Signification of the Phallus." In *Écrits: A Selection,* translated by Alan Sheridan, 215–22. London: Routledge, 1989.

Laclau, Ernesto. *On Populist Reason.* London: Verso, 2005.

Laclau, Ernesto, and Chantal Mouffe. *Hegemony and Socialist Strategy: Towards a Radical Democratic Politics.* London: Verso, 1996.

Lawrence, William Witherle. "Chaucer's *Shipman's Tale.*" *Speculum* 33, no. 1 (1958): 56–68. DOI: 10.2307/2848879.

Leicester, Jr., H. Marshall. *The Disenchanted Self: Representing the Subject in the Canterbury Tales.* Berkeley: University of California Press, 1990.

Lerer, Seth. "The Canterbury Tales." In *The Yale Companion to Chaucer,* edited by Seth Lerer, 243–94. New Haven: Yale University Press, 2006.

Lévi-Strauss, Claude. *Structural Anthropology.* Translated by Claire Jacobson and Brooke Grundfest Schoepf. Garden City: Doubleday, 1967.

Lewis, C.S. *The Allegory of Love: A Study in Medieval Tradition.* Oxford: Oxford University Press, 1958.

Lochrie, Karma. "Women's 'Pryvetees' and *Fabliau* Politics in the Miller's Tale." *Exemplaria* 6, no. 2 (1994): 287–304. DOI: 10.1179/exm.1994.6.2.287.

Lurkhur, Karen A. "Medieval Silence and Modern Transsexuality." *Studies in Gender and Sexuality* 11, no. 4 (2010): 220–38. DOI: 10.1080/15240657.2010.513251.

Manion, Lee. "The Loss of the Holy Lang and *Sir Isumbas*: Literary Contributions to Fourteenth-Century Crusade

Discourse." *Speculum* 85, no. 1 (2010): 65–90. DOI: 10.1017/S0038713409990960.

Marenbon, John. *Boethius.* Oxford: Oxford University Press, 2003.

Miller, Mark. *Philosophic Chaucer.* Cambridge: Cambridge University Press, 2004.

Millot, Catherine. *Horsexe: Essay on Transsexuality.* Translated by Kenneth Hylton. New York: Autonomedia, 1990.

Minogue, Jane Alison. "Merchants in Love and Debt: Chaucer's View in Three Tales." Unpublished paper delivered at the Medieval Association of the Pacific Annual Conference, University of New Mexico, March 5, 2009.

Muscatine, Charles. *Chaucer and the French Tradition.* Berkeley: University of California Press, 1957.

Muzzarelli, Maria Giuseppina. "Reconciling the Privilege of a Few with the Common Good: Sumptuary Laws in Medieval and Early Modern Europe." *The Journal of Medieval and Early Modern Studies* 39, no. 3 (Fall 2009): 597–617. DOI: 10.1215/10829636-2009-006.

Neuse, Richard. "Marriage and the Question of Allegory in the *Merchant's Tale.*" *The Chaucer Review* 24, no. 2 (1989): 115–31. https://www.jstor.org/stable/25094110.

Nobus, Dany. *Jacques Lacan and the Freudian Practice of Psychoanalysis.* London: Routledge, 2000.

Nobus, Dany, and Malcolm Quinn. *Knowing Nothing, Staying Stupid.* London: Routledge, 2005.

Opitz, Claudia. "Life in the Late Middle Ages." In *A History of Women: Silences of the Middle Ages,* edited by Christiane Klapisch-Zuber, 267–316. Cambridge: Harvard University Press, 1992.

Otis-Cour, Leah. *"De juro novo:* Dealing with Adultery in the Fifteenth-Century Toulousain," *Speculum* 84, no. 2 (2002): 347–92. DOI: 10.1017/S0038713400018078.

Patterson, Lee. *Chaucer and the Subject of History.* Madison: University of Wisconsin Press, 1991.

———. "Chaucer's Pardoner on the Couch: Psyche and Clio in Medieval Literary Studies." *Speculum* 76, no. 3 (2001): 638–80. DOI: 10.2307/2903882.

Pearsall, Derek. "The Canterbury Tales II: Comedy." In *The Cambridge Chaucer Companion,* edited by Piero Boitani and Jill Mann, 125–42. Cambridge: Cambridge University Press, 1986.

Pitcher, John A. *Chaucer's Feminine Subjects: Figures of Desire in the Canterbury Tales.* New York: Palgrave 2012.

Rey-Flaud, Henri. *La nevrose courtoise.* Paris: Navarin, 1983.

Ritchie, Emily Houlik. "Love Thy Neighbor, Love Thy Fellow: Teaching Gower's Representation of the Unethical Jew." In *Jews in Medieval England,* edited by Miriamne Krummel and Tyson Pugh, 101–15. New York: Palgrave, 2017.

Riviere, Joan. "Womanliness as Masquerade." *The International Journal of Psychoanalysis* 10 (1929): 303–13.

Robertson, D.W. "The Doctrine of Charity in Medieval Literary Gardens: A Topical Approach through Symbolism and Allegory." *Speculum* 26, no. 1 (January 1951): 24–49. DOI: 10.2307/2852082.

Roncière, Charles de la. "Tuscan Notables on the Eve of the Renaissance." In *A History of Private Life,* Vol. II: *Revelations of the Medieval World,* edited by Georges Duby, translated by Arthur Goldhammer, 157–309. Cambridge: Harvard University Press, 1988.

Rosenthal, Margaret F. "Introduction: Cultures of Clothing in Later Medieval Europe." *The Journal of Medieval and Early Modern Studies* 39, no. 3 (Fall 2009): 459–82. DOI: 10.1215/10829636-2009-001.

Rossiaud, Jacques. *Medieval Prostitution.* Oxford: Blackwell, 1988.

Rubin, Gayle. "The Traffic of Women: Notes on the 'Political Economy' of Sex." In *Toward an Anthropology of Women,* edited by Rayna R. Reiter, 157–210. New York: Monthly Review, l975.

Safouan, Moustafa. *Speech or Death?* Houndmills: Palgrave, 2003.

———. *The Seminar of Moustafa Safoun.* Edited by Anna Shane and Janet Thormann. New York: Other Press, 2002.

Sedgwick, Eve Kosofsky. *Between Men: English Literature and Male Homosocial Desire.* New York: Columbia University Press, 1985.

Simons, Patricia. "Manliness and the Visual Semiotics of Bodily Fluids in Early Modern Culture." *The Journal of Medieval and Early Modern Studies* 39, no. 2 (Spring, 2009): 331–73. DOI: 10.1215/10829636-2008-025.

Smith, D. Vance. *Arts of Possession: The Middle English Household Imaginary.* Minneapolis: University of Minnesota Press, 2003.

Solms, Mark. *The Hidden Spring: A Journey to the Source of Consciousness.* New York: W.W. Norton, 2021.

Somerset, Fiona. "'As just as is a squyre': The Politics of 'Lewed Translation' in Chaucer's *Summoner's Tale*." *Studies in the Age of Chaucer* 21 (1999): 187–20. DOI: 10.1353/sac.1991.0050.

Spearing, A.J. *Medieval Dream-Poetry.* Cambridge: Cambridge University Press 1976.

Stanbury, Sarah. "Women's Letters and Private Space in Chaucer." *Exemplaria* 6, no. 2 (Fall 1994): 271–85. DOI: 10.1179/exm.1994.6.2.271.

Stone, Lawrence. *The Family, Sex and Marriage: In England 1500–1800.* New York: Harper, 1977.

Strohm, Paul. "Chaucer's Lollard Joke: History and the Textual Unconscious." *Studies in the Age of Chaucer* 17 (1995): 23–42. DOI: 10.1353/sac.1995.0001.

———. *Social Chaucer.* Cambridge: Harvard University Press, 1989.

Tatlock, J.S.P. "Chaucer's *Merchant's Tale*." *Modern Philology* 33, no. 4 (May 1936): 367–81. https://www.jstor.org/stable/434286.

Thompson, E.P. *Customs in Common: Studies in Traditional Popular Culture.* New York: The New Press, 1991.

Travis, Peter. *Disseminal Chaucer: Reading* The Nun's Priest's Tale. Notre Dame: University of Notre Dame Press, 2010.

———. "Thirteen Ways of Listening to a Fart: Noise in Chaucer's *Summoner's Tale.*" *Exemplaria* 16, no. 2 (2004): 323–48. DOI: 10.1179/exm.2004.16.2.323.

Thrupp, Sylvia. *The Merchant Glass of Medieval London 1300–1500.* Chicago: University of Chicago Press, 1948.

Wallace, David. "Chaucer and the Absent City." In *Chaucer's England: Literature in Historical Context,* edited by Barbara

Hanawalt, 59–90. Minneapolis: University of Minnesota Press, 1992.

———. *Chaucerian Polity: Absolutist Lineages and Associational Forms in England and Italy*. Stanford: Stanford University Press, 1997.

Westerink, Herman. *The Heart of Man's Destiny: Lacanian Psychoanalysis and Early Reformation Thought*. New York: Routledge, 2012.

Whittock, Trevor. *A Reading of the* Canterbury Tales. Cambridge: Cambridge University Press, 1968.

Williams, Raymond. *Culture and Materialism*. London: Verso, 1980.

Zeeman, Nicolette. "Medieval Dreams." In *A Concise Companion to Psychoanalysis, Literature, and Culture*, edited by Laura Marcus and Ankhi Mukherjee, 137–50. London: Blackwell, 2014.

Žižek, Slavoj. *Enjoy Your Symptom! Jacques Lacan in Hollywood and Out*. London: Routledge, 1992.

———. *First as Tragedy, Then as Farce*. London: Verso, 2009.

———. "Leave the Screen Empty!" *lacanian ink* 35 (2010): 154–61.

———. *The Metastases of Enjoyment: Six Essays on Women and Causality*. London: Verso, 2005.

———. *The Parallax View*. Cambridge: MIT Press, 2006.

———. *The Sublime Object of Ideology*. London: Verso, 1989.

Zupančič, Alenka. *The Odd One In: On Comedy*. Cambridge: MIT Press, 2008.

www.ingramcontent.com/pod-product-compliance
Lightning Source LLC
Chambersburg PA
CBHW072044160426
43197CB00014B/2617